BROKER, TRADER, LAWYER, SPY

INSIDE THE SECRET WORLD OF CORPORATE ESPIONAGE

EAMON JAVERS

HARPER

An Imprint of HarperCollins*Publishers*
www.harpercollins.com

HarperCollins books may be purchased for educational, business, or sales promotional use. For information, please write: Special Markets Department, Harper-Collins Publishers, 10 East 53rd Street, New York, NY 10022.

FIRST EDITION

Designed by Renato Stanisic

Library of Congress Cataloging-in-Publication Data
Javers, Eamon.
    Broker, trader, lawyer, spy: the secret world of corporate espionage / Eamon Javers.—1st ed.
        p.   cm.
    Includes bibliographical references.
    ISBN 978-0-06-169720-3
    1. Business intelligence. 2. Espionage. I. Title.
HD38.7.J38 2010
364. 16'8—dc22   2009031010

10 11 12 13 14 OV/RRD 10 9 8 7 6 5 4 3 2 1

For Maureen, who promised me sixty-three years.

Contents

Prologue

The first time I met a spy was in January 2007.

I had been a reporter in Washington, D.C., for more than twelve years by that time, and I'd met congressmen, senators, ambassadors, and a president of the United States. I wrote about good guys, meeting with officials from the American Red Cross, police forces, and religious orders. And I wrote about bad guys, visiting a federal prison to interview a convicted embezzler and chatting with the infamous lobbyist Jack Abramoff at his restaurant on Pennsylvania Avenue. I thought I'd seen pretty much everything the nation's capital had to offer a reporter. But I'd never met a spy.

So I was excited as I walked up Connecticut Avenue toward Dupont Circle on that chilly afternoon. I quickened my pace, past Burberry, Brooks Brothers, and the other luxury stores that front the broad avenue. I stepped into the boxy, nondescript corporate office building that held the office of the man I was going to meet: Nick Day.

Day was in his late thirties, only a few years older than I was, but he was already a veteran of the British counterintelligence and security service MI5. He was the CEO of Diligence, LLC, a globe-spanning firm that sold intelligence services to private-sector clients. His cofounder at the firm was a fourteen-year veteran of the CIA. They had connections at the top of British and American business and intelligence, and they worked for some of the richest people in the world.

I'd spent nearly five months gathering information on Diligence at that point, and I'd been astonished at what I'd found. Day and his employees had run a months-long covert undercover operation designed to penetrate the offices of KPMG, the global accounting giant. They'd done it on behalf of a Washington lobbying firm that was in turn working for a company controlled by one of Russia's most powerful oligarchs. And they'd gotten caught.

I didn't know what to expect. I'd never been to Langley, so I imagined that a spy headquarters would look something like a cross between the laboratory of James Bond's "Q" and Batman's cave. But when I arrived on Day's floor, I walked into a reception area that looked much more like the offices of a 1990s dot-com company than a Hollywood set. Day's receptionist offered me coffee, and soon Nick Day himself came striding out from the back office. He was of medium build, with dark hair and rolled-up shirtsleeves that revealed hairy forearms. He was charming and friendly, and didn't seem the least bit fazed by the mess his company was in. I figured he'd seen worse. He led me past a row of analysts hunched over computer screens to an office that was cluttered with brown boxes. It looked as though he'd been packing files.

Day gave me a brief on-the-record interview in which he explained his company's role in the world economy. Spies, he said, are sometimes the only people who can solve a company's problems. That was intriguing enough, but I soon learned that Diligence wasn't the only company in the corporate espionage business. There are probably hundreds of firms like it around the world. Corporations, financial institutions, and wealthy individuals can hire intelligence contractors in Britain, America, Europe, Asia, and the Middle East.

In Washington alone, I discovered, potential clients have a wide menu of options to choose from. They can hire firms staffed by ex-FBI agents, ex-CIA officers, or ex–Secret Service employees. They can hire ex-British MI5 officers like Day at Diligence. There's even a spy firm made up of ex-Soviet KGB and military

intelligence officers. It's located in suburban Virginia, not too far from CIA headquarters, and I had coffee with the owner. We went to Starbucks.

I had stumbled across an entire hidden industry of spies for hire, and I was captivated.

For me, the industry I'd found represented a chance to cover something new. This was a heck of a lot more interesting than a congressional hearing, a lobbying fight, or even a corruption scandal. I began calling the spies, to see if they'd talk to me. To my surprise, most of them were happy to open up about their business—if not always on the record. I met with corporate intelligence operatives in Washington, New York, London, and Berlin, many of them veterans of the world's most elite military forces and intelligence services. I studied the history of the corporate espionage industry and learned that private-sector spying had long been intertwined with the government's own intelligence operations.

The result of that research is this book. In writing it, though, I struggled to answer the most important question about corporate spying: is it right or wrong? To be clear, corporate spying doesn't necessarily involve anything illegal or even unethical. To call people spies simply means that they use intelligence techniques or are veterans of government intelligence services.

The question of right and wrong, though, has haunted private intelligence operatives and their clients since the dawn of the industry in the 1850s. In fact, Allan Pinkerton, the man acknowledged to be the inventor of the private intelligence business, set down the first industry code of conduct in the mid-nineteenth century in order to ensure that such work would remain the "high and honorable" calling he felt certain it was. Pinkerton outlined basic rules for his agents. They would not work for defendants in criminal cases, and they would not investigate jurors, public officials, or union members. They would not work for a political party against its opposition, they would not work for "vice crusaders," and they would work only for flat fees, not for a percentage of the spoils.

Moreover, they would never investigate the "morals of a woman"; nor would they handle divorces or other cases of a "scandalous nature."

As the 1860s dawned, that was the bright ethical line of the private intelligence industry. But the line didn't hold. Many of Pinkerton's modern-day counterparts routinely violate every one of his gentlemanly commandments. The ethical line vanished so quickly, in fact, that Pinkerton's own agency became known as one of the best union-busting tools of America's corporate elite. By then, Pinkerton's sons controlled the company he had founded. Sons don't bear the sins of their fathers, it's true. But history teaches that sons don't always bear their virtues, either.

As the world's economies intertwine and different value systems collide, the ethical lines are shifting again. In London, corporate surveillance practitioners grumble about their eastern European competition. The British spies—who tail executives, eavesdrop on conversations, and obtain damaging information about their targets—complain that the eastern Europeans go too far. One British operative told me that she'd never spy on a target while he was with his children. To her, tailing an executive to his son's soccer game feels unseemly. She won't do it. But she acknowledges that there are others who will.

The way things are going in the private spy business worries some intelligence professionals. As one experienced industry operative told me, "We're just one scandal away from a government crackdown." He meant that with so much unsavory conduct going on, the industry is bound to explode into public view. The veteran CIA officer John Brennan, a deputy national security adviser in the White House, is another concerned observer. "The problem is that you do things in the service of your country that are just not appropriate to do in the private sector," Brennan told me in the months before he was tapped for his White House role by President Barack Obama. "I hope they've brought their ethics with them." At the time, Brennan was between government jobs, and sitting in a bland

office at the suburban Virginia company where he worked, which is called The Analysis Corporation. It, too, is a private intelligence firm, although it sells its services to the government, not to the private sector.

Even as it remains a largely hidden industry, the private spying business is becoming an integral part of the way companies do business around the world. The past several years have made it abundantly clear that there are far more hidden, and dangerous, secrets at work in the global economy than even many sophisticated businesspeople once thought. For nervous financiers and executives, ramping up private intelligence capability is an understandable response to the confusing and sometimes deadly situations that surround them. The global economy is a paranoid place.

What will a world shaped by that kind of corporate paranoia look like? To understand, we first need to see the private spies in the field.

Our story begins on a warm afternoon on the island of Bermuda.

Code Name: Yucca

The poor guy had no idea what he was getting himself into.

When KPMG's accountant Guy Enright stepped into the Italian restaurant Little Venice in sunny downtown Hamilton, Bermuda, in the spring of 2005, all he knew was that he was there for a lunch meeting with a man who called himself Nick Hamilton.

To set up the lunch, Hamilton had called Enright's cell phone days earlier, while the accountant was in London attending a KPMG meeting on conflict-of-interest rules. *This is going to sound really weird, but I've got something sensitive to talk to you about. Could you come to the restaurant alone?* Hamilton had told Enright he wanted to discuss important matters, and left the accountant with a vague impression that he was with one or another of the British intelligence services.

There was no way for Enright to know that Hamilton was not at all who he suggested he was. He couldn't know that several clandestine operatives were right now following him from his office at KPMG Financial Advisory Services to the restaurant, working in an efficient tag-team relay to ensure that Enright wouldn't spot anything unusual. And Enright certainly didn't notice that, among the crowd of well-dressed international businesspeople and tourists dining at Little Venice, one woman watched as he took his seat.

She, too, was working for Hamilton, and she was there to make sure Enright didn't have backup of his own.

Enright did not. He was way out of his league. The British-born executive was just like millions of other mid-level white collar workers around the world. What did he know about espionage? But his position as a senior manager in corporate recovery gave him access to documents for which a wealthy client might pay millions of dollars. Might lie for. Might steal, if necessary. And that client hired the man who called himself Nick Hamilton. Hamilton's team was a mix of American CIA veterans, former officers of the British MI5 security service, and young, adventure-seeking American college graduates.

They were corporate spies.

Over the next several months, the spies executed an extraordinary plan they code-named "Project Yucca." The covert operation, as elaborate as it became, was just one piece of a global struggle between two corporate behemoths with Russian ties. The spies were working on behalf of Alfa Group Consortium, which is one of Russia's biggest privately owned financial-industrial conglomerates, its vast holdings ranging from oil and gas to commercial and investment banking, insurance, and telecommunications. At the time Guy Enright showed up for lunch in Bermuda, Alfa Group was in a furious dispute with a mysterious Bermuda-based entity called IPOC International Growth Fund. The fight centered on which company was the rightful owner of $250 million worth of stock in a Russian telecommunications firm called MegaFon.

But the battle was much more than just a legal tussle between companies: it was a personal grudge match between two of Russia's most powerful men, and it had deep implications for the relationship between the government and the private sector in Russia. And the convoluted battle showed the world how the struggle for power inside Russia could spill over into courtrooms—and board rooms—throughout the global economy. On one side was Mikhail

Fridman, one of the youngest Russian oligarchs, who is said to be worth more than $20 billion. Fridman controls Alfa Group, and he was at loggerheads with Leonid Reiman, a former Soviet Army officer who served in Russia's government under Putin as minister of communications. Fridman and Alfa were convinced that Reiman was the real owner of IPOC, and that the company's attempt to control the MegaFon shares was a conflict of interest with Reiman's government position. IPOC, meanwhile, maintained that it was owned by a Danish lawyer, Jeffrey Galmond, who just happened to be Reiman's attorney. With powerful, and angry, men set against each other, it seemed that almost anything could happen. A former high-ranking American official involved in the affair told a reporter looking into the saga: "Be careful on this one. People get killed over stuff like this in Russia."*

The goal of the spy operation Project Yucca, then, was to help Alfa untangle the intricate global legal structure of IPOC.[1] At the time, the accounting firm KPMG was conducting an investigation on behalf of the government of Bermuda into exactly that question. Alfa's spies desperately wanted access to the investigation—what nuggets of new information had it uncovered about Alfa's bitter rival? That's why the spies targeted Guy Enright: they wanted him to turn over confidential documents at the heart of the investigation.

The spies—veterans of western intelligence services now working in the private sector on behalf of a Russian oligarch—developed a cynical plan: they would appeal to Enright's patriotism as

---

*In fact, there may have been at least one murder related to the battle between Alfa and IPOC. In early 2008, the Russian-American businessman Leonid Rozhetskin vanished under mysterious circumstances. Rozhetskin, whose attempt to sell his shares in MegaFon had triggered the corporate battle in the first place, was visiting his seaside villa in Latvia at the time of his disappearance. He has not been seen alive since. Authorities later found blood on the floor of the beach house, and discovered Rozhetskin's abandoned car. It was not clear if Rozhetskin had been killed or had faked his own death to escape the clash of the Russian oligarchs. Six months later, his wife—the model Natalya Belova—and their three-year-old son Maximillian disappeared from their London home. Rozhetskin also left behind his business partner, the Hollywood producer Eric Eisner, the son of Michael Eisner, legendary former CEO of the Walt Disney Company.

a British subject. They convinced Enright that they were working for the crown. They mentioned the sinister dealings of the Russian mafia. And before long, Enright would find himself entering the secret world of spies, hiding confidential documents under rocks in a Bermuda field for Hamilton and his team to retrieve, terrified of being caught, and believing all the while that he was helping his country.

He wouldn't find out until much later that it was all a lie.

COMPLEX LOGISTICS WENT into setting up the lunch at Little Venice in Bermuda. The man posing as Nick Hamilton was Nick Day, the charming, dark-haired, thirty-eight-year-old cofounder of the private intelligence firm Diligence, LLC, based in Washington, D.C. Years earlier, Day had started his career in the British military as part of the Special Boat Service (SBS), which operates much like the U.S. Navy SEALs. For years, the SBS motto was: "Not by strength, by guile."

His firm, Diligence, uses guile, too. And it uses the strength of an advisory board that includes some of the biggest names in global intelligence, business, and politics. Diligence boasts of its advisers on both sides of the Atlantic, including Michael Howard, a former leader of the Conservative party in Britain; Ed Mathias, the managing director of the mammoth American private equity firm Carlyle Group; and, most prominently, William Webster, a former director of both the CIA and the FBI.

Diligence's operations in Bermuda took place just a few months before the events of a far more prominent case of corporate espionage: the spying scandal at Hewlett-Packard (HP). Executives of HP hired agents to obtain illicit phone records of its board members and rummage through the household trash of reporters covering the company. The revelation of that bit of dirty trickery generated headlines worldwide, sparked confrontational congressional hearings, and prompted felony charges (which were later dropped)

against Patricia Dunn, the company's chairman at the time. But lost in all the media furor over the HP spying scandal was the undeniable fact that pilfering phone records and digging through dumpsters are among the most benign tactics in the corporate espionage playbook. Espionage gets much, much dirtier than that.

The scam Nick Day ran on Guy Enright in Bermuda was just one of 100 or more operations Diligence has launched since its founding in 2000 by Day and a fellow thirtysomething intelligence vet, Mike Baker, who had been a CIA officer for fourteen years. In this case, Diligence didn't work directly for Alfa Group. Instead, it worked for one of Washington's most prominent and well-connected lobbying firms, Barbour Griffith and Rogers. This lobbying firm paid Diligence $25,000 per month, plus expenses and, in at least one case, a bonus for obtaining a key document. The lobbyists, in turn, were working for Russia's largest privately owned bank: Alfa Bank, a subsidiary of Alfa Group Consortium.

The transcontinental struggle between the two Russian heavies was a bonanza for corporate spies, who were reaping hundreds of thousands of dollars in fees working for either IPOC or Alfa. But that meant Diligence had to move carefully—with so many spies on the case it would be hard to find sources, and harder still to determine each person's true motives. First, a team of Washington operatives from Diligence reconnoitered at the KPMG offices, trying to establish who inside the firm would have access to the key documents.

Many employees at Diligence believed they were on the right side in this battle. They felt that IPOC was the bad guy, nothing more than a convoluted set of shell companies and dummy entities that allowed Leonid Reiman to grab control of MegaFon. They couldn't wait to expose what they saw as Reiman's wrongdoing.*

---

*The IPOC saga involved a convoluted global web of companies and lawsuits. But by 2007, the government of the British Virgin Islands (BVI) concluded in a letter to the U.S. Department of Justice that "Reiman has a private beneficial interest in IPOC and its group entities." In other words, the BVI investigation concluded that Diligence had been right about IPOC's ownership all along. A Bermuda court ordered that IPOC be liquidated in 2007.

The mission would be tricky, but Nick Day, as always, brimmed over with confidence. "We have a good chance of success on this project," Day wrote in an internal memo at Diligence. "We are doing it in a way which gives plausible deniability, and therefore virtually no chance of discovery." Other, similar Diligence operations had been successful, Day noted.

Staffers at Diligence began to work the phones, pretending to be organizers of a corporate conference on accounting soon to be held in Bermuda. To keep the story straight, they talked with local hotels to find out room rates and the prices for renting a conference center, gathering convincing details to drop into later conversations. They flew to Bermuda, and treated KPMG's secretaries to rounds of drinks at local bars, probing them for information about who the key executives at KPMG were.

Still posing as event organizers, they began calling senior-level KPMG accountants in Bermuda. They told the flattered accountants that they were organizing a major conference, and they were looking for speakers. *You're such an expert. What would you say in your speech to our attendees? What a fascinating job you have! Tell me about it.* They were looking for people who would have access to documents regarding the investigation of IPOC. But not just anyone who had access to the papers would work as a source. The experienced hands at Diligence knew that only certain personality types might go along with the scheme they had in mind.

The intelligence firm was looking for people who fit one of two personality profiles, according to a Project Yucca planning memo. One personality type was a "male in his mid-20s who is somewhat bored . . . has a propensity to party hard, needs cash, enjoys risk, likes sports, likes women, is disrespectful of his managers, fiddles his expenses, but is patriotic." The memo described the second personality type as "a young female who is insecure, overweight, bitchy, not honest. Someone who spends money on her looks, clothes, gadgets. Has no boyfriend, and only superficial friends. Has a strong relationship with her mother."

Enright, the British-born accountant, didn't quite fit either of these psychological profiles, but the firm settled on him as the likeliest leaker.

Enright was oblivious of all this preparation. He didn't notice the operatives following him to the restaurant, or the spy in the dining room. And he was intrigued by what he heard from the man he knew only as Nick Hamilton. Day never said exactly who he was working for, but he hoped Enright would think he was probing KPMG to find out if IPOC had connections to the Russian mafia. After all, as a veteran of MI5, Nick Day knew exactly how real intelligence officers approach potential sources.

Day said that Enright would have to undergo a background check by the British government to ensure that he was up to the task. Day produced an official-looking—but fake—questionnaire with a British government seal at the top and asked for information about Enright's parents, his professional background, any criminal history, and his political activities. Enright provided the details dutifully.

It was what spies call a "false-flag" recruitment. To get someone to turn over secret information, a spy needs to figure out what motivates that person. Money? Sex? Patriotism? From there, spies create situations in which they can use the person's motivations against him or her. And—best of all for a spy—the payoffs don't even have to be real. You don't have to sleep with people to manipulate them with sex. You don't have to bribe them to fire them up with dreams of money. And you don't even have to be who you say you are. That's why Nick Day noted in his memo that he was looking for someone "patriotic." Guy Enright was a useful source: he loved his country. And Nick Day used that to make a fool of him.

Two weeks later, over beers at a bar, Day—still posing as Hamilton—told Enright war stories from his days in the Special Boat Service and began his charming seduction. After a couple of rounds, his questions got more specific: *What's the atmosphere like in your office? What do you know about the investigation of IPOC?* The documents from the investigation could prove crucial to the

queen's intelligence on dangerous Russian elements. Enright was no longer just an anonymous accountant. He was in a sensitive, and important, position: by the time Nick Day was done with him, Enright must have thought he was James Bond himself.

Soon, Enright was depositing confidential audit documents in plastic containers at drop-off points designated by Diligence. He turned over transcripts of interviews KPMG had conducted in the investigation of IPOC, and drafts of internal reports KPMG was preparing about the matter. Day picked out a rock in a field along Enright's scenic twenty-minute daily commute and placed a plastic container under it, creating what spies call a "dead-drop site." At appointed times, Enright slipped new material into the container, which Day later retrieved. This arrangement kept the two from being seen with one another, and from being photographed by any spies who might be working for the other side.

At one point, Enright left documents in the storage compartment of his moped, which he parked at his home. Enright told Day where he hid the keys to the moped, and when Enright left for a trip, employees from Diligence came by to collect the papers.

Diligence got hold of some of the accounting firm's most secret materials pertaining to its investigation of IPOC. It obtained a draft of a report to the minister of finance in Bermuda, dated March 24, 2005. Now Diligence knew what KPMG's investigators were thinking about the mysterious Russian company, and what conclusions the final report would probably make. In the secret global struggle between the two corporate behemoths, it was a coup. Diligence also got transcripts of confidential interviews with key figures at IPOC.

It was a huge intelligence haul for Diligence, which used it to stir up problems for IPOC. Diligence shared much of the material with its client, the lobbying firm Barbour Griffith and Rogers. It sent other information to a former Soviet military intelligence officer for help in understanding the Russian angles. It passed a copy of the draft report on to a former FBI agent, Tom Locke, in

the hope that the FBI might take an interest in IPOC. Locke, a legendary figure who had been in charge during the first weeks of the FBI's mammoth investigation in the wake of the 9/11 attacks, forwarded the report to Chip Burrus, the deputy assistant director of the Criminal Investigative Division of the FBI.

Day and Diligence took elaborate precautions to make sure Enright wasn't himself a plant or a corporate spy. In this business, one can never be too paranoid. Who knew what schemes the opposing spies were working on? After every meeting, operatives from Diligence followed Enright to his next destination. And when he left his meetings with Enright, Day followed a process spies call "dry cleaning," designed to detect whether he himself was being followed. He walked a prescribed route through several narrow choke points. That way, Diligence's employees in preset lookout positions could identify anyone who might have been tailing Nick Day.

Day knew that there were a lot of spies on contract in the battle between Alfa and IPOC. His firm worked alongside allies at other private spy firms who were hired to work other angles of the complicated case. And Day had created a detailed dossier on the long list of spy firms that he believed were working on IPOC's side of the battle, and that might at any moment be targeting his own operation.

But the most dangerous threat to any spying operation doesn't come from outside. It comes from within. On the morning of October 18, 2005, an anonymous package turned up at the front door of the offices of KPMG in Montvale, New Jersey. Inside were detailed internal business records from Diligence, including e-mails and other documents, which made it clear to managers at KPMG that their firm had experienced a terrible leak, and Diligence—a firm they had never heard of before—had access to KPMG's innermost secrets. To this day, it is impossible to say for sure who tipped off KPMG. But Nick Day suspected a recently fired employee who had access to scores of Diligence operations, including the documents dropped at KPMG.

. . . .

MIKE BAKER SETTLES into a plush armchair by the bar at the Four Seasons Hotel in Manhattan with the nimbleness of a man who has spent much of his life slipping into and out of quick conferences in posh hotels like this around the world. With spiky hair and boyish good looks just beginning to show the signs of age, at forty-eight this veteran CIA man could pass for the actor Kevin Bacon. As if to enhance his Hollywood image, Baker is wearing a black suit and white shirt unbuttoned to the point where a tuft of graying chest hair is just visible.

Mike Baker cofounded Diligence with Nick Day, and he's here to explain how the firm got its start. With a smile, he promises a boring interview.

Baker was born in England to American parents. With a father in the military, he traveled the world at an early age. In 1982, he joined the CIA, becoming a covert operative. Baker says his own exploits paralleled the priorities of the CIA during the following decades: counterinsurgency operations, counternarcotics, and counterterrorism. He loved it—the people, the travel, the operations. And he won't share any of the details. "I'm just one of those people who believe that you keep your yap shut," Baker says apologetically.

He does say that his nearly two decades as a spy taught him how the world works. "You peek behind the curtain, and you realize that there's not a one-world government, and the CIA is not out to hose the average American," Baker says. Although he worries that most people harbor conspiracy theories about the CIA, Baker depicts it as much like any other government bureaucracy—always shifting direction to please its civilian masters in Washington. "We have the most open, transparent intel service in the world. And people don't believe it."

In the early 1980s, Baker explains, the CIA was "old school," the kind of place people joined to spend an entire career. But as has

happened in other areas of American and world business, the idea of a job for life was replaced by a series of jobs in which employees pick up skills at one stop that they'll use at the next, more lucrative, stop. Baker saw a new generation of recruits come into the CIA with a different attitude. For them, the CIA would be a stopover on their way to another career. That trend was happening in other western intelligence services, too—and after the Soviet Union collapsed in the early 1990s, a flood of KGB veterans entered the global job market.

Baker says that not all those who quit the CIA left for the money. Many of his contemporaries quit in the late 1990s because they thought the CIA had become too risk averse. It was a far cry from the CIA that just ten years earlier had been running a massive secret war against the Soviets in Afghanistan, and managing other, smaller, anticommunist operations around the globe. After the Berlin wall came down, ennui plagued the spies and their bosses at Langley: *What are we fighting for now?*

In 1998, Baker went in search of something else to do. Living in London at the time, he met Nick Day through a mutual friend. Day, the son of a mathematics professor at Oxford University, had never gone to a university himself, instead opting for the military straight out of high school and then going into the British counterintelligence and security service MI5. The two men had a lot in common: Day, too, had just left the intelligence world and was looking for a place in the private sector. Over a long dinner, the two young spies got along like old friends. Soon, Baker and Day went to work together at a private intelligence firm called Maxima.

After their years in the CIA and MI5, Baker and Day had problem-solving skills, investigative talents, and street smarts that would prove to be extremely lucrative in the corporate setting. Most important, they were more aggressive than people who'd spent their careers inside the corporate cocoon. They—and the other spies then leaving government service for the private sector—approached business questions in a different way.

Say an investment firm wanted to know whether there were any problems with the rollout of a new product coming from a drug company—call it "BigPharma, Inc." The investment firm would want to know when the product would be launched, whether there were any problems with the science behind the product, and whether the executives thought it would be a blockbuster. Traditional Wall Street investment analysts would be limited to standard ways of getting information: checking corporate filings, debriefing industry experts, conducting conference calls with management, and the like.

Spies think differently. To find out what was going on with BigPharma, they might roll out a host of intelligence techniques. In a variation on the technique used to case the KPMG office in Bermuda, they might call the biggest hotel near the pharmaceutical company's headquarters, posing as potential customers, and check the dates when the hotel's ballroom might be available for an event. Which dates were free? Was the ballroom booked for a specific evening? Turning on the charm, they'd ask who had reserved it—was it the nearby pharmaceutical company? Could the pharmaceutical company be planning a party to celebrate the launch of a new product? *What's that date again?*

Then they might want to know what potential problems existed with the product. It's easy to set up an account with a job seekers' Web site like Monster.com. Posing as a potential employer, spies can set the software to show all the résumés available from people hoping to leave BigPharma. They can track how many employees of BigPharma put their résumés up on Monster.com every day. Over time, they can plot the results on a chart, and see when the number of people wanting to leave the company spikes. Are the employees looking to leave coming from the legal department? Or sales? If so, there might be a problem in that area.

To find out, the next step is to set up a dummy executive recruiting firm, and call the people who've put their résumés on the site, and offer interviews. Employees can be surprisingly candid

about their own company when they think they're interviewing for a job. They're being duped, of course, and there is no job being offered. But in the meantime, information about BigPharma changes hands.

This information exchange can run up against insider-trading laws, which prohibit trading securities based on material, nonpublic information. But many spies say that's not much of a problem: the employees talking to the fake executive recruiters are sometimes unaware of how much they're passing along. And later, while still employed by the company, they're unlikely to admit their disloyalty. What's more, the interviews are two or three steps removed from the Wall Street trader who buys or sells on the basis of the information. The trader himself may have no idea where the information came from.

Another way a spy can use a dummy corporation is to set up a fake documentary film company and call BigPharma's CEO for an interview. Many documentary films are produced by obscure firms and don't see the light of day for months, or even years, after filming. Both aspects of the process are handy for a spy: BigPharma's media relations people won't be surprised to be contacted by a small firm they've never heard of before. They might agree to the interview, and allow the phony film crew on company grounds, where the spies can film everything within camera range—labs, sales offices, documents, and more. And when the CEO sits for an interview, the makeup, bright lights, and flattering interviewer might put him off his guard. With cameras rolling, he may give far more information than he'd ever wanted to about the new product and its rollout date. Months later, the company's media representatives will have moved on to other projects, and may not stop to wonder why they never heard of that documentary film again.

It turns out that government-trained spies have all sorts of skills that are handy in the corporate arena, including surveillance, undercover operations, and the ability to blend in on the streets of a foreign country. Spies sell their services to investment firms,

companies checking up on their competitors, lawyers engaged in high-stakes litigation, corporate raiders trying to buy companies, and more.

Setting up shop in London, Baker was the only American among a crowd of former Scotland Yard investigators, former customs inspectors, and former intelligence agents like Day, all of whom were now in the private sector. Maxima's CEO played an avuncular role, schooling the two younger men on how to run a business. But after a few years, Baker and Day began to grow restless. Both men wanted to earn money—far more than their salaries at the time—and they knew that the only way to do that was to own their own firm. At the end of 2000, they quit Maxima to launch a new intelligence outfit: Diligence.

At first, Baker and Day scrambled to buy mobile phones and generate clients. They didn't have any start-up capital, but Baker recruited a former CIA colleague and Latin American specialist who had some family money to put into the nascent company. The little firm grew, soon hiring a hardworking researcher and a Russian investigator.

A few months after launching the firm, Day and Baker flew to Washington, D.C., trolling for high-powered lobbying and financial clients. Working their international intelligence contacts, they landed a meeting with the former U.S. ambassador to Germany, Richard Burt, who was then affiliated with the influential Republican lobbying firm Barbour Griffith and Rogers. Nursing a severe migraine headache that morning, Baker had to drag himself to a meeting at the firm's elegant headquarters on Pennsylvania Avenue. At the time, Barbour Griffith and Rogers represented some of the biggest companies in the world in scores of different industries, including Delta Airlines, GlaxoSmithKline, and Lockheed Martin. The automotive giant DaimlerChrysler alone was paying the firm $200,000 per year to steer it through the intricate Washington byways. Microsoft paid the firm more than $500,000 in fees that year.

Even so, Baker and Day cut the meeting short. They didn't see how the lobbying business, which was all about influencing the American government, meshed with what they were offering: global clandestine intelligence operations for corporate clients.

But Rick Burt did.

A few months later, Burt called Diligence, telling Day and Baker that his American lobbying firm wanted to buy a piece of their British spy firm. In his own career, Burt had seen how government experience could lead to lucrative business opportunities in lobbying and international finance. He'd gone from being a national security correspondent for the *New York Times* in the 1970s to a post at the State Department, leading to an appointment as ambassador to the Federal Republic of Germany from 1985 to 1989. One person who has known him for a long time says that Burt's career was helped tremendously by his second marriage, to Nancy Reagan's social secretary, Gayle Burt. Burt sat a few chairs away from President Ronald Reagan on June 12, 1987, as Reagan delivered a famous speech in Berlin: "Mr. Gorbachev, tear down this wall!"

At the end of the Reagan administration, Burt became the chief U.S. negotiator in the Strategic Arms Reduction Talks (START) with the former Soviet Union, and then decamped for the private sector and a partnership at the consulting firm McKinsey and Company.

Barbour Griffith and Rogers invested in Diligence. Suddenly, the little shop became an intercontinental firm. Burt stepped in as Diligence's chairman, although he kept his office at Barbour Griffith and Rogers. Burt's connections provided an entrée to the top of Washington society, but that access came at a cost. His abrasive style was legendary in Washington, and his verbal blunders caused some heartache for the growing company, which needed all the goodwill it could get. On occasion, for example, Burt would burst into rages at the lobbying firm. One person familiar with him says, "Rick Burt could be a very nasty piece of work."

Still, Diligence leveraged Burt's connections to its own benefit, becoming wired into the uppermost echelon of British and American business, politics, and intelligence. Eventually, Diligence's advisory board would include an astonishing array of heavy hitters:

- Judge William Webster, a former director of both the CIA and the FBI
- Michael Howard, a former leader of the Conservative Party in Britain
- Lord Charles Powell, former foreign affairs and defense adviser to the British prime minister Margaret Thatcher
- Ed Mathias, managing director of the enormous American private equity firm Carlyle Group, which specialized in buying and selling defense companies
- Thomas "Mack" McLarty, former chief of staff to President Bill Clinton
- Ed Rogers, chairman of Barbour Griffith and Rogers, a protégé of Republican political consultant Lee Atwater, and a veteran of the Reagan and the first Bush administrations.

The weave of interconnections between these men can be complicated. For example: Diligence's chairman Rick Burt has also served as a senior adviser to Ed Mathias's Carlyle Group; as a senior adviser to Mack McLarty's firm, Kissinger McLarty Associates; and as a senior advisory board member to Barbour Griffith and Rogers' client Alfa Bank, in Moscow.[2]

The overlapping relationships created a constant stream of business referrals and mutual assistance to a group of executives whose business affiliations and loyalties extend across national borders and around the world. The group was poised to take advantage of the new opportunities available in the global economy. In the coming years, Barbour Griffith and Rogers would represent clients from all over the world, including the governments of Equatorial Guinea, Eritrea, Honduras, Serbia, and Qatar. The business would

prove lucrative: Eritrea, a desperately poor country bordering Sudan in eastern Africa, for example, would sign a contract to pay the lobbying firm $65,000 per month for "strategic counsel and tactical planning" in Washington.[3]

FOR DILIGENCE, THE global network of connections paid off, and business started to accelerate. Through a contact who had formerly worked at the CIA, the Diligence team landed a high-paying assignment working for Enron, the Houston-based energy trading firm. Enron had spent years lobbying in state capitals and in Washington for energy deregulation, which would allow anyone to buy and sell electrical power just like other commodities. The huge company was politically well connected with the newly elected administration—President George W. Bush famously nicknamed his fellow Texan, Enron's CEO Kenneth Lay, "Kenny Boy"—and it was posting huge numbers. In July 2001, it reported earnings of $50.1 billion, more than triple the year before. But before long, those numbers, like much of the firm's operations, would prove nothing more than a mirage.

What no one knew at the time was that Enron was hiding more secrets than just its bogus accounting. Buried deep inside Enron was a corps of intelligence veterans, spies who reached out to Diligence for help vetting the companies that the energy giant wanted to acquire. But soon the Enron intelligence team had a much bigger idea. The company's traders could make more money if they could determine in advance when power plants would be turned off for maintenance.

Power plants can't run ceaselessly. Periodically, they have to be taken off-line for inspections and repairs. This maintenance is done at regular intervals, but not always with public notice. And when the plants go down, sometimes for days at a time, the price of electricity in an entire region can go up, following the time-tested laws of supply and demand. The less electricity in the market from the power plant, the more expensive the remaining electricity will be.

For an energy trader, advance notice of a power plant shutdown could be a powerful way to make money. Armed with a schedule, Enron traders could make bets in the energy markets based on nearly certain knowledge that electricity prices would rise, by how much they would increase, and when it would happen. These bets—a sure thing, in some cases—could be worth millions of dollars.

Enron approached Diligence with a proposition. It wanted to know when the power plants would be going on and off. Enron's intelligence officers had already developed a checklist of things a plant would do just before a shutdown. For one thing, plants tended to let the supply of coal on their property run low just before shutdown—no sense investing in expensive inventory that the plant wouldn't be using anytime soon. Also, even routine plant maintenance requires specialized employees to visit the facility. To accommodate them, plant owners frequently brought in portable toilets to set up around the grounds. And all those new workers require a place to stay. In the rural areas of Europe where power plants are frequently situated, the one or two local hotels were bound to be booked to capacity during the maintenance project.

For a spy, all these preparations are easy to detect. In late 2000 and 2001, Diligence set about gathering intelligence on as many as a dozen of continental Europe's biggest power plants. Baker won't say exactly where the plants were, but another person familiar with the operation recalls missions in France, the Netherlands, and Germany.

Baker decided that the best way to gather most of the information was from the air. So he hired small commercial aircraft typically used for mapping and surveying, and outfitted them with video cameras. Then he and his pilot flew over the plant, training their equipment on the telltale areas. *How high were the coal stacks? How did that height compare with last week? How many cars were in the workers' parking lot? More than usual?* Painstakingly, Baker overflew each location in a four-seat airplane, compiling the same kind of secret data that spies once recorded for contending governments—only now he

was doing so for one of the world's wealthiest companies.

Baker flew on many of the missions and dispatched lower-level Diligence employees on others. To avoid detection, he hired local planes and pilots in each country. Other pilots at the small airports he used might notice any foreigners hanging around. The last thing Baker wanted was pilots asking questions about the operation. As long as the locals saw the flights as a source of business, though, Baker figured that no one would worry too much about what or who they were for. After all, the operation was perfectly legal. Real estate developers, surveyors, and other specialists use aerial surveillance all the time. Baker and his pilots dutifully made sure that each day's flight plan was filed with government authorities.

Back in London, meanwhile, Diligence's team members manned the phones to gather the rest of the information they needed. Posing as potential customers, they called to book reservations in the hotels nearest the power plants they were targeting. Asking for room rates and availability weeks in advance, they could pinpoint when each hotel was at maximum capacity—or sold out. By trolling for "no vacancy" dates, they developed more data on when the maintenance was likely to happen.

Putting it all together, Diligence sent the raw data and video along to Enron's intelligence operatives, who worked out when the plants were going off-line and passed the information along to the traders doing battle in the energy markets. At first, Diligence passed along the details from every flight, but soon it settled on a system of weekly reports. Enron gained a crucial edge over the rest of the traders in the market. The work was done for a monthly retainer that represented a key, regular stream of income for Diligence. Baker declines to say how much Enron paid per month, and he says he has no idea how much money Enron made from the overflight information.

The nifty little scheme crashed to a halt in late 2001, as Enron itself collapsed into bankruptcy. Even with the moneymaking European spy flights, Enron's top executives had badly mismanaged the

company, steering revenues into numerous secret shell companies. As the firm began to unravel, Baker says he got a sudden call from his contact at Enron: "If you've got any bills outstanding with us," he said, "get them to me today, and I'll make sure you get paid."

THE LOSS OF Enron was a learning experience for the young spy firm. Baker says the message was clear: "There's a lot of information available out there." The key, he concluded, was to match a client who understands the value of information and an intelligence firm that has the wherewithal to go out and get it. And he took away one more thought: Diligence could have charged twenty times more for the information than it did. As he learned the value of information, Baker resolved not to undercut his own pricing again.

Over the next couple of years, Baker and Day traveled widely, rubbing elbows with some of the richest and most powerful people in the world. And they became close friends. Baker moved to Washington, D.C., to be near the lobbying firm Barbour Griffith and Rogers, which was still a major source of referrals for business.

By 2005, Diligence was eager to grow still further, and he was scouting around for investors to finance expansion. Ultimately, Burt provided an introduction to an Argentine private equity firm, the Exxel Group, run by a flashy buyout specialist, Juan Navarro, who was based in Buenos Aires. This Uruguayan-born investor cut a glamorous figure: he lived in a penthouse, cultivated expensive tastes, and was known for his aggressiveness. In 1991, he quit a successful career at Citibank's Argentine venture capital unit to launch his own firm, Exxel. He secured investments from GE Pension Trust, Rockefeller and Company, Liberty Mutual, and Columbia University, and began investing billions in nearly 100 companies, mostly concentrated in Latin America.

During the course of negotiations with Exxel, Baker began to feel uncomfortable about the future of Diligence. The new cash would mean big-time expansion, and new management responsibilities

for himself and Day. He says now that he was worried and felt it might be better to bring on a professional CEO who would have the experience to expand the company without wasting money. Baker disclosed to his colleagues and prospective investors such as Exxel Group that he wouldn't stay on board much longer.

Exxel Group invested in Diligence, reportedly taking a $15 million stake in it. Baker cashed out, selling his remaining 15 percent stake in Diligence to Exxel as part of the transaction. Barbour Griffith and Rogers cashed out, too. No one involved will reveal the exact numbers regarding who got what. But even if the deal valued Diligence at a relatively small amount of money, it's likely that Baker walked away from the deal with more than $1 million in cash, a tidy profit from his five-year involvement with the company.

Now it would be up to Day, running Diligence on his own, to deploy the remaining money and generate the kind of growth his new investors were expecting. Soon, his attention would turn to a new client that Baker had been working hard to sign just before leaving the firm, Russia's largest commercial bank, Alfa Bank. Alfa was already a client of the lobbying firm Barbour Griffith and Rogers, which in 2005 received $680,000 in fees from Alfa.

What's more, the lobbyists disclosed in federal filings that they didn't do any lobbying at all that year for Alfa. That's a lot of money to pay a lobbying firm that's not doing any lobbying. Often, lobbying firms are paid not to lobby—the technical definition of which is contacting public officials on behalf of a client—but to "consult," which means simply to provide advice to the client about how to handle Washington.*

Before he left Diligence, Baker says, he pushed the lobbyists

---

*That seems like a fine point, but it is a distinction with a difference. "Lobbying" expenses are required by law to be disclosed publicly. "Consulting" fees can remain private. There are many in Washington's lobbying community who argue that as much as 50 percent of all influence-peddling fees are hidden from public disclosure through the use of this loophole. If so, that would make Washington's lobbying business a nearly $6 billion industry.

to provide an introduction to Alfa. The huge Russian bank would make a great client for Diligence. Barbour Griffith and Rogers made the connection, and soon after that, Nick Day was in Bermuda fetching KPMG's documents out from under rocks.

The anonymous document drop at KPMG in October 2005 put a stop to that operation. On November 10, 2005, KPMG Financial Advisory Services filed suit against Diligence, alleging fraud.[4] But the legal complaint filed by KPMG was heavily censored. Page after page of the publicly available version of the document was left blank, simply stamped "REDACTED" in bold letters.

Perhaps the complaint was so heavily shielded from view because the company feared letting even more sensitive details of the case into the open. But perhaps, too, KPMG held back so much of its filing because the company was embarrassed at how easily an employee had been duped out of its most secret corporate work product. After all, KPMG is one of the world's largest accounting and consulting firms. It routinely handles the deepest secrets of the biggest companies in the world. What would its clients think if they knew those documents could leak out to corporate spies?

Indeed, the entire case was filed under seal, and it wasn't until months later that any of the documents began to surface into public view. At Barbour Griffith and Rogers, the move to release the documents set off panic. The prestigious firm didn't want the public or the press to know that it had been involved in the spy game.

On January 24, 2006, the firm's lead lobbyist on the Alfa account, Keith Schuette, sent an e-mail to his boss, the legendary Washington fixer Ed Rogers. Under the subject heading "Legal," Schuette wrote, "Ed: Judge has unsealed the complaint against Diligence from KPMG. It has attracted no attention thus far, but I cannot imagine that it will remain quiet forever. Neither we, nor the client are mentioned in the complaint. Current strategy if it comes alive in the press [is] for Diligence to stonewall. Will keep you posted."

"What does it say??" responded Rogers, twenty minutes later.

"Basically that KPMG was harmed by Diligence stealing materials under false pretenses etc. . . . and that they must cease and desist," wrote Schuette. "Critical issue now is KPMG's request for expedited discover[y] and judge ruling on the question of jurisdiction. If the judge accepts jurisdiction and agrees to expedited discovery, things will deteriorate in very short order. If he goes against both, then it should die a fairly quiet death."

The judge did accept jurisdiction, and permitted discovery. That is the process by which lawyers obtain testimony and documents from the other side in a legal battle. Lawyers can force documents, records, e-mails, and other material from the opponent's files onto the record. That's how Schuette's e-mail later ended up as part of the court record.

And the Diligence case did not die a quiet death.

AFTER PROJECT YUCCA imploded, Nick Day closed the Connecticut Avenue offices of Diligence, LLC, in Washington in exchange for much more modest digs. He moved his own residence to the picturesque French Alpine town of Saint-Gervais, which is only an hour's drive from Switzerland. He is still in business, although he says that fallout from the Bermuda incident—which included recriminations, resignations, and lawsuits—taught him a lesson. He and his firm have changed their ways in its aftermath. "We essentially help businesses deal with the risks of operating in challenging markets," Day says. "It's a role which government agencies don't necessarily have the resources or understanding to be able to fulfill."

Mike Baker, who left the firm well before the Bermuda operation, bounced around at other corporate intelligence firms, for a time running Prescience LLC, his own private intelligence firm serving hedge fund clients. He took on work as a Hollywood script consultant on intelligence matters and writes commentaries for FoxNews.com. He says he is working on a book. In early 2009, though, he and Day

went back into business together for the first time in years. Day's firm, Diligence, purchased Baker's firm, Prescience, and Mike Baker went to work in Diligence's New York offices at 7 Times Square.

These days, Guy Enright is working for Deloitte and Touche in London. He didn't come away empty-handed from his encounters with Nick Day. As Project Yucca wound down in 2005, Day, still in the guise of Nick Hamilton, gave Enright a Rolex watch worth thousands of dollars. Enright was led to believe it was a thank-you gift from the British government.

But that, too, was a lie.

It has never been clear who, exactly, owns Diligence, especially since several investors and owners have come and gone over the years. Day refuses to reveal who owns the spy company today. But one possible source of financial backing is one of the oldest banking families in the world, the Rothschilds.

In the spring of 2007, the British and American press reported that Diligence had received an infusion of an unknown amount of capital from a fund controlled by Nick Day's longtime friend Nathaniel Rothschild, then thirty-six years old, the wealthy son of Lord Jacob Rothschild and heir to one of the world's most famous and ancient banking fortunes. The *New York Times* once called Nathaniel "the man who may become the richest Rothschild."

By 2007, Day had become a close associate of Nathaniel Rothschild. The two men had a lot in common: they were roughly the same age, both British, and both high-living businessmen who thrived on global intrigue. The friendship was a sign of just how far Nick Day had risen, professionally and socially. Through Rothschild, Day gained entrée to a family that had long dominated European banking, and had figured out—hundreds of years earlier—the value of marrying business and intelligence.

Nathaniel is in line to become a baron, and thus the fifth in a line of Lord Rothschilds. His family's history dates back to 1744,

with the birth of Mayer Amschel Rothschild in the Jewish ghetto of Frankfurt, Germany. His roots are in England, but Rothschild maintains offices and a spectacular home in New York. He travels around the world on a private plane. Rothschild, who is known to friends as Nat, was born on July 12, 1971.

Nat's ancestor Mayer Rothschild founded a financial house, and then a family dynasty, sending his five sons to five different European capitals to open financial offices of their own. When he reached age twenty-one, Mayer's son Nathan went to England: first to Manchester, and then to London, where in 1809 he opened offices at New Court in St. Swithin's Lane that to this day serve as headquarters for the bank that bears his name. By the 1820s, Rothschild was prosperous enough to lend capital to the Bank of England, heading off a potential economic crash in London.

From their earliest days, the Rothshilds understood the importance of combining finance and intelligence. Nathanial coordinated high-stakes financial deals with his four brothers on the continent, who were based in France, Italy, Austria, and Germany. Through couriers, clients, and confidants, they developed an elaborate intelligence network that spread across Europe. Nathan Rothschild arranged for money to be shipped to the duke of Wellington's armies during their epic battle against Napoleon. In 1815, Rothschild knew of Wellington's spectacular defeat of Napoleon at Waterloo an entire day before the British government itself was informed.

In 1875, Nathan's son Lionel raised enough capital for the British government to acquire a major interest in the Suez Canal. And in 1885, Nathan Mayer Rothschild II became Baron Rothschild. Over the next fifty years, the family grew and prospered, branching into railroads, mining, and science. Two branches of the family in France became active in the wine industry, founding Château Mouton Rothschild, which produces one of the world's finest clarets; and Château Lafite Rothschild, which produces elite *premier cru* wines.

Nat is the only son of four children. He attended Eton and

Wadham College, Oxford. An extremely privileged young college student, he joined the Bullingdon Club, a rowdy all-male drinking society.

After college in 1995, he began his career in New York at Gleacher and Company, whose founder was a friend of Lord Rothschild. The same year, Nat married the socialite Annabelle Neilson, but their riotous relationship ended in divorce three years later. While in New York, Rothschild met Timothy Barakett, then just twenty-nine and a few years older than Nat. Barakett was raising money for a new hedge fund, Atticus Capital. He eventually made the young Rothschild a partner in his fund and set him loose to leverage the Rothschild family name and connections to raise money for Atticus. Nat bore down on business, and the fund achieved astonishing success until the crash of 2008, which hit Atticus, and scores of hedge funds like it, very hard.

Still, Barakett had leaped to the top of the hedge fund universe, ranking number seven in the trade publication *Alpha* magazine's survey of the best paid fund managers of 2007, with a personal take of $750 million. Another partner at Atticus, David Slager, ranked number thirteen, with single-year earnings of $450 million. Rothschild himself tied for thirty-eighth place, earning $250 million that year. In 2007, the reporter Landon Thomas Jr. of the *New York Times* quoted Peter Munk, the founder and chairman of Barrick Gold, who overcame his early skepticism and agreed to Nat's entreaties to invest in Atticus. "This kid is special," Munk told the *Times*. "It's back to when they were ruling the world."

The Rothschilds of old bestrode the globe and saw political leaders come to them for money. Nat Rothschild continues that tradition today, maintaining houses in Paris, London, Moscow, and Greece. He's said to be an adviser to the Russian oligarch Oleg Deripaska, who controls the Russian company Rusal, the world's largest aluminum company. In March 2008, Rothschild and his father hosted the Republican presidential candidate John McCain at a fund-raiser at Spencer House on Saint James's Place in London,

the lavish estate built for the ancestors of Princess Diana. Under American campaign law, foreigners can't contribute to presidential candidates, but they can host events. For the invited American donors, attendance at the Rothschild fund-raiser cost between $1,000 and the campaign maximum, $2,300.

With connections like that, Nick Day and the corporate intelligence industry he represents have circled back to a much earlier era in which private business interests deployed their own intelligence networks around the globe. And although today's corporate spies have the technology and techniques of modern espionage at their fingertips, their history is deeply interwoven with the history of capitalism itself.

PART I

From Bogus Island to Deep Chocolate

Chapter Two

A High and Honorable Calling

The story of American private intelligence begins with Allan Pinkerton, a Scottish immigrant, an American patriot, and a dogged entrepreneur who used fists, brains, and force of personality to build an empire. In the mid-nineteenth century, 27-year-old Allan Pinkerton came to the United States with his young wife, Joan, to escape the desperate poverty and unstable politics of ghetto life in Glasgow, Scotland. The couple settled in Dundee, Illinois, a dairy farming outpost on America's rapidly growing western frontier partway between Chicago and Milwaukee, Wisconsin. The town was founded by Scottish immigrants searching for work, land, and a future.

Allan and Joan survived a dangerous Atlantic crossing and shipwreck on Sable Island near Halifax, Canada; endured the theft of Joan's precious wedding ring by Indians; and worked their way across the country by boat and horse and wagon before arriving in Dundee. By 1846, Allan, a cooper by trade, had set up a barrel-making shop and employed eight men. It was good, honest work, and by any standard, Allan was a success.

One June morning, he set out by small boat for a set of islands in the Fox River, where he spent the day chopping wood to supply his small business. Making his way through the forest, Pinkerton

stumbled upon a burned-out fire pit deep in the woods, well beyond where any people should be. Something felt wrong, as if the people who had been there were hiding. His curiosity piqued, Pinkerton decided to return under cover of night to see who had been there—and what they were up to.

Crouched in the weeds, Pinkerton staked out the site. Before very long, he saw several men arrive by boat and set up a campfire. It didn't look good—a group of men this far from town must be up to something illegal or dangerous. Pinkerton returned to town and alerted the sheriff, Luther Dearborn. The mysterious campers turned out to be a group of counterfeiters. Together with a posse of men, Pinkerton and the sheriff returned to the site several nights later and arrested the entire band of criminals. At the site, they recovered a bag of tools and fake coins. Thereafter, the little patch of land was known as Bogus Island.

For Pinkerton, it was a transformational moment. Catching the counterfeiters showed his neighbors, and maybe Pinkerton himself, that he had the curiosity, patience, and intelligence of a natural investigator. Pinkerton would go on to become the world's first great private detective, and set up an agency that would bear his name and provide investigative and intelligence services to the biggest companies of his day. Pinkerton would, in many ways, invent the role of the private detective, and he served as a forerunner of today's corporate intelligence operatives.*

AFTER THE ARRESTS at Bogus Island, Pinkerton became a local celebrity. Gossips would stop by his barrel-making shop just to hear him tell the story of how he'd caught the crooks. Before long, his tale came to the attention of Henry Hunt, a general store manager in Dundee. Hunt and a shopkeeper named Increase Bosworth

---

*His tale is expertly told in James Mackay, *Allan Pinkerton: The First Private Eye* (Edinburgh: Mainstream, 1996). Mackay's account is the most comprehensive of the many biographies of Pinkerton, and it is relied on extensively here.

were worried about another ring of counterfeiters who had been passing bad notes in the area, defrauding local businessmen. The two prevailed upon Pinkerton to take on a job for them in the "detective line," as they called it.

Pinkerton agreed, and his new partners gave him what details they had. A man who had just passed a bum $10 note was having his saddle repaired at a nearby harness shop. Pinkerton, still dressed for work as a cooper, headed for the saddle shop to see what he could find out. The shop owner tipped Pinkerton off to the identity of the customer who had passed the $10 bill, and Pinkerton strolled up to him, pretending to admire his horse. He also took careful note of the stranger: gray hair, gray eyes, about sixty-five years old, gold ring on his left hand. Pinkerton struck up a conversation with him, trying to give the impression of being the kind of guy who might be a useful recruit for a shady operation. The stranger, intrigued, invited Pinkerton for a chat outside town, where no one else could hear it. He said he was John Craig, from Vermont, and he asked about Pinkerton's background and occupation. Craig thought Pinkerton might make a good pass-through for the dummy money operation, and he offered to give Pinkerton fifty $10 bills in exchange for $125 in real money.

Pinkerton scrambled back to the storekeepers for the cash. He turned it over to Craig, who left the fake bills for him to pick up later under a rock. Now Pinkerton knew that there was a counterfeit ring, and what the going rate was for the bills. But he needed to catch Craig with the bills on his person in order to make an arrest. He set up another deal, for a $4,000 purchase to be made in the lobby of the Sauganash Hotel* in Chicago. At the right instant, Pinkerton made a prearranged signal, and the local Cook County sheriff charged into the room and collared Craig.

Word of the successful undercover operation and arrest landed

---

*A little more than a decade earlier, the new town of Chicago had elected its first trustees at a meeting held in the same hotel.

Pinkerton the job of deputy sheriff of Kane County, where he worked part-time while continuing his barrel-making business. But he wasn't destined to stay a cooper much longer. In 1847, William Church, the sheriff of Cook County, offered Pinkerton a chance to move to Chicago and become deputy sheriff there. Allan and Joan Pinkerton moved to the bustling young city.

Pinkerton thrived in Chicago. The city was growing at an astonishing rate as thousands of new immigrants from Europe and the East Coast were pushing its city boundaries out into what had once been a rural landscape. In just over three years, Pinkerton became one of the most legendary lawmen in town. In 1849, Mayor Levi Boon appointed him as Chicago's first—and only—detective. It was a tough world, and law enforcement officers were called to use their fists and boots in the pursuit of a rough sort of street justice that could keep the straining city under some sort of control.

Next, Pinkerton jumped from the police force to a job at the U.S. Post Office, where he worked solving petty crimes as a mail agent. At the post office, he went undercover again, posing as a mail sorter to help nail a postal worker who had absconded with $3,738 in cash stolen from inside letters. The criminal and his brother turned out to be nephews of none other than the postmaster of Chicago himself. When the news hit the papers, Pinkerton was singled out for high praise as the best detective in the country.

Press like that can change a career, and that's what happened to Pinkerton. In 1850, he quit government service and set up a private agency with a lawyer as his partner. They called it the North-Western Detective Agency and opened a small office at the corner of Washington and Dearborn in downtown Chicago. The business began slowly and had its troubles. For one thing, historians believe that Pinkerton ousted his partner, Edward Rucker, within a year of starting the firm. But over time it became successful, and eventually it became a private intelligence juggernaut. By then, it was renamed Pinkerton's National Detective Agency. The firm would

no longer bill itself as a creature of Chicago—Allan Pinkerton signaled his national ambitions in the letterhead of his company.

In the 1850s, laws were enforced locally, county by county. There was no FBI, and the federal government didn't have much ability to track criminals from one state to another.* With the sprawling western frontier attracting all sorts of rogues and scoundrels, and improvements to transportation making it possible for them to commit crimes in county after county as they moved west, there was a desperate need for a police force. That's what the Pinkerton agency became.

But the agency didn't work for the taxpayers. Pinkerton was an intelligence agency that worked for corporate clients and wealthy individuals. It went after criminals who were causing the most damage to the biggest companies of the day: railroads, mining concerns, telegraph services. Pinkerton wasn't as concerned about crimes against people as he was concerned about crimes against property. The company's logo, a human eye above the slogan "We Never Sleep" inspired the term "private eye," still used today.

PINKERTON SOON LANDED the biggest names in business as his clients. He went to work for the American Express Company, which was beginning to transport packages containing all sorts of valuables on specially designed fast railcars. He worked for the Pennsylvania Railroad, just one of several rail clients whose nationwide scope helped push the Pinkerton name across the continent. And he worked for Western Union, which was establishing a cross-continental communications network of telegraph stations.

For the express companies, the Pinkertons tracked down stolen packages and the crooks who swiped them. For the railroads, they hunted stickup artists on the western frontier. And for the telegraph

---

*The seeds of the FBI would be sown in 1908, when President Theodore Roosevelt authorized the creation of a small corps of special agents, under the auspices of the attorney general. The new agency was named the Bureau of Investigation.

companies, they busted white-collar criminals who sent bogus information over the wires to Wall Street as part of an elaborate insider trading scheme.

In 1871, the U.S. Department of Justice outsourced much of its investigative work for the year to the Pinkertons on a $50,000 contract. The firm grew so large and successful that its mission, tactics, and organization ultimately became the inspiration for the U.S. Secret Service and the FBI itself.

For their time, the Pinkerton detectives aggressively deployed new technology and centralized information-collection techniques. Photography had been invented as recently as 1840, and Pinkerton grasped how the technology could be used in fighting crime. He invented the mug shot, and his agents were clever in getting pictures of crooks across the country. Once, they got a notorious criminal so drunk at a saloon that a bartender on the Pinkerton payroll took his picture as he slumped against the bar and grinned sloppily for the camera. That picture was soon circulated across the country and used to identify the man.

The Pinkertons understood the edge that the telegraph gave them in sending coded information across state lines. But it also gave corporate crooks new avenues for thievery.* One case set a new standard for technological innovation—and financial corruption. In 1864, a stockbroker in California was arrested for conspiring to tap telegraph lines to intercept news before it hit the markets in order to arbitrage the insider information. The *Sacramento Daily Union* of Friday morning, August 12, 1864, detailed the scheme under the headline: "Tapping the Wires for Stock Operations." A well-known stockbroker, D. C. Williams, checked into a hotel in the small gold rush town of Placerville, California, early that summer. The State Telegraph Company had offices in the same hotel, and Williams, an expert in telegraph technology, intercepted

---

*Journalists, too, were seduced by the temptation to cheat via telegraph. In his book *The Eavesdroppers* (1959), Sam Dash wrote that reporters at the *San Francisco Call* in 1899 alleged that rivals at the *San Francisco Examiner* were tapping telephone lines to steal scoops.

the messages simply by hearing the clattering of the telegraph machine and mentally deciphering the long-dash and short-dash code. That gave him advance notice of the goings-on in the region. He used the information to develop invaluable insights into upcoming corporate events that would set off gyrations in the stock market. This was enough to let him make plenty of money through insider trading on the tidbits of information that came his way. But Williams had an even more elaborate plan in mind: to bribe the telegraph agent in exchange for help intercepting information on the outcome of a crucial mining lawsuit in the Nevada Territory.

Williams planned to take over the telegraph controls when the news came through. He'd know the result of the case—and which company's stock price would soon surge—and he'd be able to keep the news from being passed on to San Francisco long enough to buy and sell the appropriate shares before anyone else knew the outcome. With his finger on the telegraph key, Williams could send fake messages down the line as he wished.

Meanwhile, the telegraph agent would help by cutting the lines to the east, preventing any messages from getting through that might tip off telegraph operators that something was up. Williams offered the man a healthy sum and an incentive bonus for his work: at least $300 if the stock scam failed, and between $700 and $1,000 if it succeeded. In today's dollars, that would be a payment of more than $20,000 for a successful outcome.

Unfortunately for Williams, the telegraph operator was an honest man who went to his boss with details of the plot. Alerted to the swindle, police investigators found letters from Williams to coconspirators in San Francisco and Virginia City, Nevada. In one missive, Williams predicted that the group could make more than $80,000 on the deal—a staggering sum in those days.

"We ought to make enough on this one thing to lay by for years to come, if necessary," he wrote. And there was no end to how many times the conspirators could pull off the scheme: "Whenever an important decision is hereafter to be given anywheres throughout the

country, we can do the same thing." The nationwide insider trading scheme never came to pass: Williams was arrested on misdemeanor charges, was unable to post bail of $2,000, and was put in jail.[1]

Williams's telegraph swindle was a rare case in which the local police made the bust on their own. But it was just the sort of new, continent-spanning crime against companies and financiers that the Pinkertons were suited to detect. In most cases, local police forces were overwhelmed by the sophistication of corporate thieves, and couldn't handle crimes beyond their jurisdiction.

The Pinkertons, by contrast, had unprecedented access to rail travel through their connections at the railroad companies. They could move around the country in ways that no force before had been able to do. They hired female detectives, a progressive move for the day, and used them to infiltrate society salons where bumbling male detectives could not go. They collected detailed files on every criminal they came across, establishing physical descriptions, habits, modus operandi, and other details for every man they tracked. The filing system was so thorough and contained so many names that for some crimes the Pinkertons could simply cross-reference a witness's description with the type of crime and pull together a list of suspects to round up. The Pinkerton corporate files from the years 1853 to 1999 are now at the Library of Congress in Washington, D.C. They consist of an astonishing 63,000 items.

Pinkerton developed a code of ethics for his operatives, to establish the boundaries of the work the company would do, and the clients it would work for. Some of the same ethical dilemmas Pinkerton was attempting to stave off still recur in today's private intelligence outfits. In his "General Principles," written in the 1850s, Pinkerton wrote that the role of a detective is "a high and honorable calling." He laid out some rules to help keep it that way:

The Agency will not represent a defendant in a criminal case except with the knowledge and consent of the prosecutor; they will not shadow jurors or investigate public officials

in the performance of their duties, or trade-union members in their lawful union activities; they will not accept employment from one political party against another; they will not report union meetings unless the meetings are open to the public without restriction; they will not work for vice crusaders; they will not accept contingent fees, gratuities or rewards; the Agency will never investigate the morals of a woman unless in connection with another crime, nor will it handle cases of divorce or a scandalous nature.

Pinkerton's modern-day successors have broken nearly every one of these rules. Pinkerton's own agency sometimes found the rules hard to follow, especially those regarding unions, and the agency became a combatant in the epic battles between labor and capital during the late nineteenth century. Despite their pro-union rules, the Pinkertons would come to be seen as the enemies of the labor movement in the United States.

OVER TIME, ALLAN Pinkerton became an expert in every type of crime that afflicted his corporate and individual clients. His book *Thirty Years a Detective* (1884)* is divided into chapters detailing the criminals he saw, including "the society thief," "hotel thieves," "steamboat operators," "confidence and blackmail," and something he called "the Boodle Game," in which con men sent anonymous letters enticing their targets to engage in financial shenanigans.†

---

*Pinkerton wrote more than fifteen books, including memoirs of his own exploits and pulp-style detective novels. He is said to have employed a squad of ghostwriters to churn out these books, which also served as publicity for the Pinkerton image. In his books, detectives were typically heroic, criminals nefarious, and clients innocent victims. They had titles like *Strikers, Communists, Tramps, and Detectives* (1878), *The Spy of the Rebellion* (1884), and *Cornered at Last: A Detective Story* (1892).

†The author Dashiell Hammett was a Pinkerton agent from 1915 to 1921, and he relied on his experiences in the agency to create the legendary fictional private detective Sam Spade in the novel *The Maltese Falcon*. Spade became the ultimate celluloid detective when he was played by Humphrey Bogart in the famous film version of *The Maltese Falcon*, but

The boodle game seems to have been a forerunner of the Nigerian e-mail scams of today. People who'd been suckered into losing money on the schemes were often so embarrassed that they didn't report the crime to the police.

The Pinkerton Agency battled corporate thieves, stalked bank robbers, and chased Butch Cassidy and the Sundance Kid and the Jesse James gang across the Wild West. During the Civil War, Pinkerton agents foiled an early attempt to assassinate President Lincoln and sent spies into the Confederacy to monitor its military strength and political developments. One of Pinkerton's agents, Timothy Webster, was hanged in Richmond in 1862 as a Union spy. He was the first American executed for espionage in nearly 100 years.

Pinkerton was already at the height of his powers in the 1850s when he sent undercover agents to nail Nathan Maroney, manager of the Montgomery, Alabama, office of the Adams Express Company, which transported goods by railcar. In 1855, Pinkerton received a strange letter from Edward Sanford, an executive at Adams. Sanford told Pinkerton that $40,000 had been stolen from a company pouch somewhere between Montgomery, Alabama, and Augusta, Georgia. Sanford's letter included key details of the company's own internal investigation, including that the leather bag containing the money had been locked when the cash went missing. With nothing to go on but the details contained in the letter, Pinkerton made an educated guess that the thief was Maroney, who would have had access to Adams's pouch keys. He mailed back his hunch.

Sanford summoned Pinkerton to Alabama and told the detective that he'd already had Maroney arrested and charged with theft. But the company had nothing other than circumstantial evidence against him, and the arrest caused an uproar among the leading citizens of Montgomery, who supported Maroney. After

the character had his roots in genuine Pinkerton exploits. Hammett didn't stay with the Pinkertons long. He grew disillusioned with what he saw as the Pinkertons' antilabor strikebreaking efforts and quit the agency.

all, Adams Express was a Yankee company and this was the eve of the Civil War. Maroney was a local man, and he had local support. He got out on bail. The situation was verging on disaster for Adams Express.

Pinkerton brought in a five-person team, including Kate Warne, who is widely credited with being the nation's first woman detective.* The group suspected that Maroney had stashed the money in a safe place until the heat blew over. They needed to figure out where the money was and prove that Maroney had stolen it. They tailed Maroney's wife as she dropped off a letter to Philadelphia, which tipped them off that she had relatives in that area. When she relocated to the outskirts of Philadelphia, Pinkerton dispatched agents to Jenkintown, Pennsylvania. One operative set up a watch-repair shop in the village as a cover operation and began gathering information on the Maroney family's activities.

Pinkerton sent in Kate Warne, posing as a society wife. Supplied with a lavish wardrobe, she played her part to the hilt, and wangled an introduction to Mrs. Maroney. Over the course of their chats, Warne pretended to confide in her, claiming that her own husband had gotten rich as a counterfeiter.

Meanwhile, Pinkerton maneuvered to have authorities rearrest Maroney, and when they did, Pinkerton placed an operative, John White, undercover in the same jail cell, ostensibly charged with forgery. Pinkerton then unleashed an elaborate scheme of psychological warfare against the hapless, imprisoned Maroney. An undercover agent was assigned to court Mrs. Maroney in Jenkintown, and to make sure he was seen with her in public. Pinkerton began to barrage Maroney, still in jail in Alabama, with anonymous letters claiming that his wife was having an affair. On her next visit to the

---

*Rumors have long circulated that Warne—an attractive widow—and Pinkerton were romantically involved. There seems to be no proof of this except that Warne was the first female detective Pinkerton hired, and she traveled the country with him for years while his wife and children stayed home in Chicago. Pinkerton praised her as one of his best detectives, saying, "Mrs. Warne never let me down." When she died, Pinkerton buried her in his family plot. His own grave is close by.

prison, Mrs. Maroney admitted she'd been out with the stranger, confirming Maroney's darkest suspicions.

Sitting right there in the jail cell was Pinkerton's operative John White, ready to serve as a shoulder for Maroney to cry on over his wife's supposed infidelity. White hinted to Maroney that it was possible to bribe the authorities to get out of jail early, and when White's "lawyer"—another of Pinkerton's actors—showed up to release him, Maroney took the bait. He begged White to help him get out, too, no matter how much it cost. Maroney was desperate to reach his wife. White agreed to help once he'd gotten out of jail, and he encouraged Maroney to get word to his wife that he'd need the stolen cash for bribe money. Maroney sent a message to his wife to dig up the money from its hiding place and give it to White, who Maroney thought would bring it to Alabama and help arrange his release from prison.

When she got the message, Mrs. Maroney wasn't sure that the scheme was a good idea. After all, Maroney was under suspicion of theft, and getting caught with the cash might seal his fate. But Pinkerton had foreseen that Mrs. Maroney might balk, and had a plan to encourage her along. The anxious woman turned to her new best friend and asked what to do. Kate Warne advised her that paying the money was the best plan. The couple could head out west with their booty, and escape the Alabama authorities.

When Mrs. Maroney handed the money over to White, only $400 of the total amount stolen was missing.

In late 1855, Maroney went on trial in Montgomery, White never having returned to release him. He was shocked to see White called to the stand to testify against him. Realizing he'd been set up and the state had all the evidence it needed to convict him, Maroney pleaded guilty, and was sentenced to ten years in prison. Adams Express put the Pinkertons on an annual retainer, and the Maroney case led to a wealth of new business for Pinkerton.

As THE NATION collapsed into the Civil War, the Pinkerton Agency was the premier intelligence operation in the country. It had a nationwide force in place, and had developed unparalleled investigative techniques. An avowed abolitionist who worked to spirit escaped slaves to Canada, Pinkerton even helped raise money for the militant antislavery agitator John Brown's escape from lawmen. When hostilities broke out in 1861, Pinkerton was well positioned and motivated to serve the Union. He knew President Lincoln—who, as a lawyer and budding politician, had drawn up Pinkerton's contract with the Illinois Central railroad in 1855—and he was close to an energetic young railroad executive named George McClellan.

When McClellan reentered military service (he had once been at West Point) to lead the Ohio state volunteers, he summoned Pinkerton to his side as the head of a military "secret service." In those days, there was no separate intelligence service, and individual military leaders gathered battlefield and political intelligence on their own. Using the nom de guerre "E. J. Allen," since by then "Pinkerton" had become almost synonymous in the public imagination with detective work, the great investigator entered military service.

There's no question that Pinkerton was an American patriot and a true believer in the Union cause. He'd put his career and life on the line more than once to help slaves escape to freedom. But much like his contemporary successors, Pinkerton was a private intelligence contractor who found war a profitable business. In his comprehensive history *The Eye That Never Sleeps* (1982), Frank Morn notes that Pinkerton earned what was then a princely sum of $38,567 for his government work between September 1861 and November 1862. After the war, he wrote in a letter to his son that he had been relatively poor before combat began, but that during the war, he "amassed considerable money, which was all invested in property of one kind or another in Chicago."

To this day, selling private intelligence services to the

government in wartime can be a profitable enterprise. An entire industry has evolved around it, and many of these enterprises have headquarters outside Washington, D.C., where the other "Beltway bandits" set up shop selling services to the feds. Among the intelligence contractors of today are well-known names such as Booz Allen Hamilton, with 19,000 employees and more than $4 billion in annual revenue, which depends on consulting work for the U.S. intelligence community. At the other end of the scale is the relatively small corporation Abraxas, which, the *Los Angeles Times* revealed in 2006, creates fake identities and dummy companies for undercover CIA employees around the world. Some of today's intelligence contractors have gotten into trouble. The CEO of an obscure contractor, MZM, was found in 2005 to have paid more than $1 million in illegal bribes to a powerful congressman in exchange for classified contracts. And the role of the security contractor Blackwater drew attention during congressional hearings in 2007 on the conduct of the firm's employees in Iraq, who had been accused of murdering innocent civilians.

But first there was Pinkerton.

AFTER LINCOLN WAS elected president of the United States in November 1860, planning began for his triumphal journey from Illinois to the capital. Cities all along the rail route offered the president-elect the chance to speak to large, adoring crowds. But the route was scheduled to go south from Philadelphia to Baltimore, Maryland—an area with thousands of people, known as copperheads, who sympathized with the South. At that moment, it wasn't clear whether Maryland would end up in the Union or as a Confederate state. Debate raged in the state capital at Annapolis. Lincoln would have to traverse this dicey geography on his way farther south to Washington, D.C. Samuel Morse Felton, the president of the Pennsylvania Central Railroad, was in charge of organizing the logistics of the trip, including arranging for special presidential

trains and setting schedules. He called on Allan Pinkerton, saying he'd heard that Maryland's secessionists were planning violent reprisals if the state voted to stay in the Union.

Pinkerton put together a plan to protect the president-elect. James Mackay has laid out the detailed preparations in his book *Allan Pinkerton: The First Private Eye.* The Pennsylvania Railroad organized rail workers and drilled them as a kind of a railway militia. Concerned that copperheads would try to burn train bridges, the workers covered the bridges with coats of fresh paint and fireproof materials. Felton sent men to infiltrate the Maryland militia, to figure out which units might stay loyal and which tilted toward the Confederacy.

Meanwhile, Pinkerton sent in a top team of detectives, including Timothy Webster, Hattie Lawton, and Pinkerton's own assistant, Harry Davies. Pinkerton trawled the bars of Baltimore using an undercover alias—"J. H. Hutcheson" of Charleston, South Carolina— looking to identify copperheads and their supporters. At the same time, Davies befriended one transplanted southerner during nights of carousing at Anne Travise's house of prostitution in Baltimore. The man bragged to Davies that he was plotting with a recent immigrant to assassinate President-Elect Lincoln as his train rolled through town. Webster enlisted undercover in the Confederate militia, and heard that it, too, was planning an assassination.

This was enough to convince the team that Lincoln would be in real danger as he passed through Baltimore. Eventually, Pinkerton and his team ferreted out the details of the plot—a small band of men would strike at the Calvert Street train depot. Lincoln heard similar rumors of a plot against him from law enforcement agents as well, and weighed whether to travel to Baltimore as planned or skip the city on his way from Harrisburg, Pennsylvania, to Washington, D.C. As Lincoln's train left Harrisburg, the American Telegraph Company cut all the telegraph lines running out of the city. That shut down communication into and out of Harrisburg, but it also prevented any southern spies from alerting colleagues in Philadelphia and Baltimore that the president-elect was on the move.

Pinkerton knew that the presidential train would be an irresistible target. He decided to bring Lincoln to Washington ahead of schedule on a regular passenger train, instead, and roll the presidential train though on its regular timing as a decoy. Incredibly, he left Mary Todd Lincoln and her sons aboard the decoy train. Perhaps that was to lend a sense of realism to the procession, or maybe this was simply an era in which no one could contemplate that the assassins might strike at a woman and children.

The undercover Pinkerton agent Kate Warne rented the two rear sleeping cabins of the regular southbound passenger train out of West Philadelphia, telling ticket agents that she needed to transport her brother, who she claimed was an invalid. Felton and a small squad of Pinkertons spirited Lincoln into the cabin. Allan Pinkerton stood by Lincoln's door, and handed the tickets to the train conductor, never revealing who was in the cabin with him.

Pinkerton deployed agents along the train's route, to watch for saboteurs trying to blow up the tracks or assassins preparing to assault the train. They waited in preset positions with lanterns to signal the train that all was well in each sector. Allan Pinkerton stood on the rear platform monitoring progress, sector by sector. The train left Philadelphia late in the evening, and pulled into Baltimore at 3:30 A.M., where it paused at the platform. This stop was the moment of highest danger. Only a few armed Pinkertons stood between the roiling population of Baltimore and a vulnerable Abraham Lincoln.

All they heard, though, was a drunk on the platform singing "Dixie" at the top of his voice. After an agonizingly long wait at the Baltimore station, the train rolled on to Washington, arriving at 6 A.M.

Later, when the decoy presidential train rolled into Baltimore, a menacing crowd of thousands gave lusty cheers for Jefferson Davis and the Confederacy. But all they could do was holler.*

---

*The security contract for Lincoln was not to last long. The Pinkertons were not on duty the night he was assassinated.

. . . .

THE PINKERTONS STAYED in government service throughout the Civil War, and the company continued to operate its corporate service out of its Chicago offices. The Pinkerton precedent of intertwining private-sector intelligence agencies with government service continues to this day.

Allan Pinkerton went to work for General George McClellan's army of Ohio, taking the rank of major. He turned to Timothy Webster, one of his most trusted agents, to help infiltrate the Confederacy. An Englishman who'd begun working for Pinkerton in 1853, Webster was dressed in the classy outfits of a dapper Brit, posing as a rebel-loving copperhead. At this point, the British were teetering toward full diplomatic recognition of the Confederate government, which would have been a blow to Union hopes for reconciliation.

Webster set up shop in Baltimore and cultivated copperhead contacts. He soon met the members of a secret society of Confederate loyalists called the Sons of Liberty, and heard from them about plans to stir up trouble for the federal government in Maryland. Thanks to Webster's spying, Pinkerton agents pinned down the date of a large copperhead gathering. Webster himself, still undercover, was one of the keynote speakers, haranguing the audience with anti-Union rhetoric. But just as he reached fever pitch, Allan Pinkerton, a squad of detectives, and dozens of federal troops burst into the room and arrested the leaders of the plot.

Later, Webster made his way south, and reached out to the Confederate government, brazenly offering his services as a spy against the North. The Confederates employed him, giving him access to high echelons of their government and all kinds of Confederate facilities.

Now working as a double agent, he compiled detailed reports on the military installations he saw, including fortifications in the strategically significant town of Yorktown, Virginia, which sits at the southern end of Chesapeake Bay and might have offered

invading waterborne Union troops quick access to the Confederate capital, Richmond. The fortifications, he wrote, were "of split-pine logs with a 64-pounder [cannon] with a traverse of 180 degrees," and the town's landing was "in front of a hill with a slope of five feet above the beach." He also included the price points for various goods in the town, giving the Union military leaders a sense of the troubled economy there.

Despite this detailed and accurate reporting—which he risked his life to deliver—many historians have highlighted Webster's one great failure, which was also the signal failure of the Pinkerton agency during the war. Webster guessed in his reports that the Confederate troops near Richmond numbered 116,430. But it appears that his estimate was too high by far—there were actually 40,000 fewer troops in the area. That miscalculation may have contributed to General McClellan's reluctance to attack the southern force. That in turn led to intense political antagonism between McClellan and Lincoln, who was pressing for an onslaught against the Confederate positions.

Webster's bravery, though, is unquestionable. He continued to send back detailed reports until a slipup by a separate team of Union spies in the South revealed Webster's identity as a Pinkerton. Webster was arrested, and on April 28, 1862, hanged for espionage in front of thousands of spectators on the Richmond fairground.

In his last message from his cell, Webster told a female Pinkerton agent who had come to visit him, "Tell the major I can meet death with a brave heart and a clear conscience."*

WHEN THE WAR ended, the industrializing North once again offered opportunity for corporate espionage. The Pinkertons would

---

*After the war, Allan Pinkerton had Webster's body removed from its grave in Richmond and reburied in northern soil. He also erected a monument to Webster in his own family cemetery.

again use undercover techniques in the late 1870s, under circumstances almost as dangerous as those faced by Timothy Webster.

The postwar era was a time of violent unrest in the anthracite coalfields of Pennsylvania, where child labor, unsafe working conditions, and an economic depression in the middle of the 1870s combined to provoke violent strikes by miners and brutal reprisals by management. Illiterate, poverty-stricken foreign immigrants vied with each other for work in the mines, and organized themselves into warring camps along ethnic lines.

Amid the chaos, some Irish-Catholic immigrants created a secret society they called the Molly Maguires. Historians aren't quite sure where the name came from, although the organization seems to have had roots in secret societies in Ireland through which poor tenant farmers waged secret class wars against English landowners. There are those who believe that the Mollies never existed at all, and the society left almost no records for historians to examine. Legend holds that "Molly Maguire" herself was a poor widow whose cause was taken up by the local workingmen. Or she could have been a fiery Irish lass who led nighttime raids on wealthy landlords in Ireland. No one knows.

In coal country, the Mollies became a violent and vindictive gang motivated by both criminal agendas and the class war. In their lively account of the saga in their book *The Pinkerton Story* (1951), James Horan and Howard Swiggert wrote that the Mollies were believed to be responsible for numerous crimes in the area, including these over just a two-month period in 1870: ambushing a mining foreman, shooting a merchant, beating up a bridge watchman, beating a mine superintendent, and murdering a mine boss.

By 1873 Franklin Gowen, the president of both the Philadelphia and Reading Railroad and the Philadelphia and Reading Coal and Iron Company, had had enough. He wrote to Allan Pinkerton and asked him to come to Pennsylvania. Gowen's concern was not so much for the lives of the men on both sides of the fight as for the fate of a

business venture. Gowen was diversifying out of the railroad business and into the coal business. The Reading railroad had purchased enormous tracts of land, and planned to transport the coal mined from the land on its own rail lines. But the crime wave was bad for business. Gowen tasked Pinkerton with bringing down the Mollies.

Allan Pinkerton told Gowen that the operation had to be conducted with the utmost secrecy. He didn't want anyone other than Gowen to read the Pinkerton reports, and he didn't want the company to keep any records that would show it had hired the Pinkertons. He knew the Mollies had deep contacts inside the company, and might even be able to read Gowen's own documents. Pinkerton began putting together a plan to infiltrate the Mollies with one of his own men. He knew he'd need an Irish-Catholic immigrant capable of passing as a hardened miner. And the recruit would have to be able to function even while fearing for his own life. Pinkerton settled on James McParland, a thin, red-haired twenty-nine-year-old immigrant from Ulster who had just begun work as a detective.

Pinkerton told McParland he could refuse the mission with no penalty to his career, but McParland agreed to the job. To keep up the secret, McParland left the Pinkerton service, and took the cover name "James McKenna." Posing as an out-of-work immigrant, he made his own way to the coal country. He began to frequent local saloons, drinking heavily and spouting off publicly against English landlords. In Pottsville, Pennsylvania, he settled into the Sheridan House, where he bought a round of drinks and impressed the locals with his singing voice and dancing skill. The owner of the saloon, charmed, gave McParland a letter of introduction to Muff Lawler, who was the leader, or "body master," of the Mollies in Shenandoah.

McParland told Lawler and his crew that he had been affiliated with secret societies in Ireland but had been out of contact for some time. He explained his ready access to cash by telling them it was the spoils from a murder in Buffalo, New York. And he covered his need to duck away frequently to meet with his Pinkerton

supervisor by explaining that he was a counterfeiter and needed to meet a contact. He would show off real money to his new friends, telling them that it was his counterfeit stash and daring them to spot any imperfections.

Eventually, McParland landed a real coal mining job, hauling twenty tons of coal in each ten-hour day. And on April 14, 1874, McParland came up for formal initiation into the Molly Maguires. The local group met at Muff Lawler's house, and McParland waited downstairs under supervision of a Molly officer. McParland couldn't be sure that he was really there for an initiation at all. Could the Mollies have figured out that he was a spy? Could they have a spy of their own inside the sprawling Pinkerton organization? It was impossible to be sure. But shortly he was led into a room upstairs, where he knelt down, swore an oath, made the sign of the cross, and paid the treasurer $3.

McParland remained in the society, before long as elected secretary of his local chapter, through 1875, dodging requests that he kill or commit crimes, and narrowly escaping discovery. The brutal Mollies would surely kill him instantly if they discovered that he was a Pinkerton spy.

Tension rose as the company sent in scab labor to break a miners' strike. McParland talked his fellow Mollies out of blowing up a railroad bridge across the Susquehanna River, but despite his efforts toward peace, agitators still managed to burn a telegraph office and derail a train. McParland sneaked off to meet his Pinkerton supervisor and advised him to send in a force of police to control the area. He had already requested that the Pinkertons have one man arrested—if only to keep him safe from the Mollies, who wanted him dead. McParland broke away for a trip to Chicago to debrief Pinkerton on the operation, which had now been under way for a year and a half.

McParland wasn't able to prevent the Mollies from spiraling into an increasingly violent rampage. He could speak out against some proposed killings, but if he opposed every crime that was planned,

he'd arouse the suspicion of the gang. Despite McParland's best efforts to talk them out of it, Molly gunmen shot a man named Bully Bill Thomas as he stood tending his horse in a stable. But they botched the job, and Thomas survived. Then they turned their attention to Benjamin Yost, a night watchman who had earned their enmity by arresting several Mollies for minor infractions. The Molly killers Hugh McGehan, James Boyle, and James Kerrigan lay in wait for Yost at two o'clock in the morning, when they knew he'd emerge from his house to climb a ladder on the sidewalk and put out the street lamp. McGehan fired his pistol in the darkness, and Yost collapsed. A man working nearby rushed to his side, and Yost, dying from the gunshot wounds, was able to tell him that the killers were Irish. What's more, he'd seen them in a saloon earlier in the night. He even ruled out some suspects before he died at 9 A.M.

McParland didn't know who the killers were, but he thought he could figure it out. He carefully gathered evidence. He asked to borrow a pistol, and was given one that matched the caliber of the murder weapon. He pulled together bits and pieces of information about who had been on the scene at the time of the shooting. He also picked up word of yet another planned killing, this time of the mine boss J. P. Jones, and was able to get word to the Pinkertons to spirit Jones out of town until the danger passed.

McParland bided his time even as Molly gunmen killed one man at a fire department picnic and engaged in a gunfight with another target. Soon after that, Mollies proposed killing a mine boss, Tom Sanger. There were getting to be so many murder plots that McParland, still undercover as "James McKenna," couldn't warn the Pinkertons in time to head off each one. Molly assassins hit Sanger before McParland could do anything about it. When the mine boss Jones, thinking that the threat to his life had passed, returned to the area, three Mollies shot and killed him on a train platform in front of 100 witnesses. They got away.

McParland wrote up a detailed report for his Pinkerton bosses

about each murder, listing the killers and their accomplices. He was convinced he was doing the right thing. After all, the reports would be evidence for eventual court proceedings against the murderers.

Allan Pinkerton, writing from Chicago to his lieutenants on the scene, worried that the local authorities would never be able to get a conviction in counties heavily populated by Irish Catholics who supported the Mollies. Pinkerton advised his men to put together a vigilante party of their own to murder the Mollies and be done with them. That plan was too overt, and the Pinkertons in Pennsylvania developed a more hands-off solution. They printed up a handbill with the names of 374 Mollies and began circulating the document among the population. On December 10, a crowd of masked men broke into a home and opened fire on Mollies living there, killing Charles O'Donnell and his sister, Ellen McAllister, and wounding two others who escaped during the firefight. It's clear that the Pinkertons hoped someone would take the law into his own hands and start killing Mollies, but it's not clear if they arranged these particular killings.

McParland may not have known all the details, but he suspected that his own organization had somehow provoked the killings. He was horrified that his work had led to the killing of an innocent woman. He dashed off an angry letter to his boss: "As for the O'Donnells, I am satisfied they got their just deserving," he wrote. "I reported what those men were. . . . Now I wake up this morning to find that I am the murderer of Mrs. McAllister. What had a woman to do with the case[?]" McParland tendered his immediate resignation. "I am not going to be an accessory to the murder of women and children."

Allan Pinkerton convinced his valuable agent that the detective agency had nothing to do with the murders, and talked McParland into staying in his undercover position. Suspicion was swirling. The Mollies wanted to know who had circulated the handbill. How did that person get a list of Mollies? There must be a traitor in their ranks. When someone accused McParland of being the traitor, he

bluffed his way out of the situation once again, demanding a full internal investigation by the Mollies and a trial of his case, and loudly proclaiming that he'd prove his innocence.

Told that a local priest had fingered him as a detective, he went to the church and confronted the priest. Still, he noticed that he was regularly being tailed by armed Mollies, and he heard a rumor that leaders had ordered his killing. McParland decided he couldn't bluff his way out any longer. On March 7, 1876, he boarded a train heading north, with a Pinkerton captain keeping watch over his train car. McParland's run as an undercover Molly was done, almost two years after he'd been sworn into the murderous secret society.

But McParland's role in breaking the Mollies wasn't done: Pinkerton asked him to take the witness stand in court. That would expose his real name and identity, and possibly subject him to retaliatory violence from the Mollies. McParland agreed— after some persuasion—to testify in public. During the trial for the murder of Yost, McParland made his first appearance on the witness stand—giving the Mollies the first indication of how badly their organization had been penetrated. Here was a man they knew as a drunken brawler, transformed into a clean-shaven, articulate, well-dressed detective. One contemporary newspaper account described the astonishment of the Mollies as they realized what had happened. "Carroll was as if struck by lightning. Boyle shook like an aspen as the prosecutor announced, 'We will produce to you the full and complete confession of James Carroll and Hugh McGehan of their part in this murder made to James McKenna, a detective.'"

Eventually, twenty Mollies would hang for their crimes, with McParland's testimony serving as the crucial evidence to break the gang's back.

McParland lived a long life, and went on to become one of the Pinkerton Agency's most legendary detectives. He was still solving cases of mine-related violence in Idaho as late as 1906. But Franklin Gowen, who had started the whole Molly case, met a much

different fate. The railroad company came close to failure, and Gowen was pushed out of its management. He became a private lawyer, and in 1889 he was summoned to Washington, D.C., as part of a case against Standard Oil. There, in his room at Wormsley's Hotel, he shot himself.

The Pinkertons thought his death might not be suicide at all, and investigated it as a possible hit by the Mollies. But despite their suspicions and a thorough investigation, they came up with no evidence that it had been anything other than a sad man alone in a hotel room, far from home, with a gun.

THE PINKERTONS HAD their share of casualties in their ongoing war against the enemies of their clients. The Adams Express Company hired the agency to track down a group of outlaws known as the Jesse James gang: former Confederates who had been robbing trains and banks across the middle of the country. In 1874, two Pinkerton detectives—Louis Lull and Joseph Wicher—were killed by the Jesse James gang. These brutal, execution-style killings seem to have unhinged Allan Pinkerton. He wrote to his deputy, "I know that the James Youngers [The Youngers were four brothers who made up the core of the James gang, along with Jesse's brother, Frank] are desperate men, and that when we meet it, it must be the death of one or both of us. . . . My blood was spilt, and they must repay, there is no use talking, they must die."

The Pinkertons deployed their private army against the James gang, tracking them to their family farm in Missouri. They surrounded the place, nicknamed "Castle James" by the locals, and prepared for battle. What they didn't know was that their own heavily armed band had attracted notice. The James brothers had skipped town, leaving their mother, Zerelda; her husband (who was not the James boys' father); and the couple's two children, who were half siblings of the James brothers.

Someone from the Pinkerton side—exactly who was never

determined—lobbed an early type of hand grenade into the building, and Zerelda's husband pounced on it, skittering it into the fireplace. The device exploded, lacerating Zerelda's arm and wounding
the James brothers' eight-year-old half brother, Archie, who died
soon afterward.

Following this incident, the Pinkertons suddenly became bad
guys in the eyes of the public. In the remnants of the Confederate south, the agency was seen as the heavy-handed enforcer of
the northeastern moneymen who ran the railroads and banks. The
James gang had captivated the public, since their targets tended
to be large corporate concerns, and only rarely individuals. The
local papers denounced the Pinkertons' tactics, and the pulp press
churned out homages to the glamorous James boys. The Pinkertons never caught the James gang. Jesse James would be killed by
a traitor within his own ranks in 1882. Frank James surrendered
to authorities a few months later. He lived into his seventies, and
died in 1915.

Allan Pinkerton didn't outlive Jesse James by long, dying of
a tongue infection in 1884. He left the company in the hands of
his two sons, Robert and William. The sons had different priorities from their father. He was an immigrant, but they were first-
generation Americans. He had been raised in poverty, but they
were the sons of a wealthy man. He built a company with his bare
hands, and they inherited one. Before long, the company began to
depart from the code of conduct established by Allan Pinkerton in
the early days, taking on more overtly antiunion work.

The brothers' first major test came soon enough. In 1892, a labor
strike loomed in Homestead, Pennsylvania, just outside Pittsburgh.
The executive in charge was Henry Clay Frick,* an overseer with
the Carnegie, Phillips Steel Company. Instead of going to the local

---

*Frick's partnership with Carnegie, though severed after the Homestead strike, was lu-
crative. The union-breaking industrialist built an enormous mansion on Fifth Avenue in
New York City, which is now the home of the Frick Collection, a museum dedicated to old
masters including Rembrandt, Goya, and Titian.

police to handle the trouble, Frick turned to the Pinkertons. More than 300 Pinkerton men traveled to Homestead by barge, taking fire from armed strikers on the riverbank as they attempted to land. The Pinkerton men, pinned down on their barges, fired back, setting off an intense firefight with the strikers. The fighting lasted twelve hours, and three Pinkertons and ten strikers were killed. Exhausted and unable to retreat, the Pinkertons surrendered.

The incident became a flash point in the American labor movement. Workers denounced the Pinkertons as hired killers and called the shootings the "Homestead massacre." Congress held hearings, weighing whether or not private firms should be allowed to wield police authority without government oversight. Should bands of armed men be allowed to cross state lines? Were the Pinkertons modern-day Hessian mercenaries? Could they be a threat to national sovereignty?

Still, the Pinkertons saw themselves as the victims. In prepared testimony before the House Judiciary Committee in July 1892, Allan's sons Robert and William Pinkerton said their men had acted legally:

After the surrender all our men, including the wounded and helpless, were brutally beaten and robbed by the strikers, and the leaders made no real or honest effort to protect them. Our men were robbed of watches, money, clothing, in fact, everything, and then mercilessly clubbed and stoned. Conners, unable to move or defend himself, was deliberately shot by one of the strikers and then clubbed. Edwards, also wounded and helpless, was clubbed by another striker with the butt end of a musket. Both died, and subsequently another watchman became insane and committed suicide as a result of the fearful beating after having surrendered. All our men were more or less injured. The acts of the strikers, after our men surrendered, would be a disgrace to savages. Yet, because done in the name of organized American labor,

sympathy, if not encouragement, is shown for such deeds by part of the press and by political demagogues.[2]

These protests didn't register with the politicians on Capitol Hill. In 1893 Congress passed the federal Anti-Pinkerton Act, which began the company's long decline in the popular imagination. The Pinkertons were reduced from heroic detectives to oppressors of the workingman. The Anti-Pinkerton Act is still a federal statute, stating:

> An individual employed by the Pinkerton Detective Agency, or similar organization, may not be employed by the Government of the United States or the government of the District of Columbia.

That language has new resonance now: it has been cited by opponents of controversial U.S. government military contractors working in Iraq, such as Blackwater (now known as Xe), Custer Battles, and Triple Canopy.

Despite the disaster at Homestead, the Pinkerton Agency had a long life. It prospered financially under the leadership of Allan Pinkerton's sons.* The agency found lucrative work around the turn of the century, infiltrating labor unions for corporate clients; and James McParland, who'd succeeded so spectacularly against the Mollies as a young man, now served as the head of Pinkerton's Denver office, deploying newer agents in undercover operations against labor. McParland ran the entire western division of the Pinkerton agency, but his critics claim that he conducted a cynical operation, positioning his spies in leadership positions in the regional mining unions, where he could both obtain intelligence on the labor activists, and, some said, even

---

*The sons weren't as liberal as their father in at least one respect: they discontinued the use of female detectives.

order provocative union actions that in turn generated ever more lucrative business from the mining concerns.

In an era of easier transatlantic travel, made possible by the introduction of the steamship, the Pinkerton brothers also became global operators, hunting down suspects for clients in London, in Paris, and across Europe. Robert's son Allan Pinkerton II served in World War I and then took over the company from his father in 1923. Allan II's son, Robert Pinkerton, took over in turn in 1930, renounced antiunion work entirely after yet another series of bruising hearings on Capitol Hill in the 1930s, and took the company public in 1965. He died on October 11, 1965, and was replaced by the first non–family member since the company's founding more than 100 years earlier.

Throughout most of the twentieth century, the Pinkerton Agency receded from its dominant position in the national consciousness. Several competitors, including the Thiel Detective Service Agency, formed by a former Pinkerton detective, George H. Thiel, began to obtain market share. The Pinkertons never forgave Thiel for launching a competing firm. Another up-and-coming competitor was the William Burns International Detective Agency. All the firms dabbled in strikebreaking to some degree, but that work began to wane after the 1930s.

In 1999, the company Allan Pinkerton founded was sold to Stockholm, Sweden-based Securitas AB, a 250,000-employee security services company based in Stockholm, Sweden, with offices around the world. Pinkerton's operates today as a subsidiary of this Swedish conglomerate; it is now called Pinkerton Consulting & Investigations.

It's a long way from Bogus Island.

CHAPTER THREE

For the Money

At the dawn of the twentieth century, the Department of Justice had no investigators of its own. Humiliatingly, it had to borrow agents from the Secret Service every time it needed to conduct an investigation. There was no national police force, and early efforts to create a federal bureau of investigation were mired in controversy. The government's impotence created the market filled by the Pinkertons. Congress, for the most part, was happy with this state of affairs: in the early 1900s, the nation's politicians were suspicious of the "secret services," or what they called "black cabinets," that governments around the world used to conduct espionage on their own citizens.

The conduct of the actual Secret Service didn't help matters. In one famous case, the federal agents conducted surveillance on a Navy midshipman who'd run away with a married woman. That set off howls of protest on Capitol Hill, where lawmakers resented the idea of federal investigators' being used as a kind of morality police.

The debate began to change in 1906. Attorney General Charles Bonaparte decided he needed a police force of his own, as the situation was becoming intolerable. In 1906, he had to borrow sixty agents from the Secret Service. The next year, he'd borrow sixty-five. This borrowing was getting expensive, and Bonaparte resented

the fact that he didn't have control over the investigators working
for him. In a missive to Congress, he alerted the legislators to "the
anomaly that the Department of Justice has no . . . permanent detective force under its immediate control."

President Theodore Roosevelt, eager to expand his executive
authority, leaped into the debate. He dismissed the worries of the
civil libertarians in Congress, writing, "There is no more foolish
outcry than this against 'spies'; only criminals need fear our detectives." Roosevelt, always blunt, said that Congress was reluctant
to create a detective force because the congressmen feared they
would become targets of investigation. That accusation didn't sit
well with members of Congress.

Attorney General Bonaparte had to proceed carefully in July
1908, when he reorganized his staff and appointed Chief Examiner
Stanley W. Finch to head a small group of special agents. That
was against the will of many in Congress, but Bonaparte's special
force managed to survive heated debate on Capitol Hill. The force
would grow to become the Federal Bureau of Investigation.[1]

With the rise of the FBI as a national police force, the need for
private corporate detective services gradually dwindled, and the
Pinkertons were forced to consolidate, maintaining a core business
around their still profitable activities: keeping watch against corruption at horse-racing tracks, chasing jewel thieves, and providing uniformed guards for corporate plants.

Although this era was the heyday of the fictional private eye,
such as Sam Spade, the years of the two world wars and the early
cold war saw increasingly centralized national investigative and intelligence capability under control of the federal government, not
the private sector. From the founding of the FBI to the creation of
the Central Intelligence Group in 1946 (it became the Central Intelligence Agency in 1947), the government was consolidating ever
more intelligence and investigative power in its own hands.

In those days, private eyes were better known for working on
their own, cultivating a disdain for law enforcement, and sometimes

using illicit tactics to solve cases. And those cases were often small-time stuff: missing people, insurance fraud, and divorces—lots of divorces.

But even as companies ceded their defense against criminals to government authorities, many found they still needed offense: intelligence-gathering operations against their competitors. Corporate espionage never went away. It just went farther underground.

WITH NEW TECHNOLOGY, the spying became ever more sophisticated. The investigator Sam Dash* chronicled the rise of corporate espionage involving bugging and wiretapping during the early twentieth century in his classic book *The Eavesdroppers*. He found corporate spying in small towns and in the nation's capital. In Toledo, Ohio, in 1932, for example, investigators came across an extensive wiretap setup in a hotel room next to the headquarters of an agricultural group, the Farmers' Producers Association. This group had been discussing boosting the price of milk, and the evidence showed that the room had been bugged for days. As a result, somebody had advance warning of the price increase, although it's not clear who ordered the spying. (Today's commodities traders still use esoteric intelligence techniques to get advance information on market pricing—in a later chapter, we'll see that they're now using satellites to gather intelligence.)

In Washington, D.C., Dash wrote, a "raiding squad" from the Federal Communications Commission (FCC), acting on a tip in 1935 or 1936, found wiretapping equipment in a building near the brand-new Supreme Court building. The wiretappers had been using the equipment to listen in on the phone lines of Supreme Court justices. The spies were never found—not surprisingly, they didn't turn up to collect their equipment from the government

---

*Dash would go on to fame as the co–chief counsel of the Senate Watergate committee nearly two decades later.

agents—but one member of the FCC team concluded that the wiretapping was paid for by a "major private business concern" that had an interest in a case before the Supreme Court.

Across the street, members of Congress were also targets of spying. A Senate investigation revealed that a police lieutenant in Washington, D.C., Joseph Shimon, had tapped the telephone of Senator Josiah Bailey of North Carolina, a Democrat who was chairman of the powerful Commerce Committee. The question for investigators: Why did Shimon do it?

They found that the police lieutenant wasn't working for the metropolitan police department when he'd tapped the lines; he was working on his own. Shimon had carved out a unique niche within the department. Although he was a police officer who reported each morning for roll call, he was assigned much of the time to a special investigative unit of the U.S. district attorney for the District of Columbia. He had no full-time boss, and no one in the police department knew where he was each day. By 1946, Shimon had been a lieutenant for less than five years, but he was often free to spend his time as he pleased.

And what pleased Shimon was making money on the side. As the Senate investigation concluded, Shimon was doing freelance spying for paying clients.

Shimon's saga gets complicated, but the layers of corporate and political intrigue are crucial to understand. They underscore just how valuable a particular piece of intelligence can be in a corporate setting. The information from one wiretap, placed on the right phone at the right time, can be worth billions of dollars. As a result there were—and probably always will be—people willing to pay for the tapping, and people willing to conduct it.

In 1945, Senator Bailey's Commerce Committee held hearings on the All-American Flag Lines Bill, which would have rolled all the major American air carriers into one national airline. Executives at Pan American Airways were desperate for information on the hearings. Pan American was pushing for the bill, which would be likely

to put it in control of the most lucrative market in the world, the United States. It was going head to head with the powerful billionaire Howard Hughes and his Trans World Airlines (TWA), which opposed the bill. Pan Am wanted to know how much influence TWA had to block the proposal in the congressional committee. It had more questions than answers. *What is Bailey going to do? Who is he talking to? Does our All-American proposal stand a chance?*

Lieutenant Shimon went to work—on his own, without police supervision—for a private detective who in turn had been hired by Sam Pryor, a vice president of Pan American. In effect, Shimon provided the espionage component of Pan American's Washington lobbying strategy. But that's not what he told his fellow officers. Since wiretapping was a labor-intensive business—someone has to sit there all day to monitor the recorders—Shimon recruited several other cops to work on the case with him, explaining the wiretapping as a hush-hush investigation for a legitimate congressional inquiry.

Shimon's team tapped the phones of Senator Bailey's apartment complex in Georgetown, pulling into the garage of the building and setting up camp in the basement for long hours of eavesdropping. It was boring work, but the men found one way to spice it up. One participant brought a "young lady" to the basement to "keep Shimon company" while he waited.

Shimon's little group also tapped phones at the luxurious Occidental Hotel, where the freelancing cops listened in on the conversations of a TWA lawyer who had traveled to Washington for the hearings. The attorney used his hotel phone to coordinate strategy, and those listening to the recordings of his calls had advance notice of TWA's every move. Pan Am now knew what its rival TWA was thinking and what the chairman of the committee was planning. This was a tremendous tactical advantage. But still it wasn't enough. The All-American Bill never passed.*

---

*Merger talks between the two airlines would continue in one form or another for decades, resuming again in 1962 and 1990. Pan Am eventually collapsed in 1991.

Two years later, Shimon was at it again. This time, Senator Owen Brewster of Maine, a Republican, used his Senate War Investigating Committee to hurl incendiary charges at Howard Hughes. Brewster alleged that Hughes's company had collected $40 million from the government to develop a prototype aircraft that had never been delivered. He said this was fraud, and he hauled Hughes before the committee to defend himself. The testimony set off a media frenzy, as Hughes confronted Brewster and his Senate colleagues—on national television. Hughes made his own counterallegations, charging that Brewster had secretly promised to call off the investigation if Hughes would agree to merge TWA with Pan American.*

As the fireworks exploded on television, Shimon's small group quietly recorded phone conversations of TWA lawyers staying at the Carlton and Mayflower hotels in Washington. Once again, Pan Am executives would have the inside track on their opponents' strategy. And once again, it wasn't enough.

By the time the hearings ended, Hughes was seen nationwide as an honest businessman who'd taken on the corrupt Washington elite. Brewster's reputation was damaged, and Hughes drove home his victory a few years later, financing an aggressive Republican Party challenge that ousted Brewster from the Senate. Brewster died in 1961. Hughes lived until 1976 and became more involved in private espionage of his own, eventually becoming so suspicious of his enemies, real and imagined, that after 1950 he dropped from sight to live as a terrified recluse.

As for Lieutenant Shimon, in 1950 he was dragged in front of a hostile Senate investigating committee, where he denied running the wiretapping operation. His fellow cops, however, gave detailed accounts of the operation in a public hearing. A federal grand jury investigated Shimon in 1950, but did not indict him. It seems his

---

*The moment of high drama became the climactic scene in a 2004 movie called *The Aviator*, starring Leonardo DiCaprio as Howard Hughes and Alan Alda as Senator Brewster.

career continued, unscathed by the controversy: by 1960, he had been promoted twice, and he eventually became an inspector in the Washington, D.C., police force.*

DESPITE THE HIGH drama of the Shimon case, the wiretapping itself was standard stuff. Shimon or his associates walked up to basement phone boxes and installed their taps right on the premises. All they needed to know was which cable to tap, and they got that information by calling the phone company and posing as repairmen out in the field. Helpful but clueless receptionists at headquarters always gave them the wiring details they needed.

But the ambitions of the wiretappers were growing ever more sophisticated. On February 11, 1955, a group of investigators, including two city detectives and two inspectors for the telephone company, knocked on the door of a midtown Manhattan apartment building and stumbled upon a wiretapping operation capable of bugging any one of 100,000 telephones in the neighborhood. The discovery set off a chain of events that would embarrass some of the most important companies—and some of the wealthiest people—in America.

The apartment building was conveniently situated just around the corner from the telephone office, and conspirators had strung a cable between the two.† With the help of a twenty-nine-year-old phone company employee, Walter Asman (who wore his hair in a stylish pompadour), the eavesdroppers had managed to assign apartment 4W at 360 East Fifty-Fifth Street ten fictitious phone numbers. Using those lines, they were able to tap ten telephones at

---

*Shimon continued his decades-long career as a wiretapper. In 1962, he bugged yet another attorney's room at the Mayflower Hotel, and was indicted and convicted on charges resulting from the incident, although the conviction was reversed on appeal. He pleaded guilty to two misdemeanor charges, according to *The Intruders*, a book written by Senator Edward V. Long in 1967, following his Senate investigation into illegal wiretapping.

†The address of the New York Telephone Company office was 228 East Fifty-Sixth Street. There is a Verizon telecommunications facility in the same building today.

the same time. When police got into the apartment, they discovered that it was equipped with automatic tape recorders for continuous recording. Two men and two women were found operating the machines, tapping phones in as many as ten different New York City exchanges, then known by their mid-century names, including the prestigious exchanges Murray Hill 8 and Eldorado 5.

In his book, Dash explained that the covered area included "large law firms; gigantic businesses and financial houses; major publishing companies; aristocratic hotels patronized by the wealthy and the famous; fashionable apartment houses; and other subscribers who daily on the telephone made decisions, plans, and compacts, the knowledge of which was priceless to competing or adversary interests."[2]

The taping had been going on for years.

Initially, the investigators didn't do much about their discovery, simply ordering the tappers to knock it off. Police forces in those days were themselves heavily engaged in quasi-legal wiretapping, and wouldn't have wanted any undue publicity about the practice. And no one at the phone company wanted the public to find out just how easy it was to listen in on telephone calls. One of the investigators told the wiretappers that the team would come back the next day, and he wanted all the equipment out of the apartment by then.[3] It looked as though the tappers might get away with it.

But the raid didn't remain secret long. An anonymous tipster alerted a private citizens' crime fighting group, the New York City Anti-Crime Committee, which in turn alerted the New York state legislature; and the media excitedly pushed government officials to launch an investigation into the goings-on in apartment 4W.

It turned out that the tenant in the apartment was thirty-year-old Warren Shannon. An employee of the telephone company, Carl Ruh (also thirty years old), was involved in the plot as well. But those two were junior players. They reported to a tough-looking, heavyset fifty-two-year-old attorney and private eye, John Broady,

who hired the wiretappers and encouraged the scheme.* Broady was already infamous, having been indicted twice during the 1940s on wiretapping charges, and this new case would mark the fedora-wearing lawyer as one of the most legendary wiretappers of the twentieth century.

Investigators found that five active wiretaps were secured to the lines of executives of the pharmaceutical company E. R. Squibb and Sons—today, Bristol-Myers Squibb—and it was apparent what the tappers had been up to: "The circumstances make it clear that business intelligence may have been the reason behind them," William Keating, counsel for the New York City Anti-Crime Committee, told a reporter for the *New York Times* several days later.†⁴

Court testimony revealed that Broady's biggest client was Charles Pfizer and Company, the corporate parent of today's pharmaceutical giant Pfizer. Its executives worried that their corporate secrets were leaking to competitors. They hired Broady to tap the phones of several of their own employees, paying him $60,000 (a hefty sum at the time) for the project.

Working closely with Pfizer's general counsel, Broady learned that the company was having trouble securing a patent for tetracycline, a cutting-edge antibiotic, that has been used in years since to treat many kinds of infections, from gonorrhea to acne. The development of this chemical was a significant breakthrough, but Pfizer's patent application was stalled. Executives muttered darkly that a rival drug company, Bristol-Myers, must be holding up the process, and that this competitor had been selling illicit tetracycline to a third company, Squibb. Broady placed taps on the phones at Squibb, hoping to find out what it was doing to block Pfizer's patent. He also had an accomplice tap long-distance phone lines that ran all

---

*At the subsequent trial, Broady's lawyers insisted that the real figure behind the wiretapping scheme was a private detective named Charles Gris.

†Broady also tapped other phones, including those of the St. Joseph Lead Company, the Knoedler art gallery, the chairman of the board of Pepsi-Cola, a prominent lawyer, and a publishing company, according to *The Intruders*.

the way to the Bristol-Myers headquarters in Syracuse, New York.

Broady met with Pfizer's general counsel once a week, near the entrance to the Holland Tunnel, as his spying activities got more and more elaborate. At one meeting alongside the traffic-choked entrance to the tunnel, the corporate lawyer handed Broady a list of about fifty employees and asked him to check their living standards, friends, and work habits. A government investigation later found that Broady's reports became so detailed that Pfizer executives didn't have time to read through all the intelligence he produced. The company asked him to condense the reports to just the most important findings.[5]

No one knows what Broady discovered during his elaborate eavesdropping scheme, but Pfizer won the fight over tetracycline, securing the coveted patent on January 11, 1955—just a month before authorities uncovered the wiretapping conspiracy.[6]

The whole matter ended badly for Pfizer, though. As a result of other activities unrelated to the wiretapping, the feds concluded that Pfizer had submitted false and misleading information to the U.S. Patent and Trademark Office, and that it had colluded with five other antibiotic manufacturers to keep competitors out of the business and attempt to monopolize the market. The Federal Trade Commission (FTC) mandated that Pfizer and another company grant nonexclusive licenses at specific royalty rates to any qualified American company that applied to sell tetracycline. Indeed, the entire tetracycline industry became a magnet for allegations of wrongdoing: the FTC conducted investigations in the late 1950s, and the Department of Justice investigated again ten years later.[7]

Not all of Broady's work involved advanced science and corporate intrigue. In a subsequent trial, the millionaire John Jacob Astor testified that he'd hired Broady in the early 1950s to tap the phones at his own posh apartment at 598 Fifth Avenue in Manhattan. Astor, whose father had perished in the sinking of the *Titanic* in 1912, needed evidence in his divorce from his second wife. He hired Broady to tap the phones not only in his apartment

but also in the home of the private investigator his wife had hired during the bitter marital battle. Their divorce became final in 1954.

Broady also trolled the phone lines for juicy secrets, which he used to generate divorce clients for himself. In one case, he tapped the line of a famous burlesque dancer, Ann Corio, hoping to learn who she was sleeping with—and sell that information to the wives of the unlucky men.*

During his trial, Broady denied that he'd been a party to the wiretapping scheme. He claimed that he had used the apartment for a different purpose. He spun an elaborate tale, claiming that he'd been working on a secret investigation of a Chinese air force general who had stolen $7 million from the Republic of China. On the witness stand, Broady burst into tears, saying that he feared for his life, and that one of his employees had been killed by the Chinese.

"I didn't want them to knock me off like they did my man," he blurted out. "I have a wife and kids."[8]

The jury didn't buy the story. Broady was convicted and sentenced to two to four years in a New York state prison, stripped of his private investigator's license, and barred from practicing law.[9]

If Broady was one of the quintessential private eyes of the mid-century on the East Coast, the ultimate investigator on the West Coast was Hal Lipset, a detective based in San Francisco, who was active for several decades after Broady's misadventures in New York. Lipset's work has not been forgotten. One of today's leading corporate detectives told me, "If you want to understand this industry at all, check out Hal Lipset. We're all still copying him."

---

*Corio had a long career on Broadway and as a B-movie actress, appearing in films such as *Swamp Woman* (1941). Neither she nor the critics took her films seriously. "I was the Queen of the Quickies," she once said. "Those pictures weren't released, they escaped."

Hal Lipset applied new technologies to the science of bugging. Now, instead of phone taps or microphones with wires attached, investigators could use transistor technology to place wireless microphones almost anywhere they wanted. Moreover, Lipset argued that secret recording wasn't an invasion of privacy—but a way for good citizens to protect themselves against fraud and government abuse.

Lipset was an accomplished detective, a great storyteller, and something of a showman. He was purely a private detective—he had almost no interest in the outcome of his cases with regard to law enforcement. "Judgments belong in a court of law," he told his agents. "Our job is to earn the fee."[10] But he didn't look the part of a hard-boiled detective at all. In his later years, his receding hairline, thick glasses, and gentle expression made him look more like a doting uncle than an aggressive investigator.

By the mid-1960s, Congress had become increasingly concerned about the rise of a private eavesdropping industry that used bugs and telephone taps on citizens across the country. Senator Edward V. Long of Missouri launched an investigation to find out if Americans' privacy rights were being trampled by new technology, and he turned to Lipset as his star witness. Lipset accepted the invitation to testify before the committee, hoping to make the case that the new technology was not scary at all. What Lipset didn't understand was that his dramatic testimony would have just the opposite effect, showing a startled public just how far bugging technology had come.

Shortly after 10 A.M. on February 18, 1965, Long convened a hearing in the Senate office now known as the Russell Building. Long's chief counsel had let Lipset into the hearing room early to make a few preparations. Lipset began by introducing himself to the Senate committee, mentioning that he'd served as a captain in the army's Criminal Investigative Division during World War II and had been awarded the Bronze Star. He held up a series of items from the table in front of him, each of which he said was

in common use by private detectives: a microphone hidden in a package of cigarettes, a wristwatch microphone, and a tie clasp microphone.

Then he held up a martini glass. "It is missing a special ingredient, an olive the senator is holding there," he said, gesturing toward the chairman. "That is a transmitter unit and the toothpick is the antenna. That is a complete transmitter and will work when covered over with liquid that fills the glass."

The senators were fascinated. Though more than a few of them were familiar with martinis, they'd never seen an olive like this one.

"How far will it transmit?" asked Long.

"That should be good for a block," Lipset responded.[11]

And, by the way, Lipset told the committee members, he'd bugged their conversations during the hearing. The mike was hidden in a vase of flowers he'd placed on the rostrum where the senators sat.

"When you made your opening remarks we caused that to be recorded by using the transmitter concealed in the rose flowers in front of you," Lipset said. "And we will play back a little bit of your opening remarks right now."

Feigning surprise, Long said, "Be sure it is just the remarks I read for the record."

The implications were tremendous. Thanks to the miracles of science—a mixed blessing—private investigators and corporate snoops could now listen in on a conversation without being in the room, and without needing to run a physical wire onto the premises. Voices could be taped from as far as a block away. Almost any conversation anywhere was recordable.

People in the media, too, were fascinated. The new technology caused a stir. "To think that the martini, to which the harried man turns for solace and comfort, should now turn on *him*," wrote Art Hoppe, the reigning humorist at the *San Francisco Chronicle*. "A splendid development," proclaimed the columnist Russell Baker of

the *New York Times*. "With his olive, an agent can pick up disloyal comments during the cocktail hour."[12]

Lipset became one inspiration for the character Harry Caul, the paranoid bugger played by Gene Hackman in the 1974 movie *The Conversation*.* And although Lipset didn't want Americans to become even more frightened of bugging technology, he couldn't help seizing an opportunity to make a buck: he accepted the director Francis Ford Coppola's offer to serve as a consultant on the movie.

IT WAS THANKS to the U.S. government that Lipset had become a spy in the first place. In a pattern that's still being repeated today, Lipset got his training from the U.S. Army before going into the private sector. During World War II, he was responsible for rooting out criminal behavior by American soldiers on the battlefield and in U.S.-occupied areas of Europe. He told tales of chasing down soldiers who'd killed civilians, looted villages, and committed other crimes. In one case, he investigated a brutal crime in which a twenty-year-old woman leaped from a second-story window to escape from two American soldiers who tried to rape her. The men shot and killed her where she landed.

In another case, recounted by Patricia Holt in her biography of the detective, Lipset said that the army's criminals weren't always the smartest crooks, but they could be brutal:

A Belgian couple was found leaning against each other in a sitting position on their bed, with a trail of bullets from

---

*Things didn't turn out as well for Senator Long. Many believe that his years-long investigation of bugging and wiretapping annoyed the FBI's powerful director J. Edgar Hoover, who wanted its use of such technology to remain a closely guarded secret. Whether Hoover leaked the material or not is unclear, but soon two media outlets ran allegations that Long had received tens of thousands of dollars in payments from a lawyer connected to the Teamsters boss Jimmy Hoffa, who was then in prison. *Life* magazine alleged in 1967 that Long had run the hearings on bugging mainly as a way to find evidence to clear Hoffa of his conviction, in 1964, for jury tampering. Long was defeated in a primary and resigned from the Senate on December 27, 1967.

an automatic rifle moving up the right arm of the woman, through her shoulder and neck area into her husband's shoulder and neck area and down his left arm. They had been killed in this manner by a GI looking for jewels. He had mistaken them for the jewelers who lived next door. He thought they were lying when he killed them and took some of the woman's heirloom jewelry, which we later found sewn into the lining of his backpack.[13]

Crimes like these left a lasting impact on Lipset, who for the rest of his life kept every file and report from his World War II days—along with every grisly crime scene photo of hacked and mutilated bodies—locked in his attic in San Francisco.

But another lasting legacy of World War II was the rigorous training the army gave him. Although Lipset grew frustrated with the bureaucracy and petty corruption of the officers he worked for in the service, he appreciated their methods and attention to detail. The record-keeping system he used in private practice and even the format of his reports resembled systems he'd followed in the army.

The army taught Lipset almost everything he needed to know to become a private eye, including how to search a crime scene without disturbing evidence, how to interview witnesses, and how to analyze documents. Thanks to exacting supervisors, he also learned how to use ethyl alcohol to test for blood, how to take fingerprints, how to detect gunpowder burns, and how to make a plaster cast of a tire print. In one training exercise, instructors sent students into town to spend thirty seconds in front of a store window, and then turn around to be quizzed by an officer on the exact details of the display. How many objects were there? How many inches away from one another were they? What color was the backdrop?

Lipset was also taught how to conduct surveillance, with teams of investigators leapfrogging the suspect or bracketing him, with

one in front and one behind the target. The importance of attention to detail was relentlessly hammered into each trainee.

In the 1970s, Lipset was a wealthy man, working for San Francisco's most prominent law and financial firms. He was at his most powerful during a project his biographer Patricia Holt called "the case of the elusive entrepreneur."

In 1973, Lipset received a call from Creative Capital, a venture capital company based in New York, which wanted his help in unraveling a bad investment. Creative Capital—along with an entrepreneur, Paul Maris—had invested $3.5 million to buy a garment manufacturing business: the Alvin Duskin Company in San Francisco. But now, as CEO of Duskin, the stylish, dark-haired, thirty-five-year-old Maris was running behind on his debt-service payments and spending a lot of money on the company, putting several members of his family on the payroll, and giving expensive Mercedeses, Maseratis, and Ferraris to his executives. Creative Capital felt Maris had become a bad investment and wanted to force him out of the company. But when representatives of the board of directors attempted the ouster, Maris threatened to punch them in the nose.

Creative Capital hired a law firm to obtain restraining orders and Lipset's firm to plan a more forceful corporate ouster. To prepare for the takeover, Lipset hired twenty operatives and developed a written plan for going into the garment company and forcing Maris out. Lipset also retained a six-foot-six bodyguard for the CEO of Creative Capital, in case Maris became violent during the confrontation. Lipset said: "The dress factory was a big building with half a dozen floors. We knew we would have to keep people from moving around and telephone calls from going out. It was the same as securing a whole building, as you would do in an army or police action."

He planned the attack for a Thursday. That morning, Lipset strode onto the property and planted agents in the parking lot at the back of the building to keep employees from getting into

their company-owned cars. He placed one man on the front door, one man on the elevator, and a man on each stairwell to keep employees from moving from floor to floor. Another agent guarded the computer room to keep Maris or his executives from destroying records.

Arriving on the executive floor, Lipset stepped out of the elevator and told the switchboard operator to step aside for one of his detectives, who would handle all inbound calls for the rest of the day. Lipset's team went through the floor office by office, stopping at the key executives' locations with court documents ordering them to be fired. Each one was replaced by an executive handpicked by Creative Capital who began the tedious process of figuring out where the garment company's money had been going.

Lipset and his remaining team burst into Maris's suite last, confronting the surprised entrepreneur at his desk.

"What is it?" he asked.

"Paul Maris," Lipset intoned, "I'm here to serve papers on you."

"Oh, you're trying to scare me. OK, go ahead. I've got the best law firm in San Francisco, so just try it."

"Mr. Maris," Lipset replied, "I'm serving these documents on you in addition to a complaint allowing Creative Capital to take over this company. These papers specifically restrain you from removing any company property. You are not allowed to take your company car when you leave. You are not allowed to take business papers from this office. You are not allowed to take printouts from the computer room. You are not allowed to take plans from the designing room. You are not allowed to take any samples, and furthermore, according to paragraph 16 of this order, you are restrained from discussing this matter with any employees until this case is heard in court."[14]

After some back-and-forth bickering about what he was allowed to take from his office, Maris left—without throwing a punch.

In the aftermath, Creative Capital kept Lipset on the case—

trying to find out if Maris was violating the court order by meeting with company employees or was still in possession of any company property. Lipset sent a woman operative to tail Maris, and she followed him to the Stanford Court Hotel on San Francisco's posh Nob Hill. With cable cars clattering up the hill nearby, the operative began taking clandestine pictures of Maris and the people he was meeting with. But Maris and the others spotted her, closed in, and grabbed her wrists. They snatched her camera and pulled out the film, ruining the surveillance images.

Shortly after that unpleasant episode, Lipset got another surprise: Maris was suing him for $5 million.

Planning to fight back, Lipset demanded that Creative Capital tell him everything it knew about Maris. The CEO of Creative Capital told Lipset that he'd had Maris checked out by a prestigious investigative firm, Proudfoot Reports, which was based on the East Coast and was headed up by a former FBI agent. Proudfoot reported that Maris was on the up-and-up. He went to a filing cabinet and turned over a copy of the investigative report on Maris.

Lipset scanned the report by the Proudfoot team, and felt that something was wrong. The document listed Maris's army career but didn't identify the unit he'd served with. It included a list of stocks that he held, but they were all in privately held companies, with no addresses listed. It said Proudfoot had checked with the schools Maris had listed on his résumé, and the information checked out. But the document didn't list the name of the registrar Proudfoot's investigators had spoken to, which Lipset knew his own operatives would include as a matter of accuracy.

Lipset realized that Maris was not who he said he was. He insisted that Creative Capital hire him to figure out who Maris really was.

Creative Capital's CEO scoffed at the idea. His investigators at Proudfoot were top-notch. Why would he want to hire Lipset to redo their work? Lipset was probably just trying to generate more fees. The conversation ended badly, with Lipset and his client shouting at each other. The stressful operation and the new lawsuits were getting

to them both. Lipset announced that he'd conduct the investigation on his own dime, and stormed out of the CEO's office.

Lipset was burning money, desperate to fend off Maris's $5 million lawsuit. He deployed his own network of investigators to find out who Maris really was, starting in Philadelphia, where Maris claimed to have been born. Lipset had an investigator check for a birth certificate and school records—on his résumé, Maris said he'd attended John Bartram High School in Philadelphia and Baldwin Wallace College in Ohio. Lipset's detectives fanned out to both campuses. Next, Lipset had another colleague check Maris's military record in Washington, D.C.

The investigator in Philadelphia could find no records of Paul Maris at either the high school or the college. Maris's old address was a vacant lot in an African-American neighborhood. Maris, who was white, probably hadn't grown up there, the investigators figured. The Washington end of the investigation came back empty, too. Maris had never served in the army at all.

What's more, Lipset found that Maris, his wife, Lillian, and his father had similar Social Security numbers, each just one number higher than the last. He knew that couldn't be a coincidence. But his team of investigators still had no idea who Maris was. They developed a working theory: he'd changed his name from something he felt sounded too ethnic, like Maresh or Mariscal.

So Lipset called Patrick Murphy, the former FBI investigator at Proudfoot, to find out what he knew. Over the phone, Murphy said he remembered Maris well, he'd checked Maris out, and everything was fine.

But, Lipset wanted to know, did the investigators check where Maris had gone to school?

Murphy said he had, and he'd spoken to a registrar at the school who confirmed Maris's dates of enrollment.

Now Lipset knew that Murphy was lying: the schools did not have a record of Maris. But why would this private investigator be in on the cover-up? Lipset couldn't figure it out.

The six-foot-six bodyguard who'd accompanied Creative Capital's CEO had the final piece of the puzzle. The bodyguard's name was Ed, and he was a former narcotics investigator with an entrepreneurial streak of his own. He knew Maris was a valuable prize, and he demanded that Creative Capital pay him thousands of dollars to reveal what he knew. The company paid Ed off, and he said he had heard from his buddies in the federal marshals' service that Maris was actually a gangster from New Jersey. Years earlier, he'd testified against the Mafia, and he'd been offered a spot in the government's witness protection program.

Maris, it turned out, did have a fake identity—one that had been created by the FBI itself. Eventually, Lipset found out that Maris's real name was Gerald Zelmanowitz. The Mafia had a contract out on his life.

Zelmanowitz was a stock cheat who had been born in Brooklyn and whose testimony against the Mafia capo Angelo ("Gyp") De-Carlo had put DeCarlo behind bars in 1970.[15] Zelmanowitz, who described himself as a "securities analyst," told the court that he'd seen DeCarlo's associates brutally beating an insurance broker who had fallen behind in loan payments to the Mafia. The broker later died under suspicious circumstances, and the government thought he'd been murdered. Zelmanowitz's testimony was one of the keys to the case. During the high-stakes proceedings in a courthouse in Newark, New Jersey, the feds went to great lengths to keep Zelmanowitz safe. He was escorted into and out of the courtroom by four federal marshals, and every person in the courtroom was screened for weapons by a metal detector. In those days, such screening was rare enough to be noted prominently in the newspaper.[16]

Still, Zelmanowitz exuded the confidence of a veteran con man on the witness stand. Under cross-examination, he said he'd earned $1 million over five years in a complicated Mafia-backed stock scheme. Zelmanowitz was used to living high. He and his wife drove new Cadillacs, his home was crammed with expensive

furniture, and he was in the habit of flying back and forth to Europe to tend to his secret Swiss bank accounts.

He readily admitted that he'd filed no tax returns and paid no taxes on his ill-gotten gains. Asked why he hadn't paid taxes, he responded blithely, "I didn't file because I stole the money, and had no job, and couldn't show how I earned it."

The mobster DeCarlo and his associates weren't about to forget Zelmanowitz, but by 1973, they had no idea where he was. That's why "Maris" was so angry when Lipset's operative took pictures of him in the hotel lobby in San Francisco. And it's also why the private investigator Murphy had returned a clean, but unverifiable, report on Maris. Murphy was helping his former colleagues at the FBI maintain Zelmanowitz's fictional identity lest the mob find him and kill him.*

In the end, Creative Capital got its company back, Lipset got out of the lawsuit, and Creative Capital was stuck with the bill for his extra investigation. "Maris" disappeared from sight in 1973, relying once again on the FBI to build a new life for him somewhere else. On the lam that year, Zelmanowitz called a reporter, but refused to say where he was calling from.

"My whole entire cover is being destroyed and torn apart," Zelmanowitz said. "At this moment, I am traveling very far and very fast."

Lipset noted that Zelmanowitz sued the FBI for $12 million for failure to protect his identity, but he lost that case, too.

IN THE CREATIVE Capital saga, Lipset had a client who had been wronged. But not all his clients were so virtuous. Like many of

---

*Murphy later refused to tell a reporter for the *New York Times* whether or not he'd misled his own client. He would say only this: "If the government had decided that they were going to keep someone secure, I don't think that I would be the one to blow him out of the water."

today's corporate intelligence operatives, Lipset was happy to work for anyone who would pay. By his own account, he didn't flinch when he was asked to work for Jim Jones, the founder of Peoples Temple, the infamous religious cult in San Francisco. At the time Lipset went to work for him, Jones was still masquerading as a Christian preacher, although there were already rumors that some of his followers were being held against their will.

This case would end in a spectacular tragedy in 1978, when the insane Jones ordered the followers who had come with him to the jungles of Guyana to kill themselves with poison. More than 900 church members—men, women, and children—died there. While the suicides were going on at the jungle settlement, some of Jones's followers drove a truck to a nearby airstrip, opening fire and killing a United States congressman and several reporters who were trying to leave Guyana after conducting an investigation of the cult.*

The horrific tragedy didn't seem to weigh on Lipset's conscience. In an interview conducted for Patricia Holt's biography, Lipset said his work for Jim Jones began in the late 1960s, when Jones began to feel that he was under threat of assassination. Lipset went to Jones's facility in Ukiah, California, and offered some advice: how to set up a defensive perimeter around the church, how to avoid driving on the same roads twice, and how to avoid repetitive schedules. Lipset passed along other basic security tips to Jones, including how a security team could serve as bodyguards, each man responsible for keeping his eyes on a certain sector so the team could maintain 360-degree awareness of people around the preacher. Lipset said that Jones didn't seem crazy in those early days.

But when pressed on whether he felt it was right or wrong to work for a man like Jones, who was facing allegations that he deprived his followers of their freedom, forced odd sex practices on

---

*My father, Ron Javers, was a reporter with the *San Francisco Chronicle* traveling with the murdered congressman, Leo Ryan. He was wounded during the shoot-out in Guyana and later was the coauthor of a book on the Peoples Temple, *The Suicide Cult: The Inside Story of the Peoples Temple Sect and the Massacre in Guyana*.

them, and confiscated their money, Lipset responded with a blithe comparison of Jones to the U.S. Army, in which he'd served, and to the Catholic Church.

Asked if he would work for a group if he knew the people in it had lost their ability to make choices for themselves, Lipset said:

> It's a matter of degree. I see people giving up their choices every day. . . . If you're a soldier in the Army, you give up even more freedom—that's because you wanted to when you joined up. You made the decision. That's your business. It's certainly none of *my* business.

Applying that stunning moral analogy allowed Lipset to work for just about anybody who could afford his services. It's a trend we'll see over and over again in the corporate intelligence business. Though clients as evil as Jim Jones are rare, today's operatives are selling the talents they developed in government intelligence careers to any client: corrupt companies, Russian oligarchs, Middle Eastern sheikhs—anyone, really, who can afford to pay.

Lipset put it this way: "I'm in it for the money."

The Man Is Gone

Hal Lipset began as a small-time private eye, presiding over a tiny firm operated out of his house in San Francisco, and his outfit was a far cry from those of his predecessors at Pinkerton and elsewhere. Later in the twentieth century, corporate sleuths would once again build much more elaborate intelligence empires—some would become intertwined with United States government intelligence, offer their services to the nation in times of crisis, work the opposite side of the street for foreign governments, ride the ragged edge of morality, and grow extraordinarily wealthy.

The first claimant to the Pinkerton legacy was International Intelligence, which was often referred to as Intertel and was known as the "private CIA" of the reclusive billionaire Howard Hughes. Intertel terrified the Nixon administration, which worried that it was being used by the Kennedys to help elect Teddy Kennedy as president. In just a few years after it was founded by veterans of Robert Kennedy's Justice Department, Intertel had extended its reach into the worlds of Hughes, the Kennedys, Richard Nixon's incompetent plumbers, vicious Mafia figures, and the elusive CIA. As a result, its history has become something of a touchstone for conspiracy theorists, many of whom have concocted elaborate fantasies about Intertel and the dastardly deeds of elites controlling

the world. Much of that is no more than fantasy, or fiction. But Intertel did exist, and for about a decade it was involved in some of the country's most secret episodes.

Howard Hughes was an oilman, a Hollywood bon vivant, and an aviator. He lived in Texas, Las Vegas, and the Caribbean, among other locales around the world. But today, his last remaining secrets can be found in an unlikely place: the small town of Fairfield, Pennsylvania, amid the rural countryside just north of the Mason-Dixon Line. Here, alongside 400 acres of soybeans, sit a small brown farmhouse, two silos, and a barn. Intertel's founder, Robert Dolan Peloquin, and his wife, Peggy, live here.

Peloquin, who is nearly eighty, is an imposing man: tall, with a firm handshake, swept-back white hair, a welcoming manner, and a deep voice edged with a southern Massachusetts accent. He relishes telling stories about the old days. Peloquin was once an intelligence officer at the National Security Agency and a Mafia hunter at the Department of Justice. In later years, there were Christmas-morning requests from Howard Hughes, sudden trips to Switzerland to track down a con artist, and jaunts to the Caribbean to play Twenty Questions with Merv Griffin. (Griffin, a famous entertainment executive and talk show host, kept the topics focused on Hollywood, and so usually won the games.) Robert Peloquin was one of the world's greatest corporate spies.

He began his career, like so many other corporate spies, in the military. After graduating from Georgetown University at the beginning of the Korean War, Peloquin entered the navy. He figured it would be easier duty than slogging through the mud in the army. But after midshipman school at Newport, Rhode Island, he was assigned to Norfolk, Virginia, and a navy unit called the beach masters—an amphibious force designed to take charge of beachheads during the first wave of any invasion, making sure that the troops and matériel got forward as fast as possible. Peloquin didn't like what he saw of the beach masters. This was a first-wave invasion force training to go to war in Korea. Its commanding officer,

whose name was Peterson, had been a hero in World War II—
wounded seven times in action. The unit drew many of its enlisted
men straight from the brig at nearby Camp Allen: these men had
been told that they could either rot in a navy jail or report to the
beach masters. To Peloquin and his fellow ensigns, it seemed that
the unit was being stocked with cannon fodder, and led by a man
who wouldn't hesitate to charge into the most brutal combat. Peloquin came to a conclusion: "If I hang around this place, I'm not
gonna live long."

But how to get out of this assault unit? Peloquin solved the
problem by deploying two talents he would rely on for the rest of
his life: an ability to curry favor with important older men and a
talent for job hopping ever upward.

His boss, Peterson, had a problem that Peloquin could solve. The
bad seeds and ex-cons in his unit were racking up courts-martial at
an astonishing pace. And the Uniform Code of Military Justice—
which was then new, and which governs the way military personnel
should be tried and punished—was causing Peterson fits. He was
of the old school and didn't understand how the new rules worked.
He sent Peloquin to the Naval Justice School in Newport, Rhode
Island, far from the fighting in Korea. On returning to the beach
masters, Peloquin helped solve Peterson's backlog of court-martial
cases. From then on, Peloquin recalls, "I was kind of his boy."

After seeing some combat at Inchon in Korea, Peloquin took
advantage of a navy loophole and went to law school without prom-
ising extra years of service in return. He spent a few peaceful years
at Georgetown Law, and after graduation received orders to join
a destroyer in Pearl Harbor. Peloquin protested to his superiors
that the bar exam was just a few months away—why send him to
Hawaii before he had passed the bar? The answer was clear. Navy
rules required only that he graduate from law school to practice
law in the navy. He didn't have to be a member of any bar. Passing
the bar, as far as the navy was concerned, was his own business, to
be conducted on his own time.

Peloquin didn't like that answer. He resigned from the navy. During his time in law school in Washington, Peloquin had reported to the same navy facility that also housed a supersecret code-breaking and electronic eavesdropping entity: the National Security Agency. It was so covert that its acronym, NSA, is still jokingly said to mean No Such Agency. The NSA happened to be just down the hall from Peloquin's navy office. He worked his connections there, and landed a job in 1954.

Peloquin found the work fascinating. It was his first exposure to the world of intelligence. He worked in the security office, helping to vet and investigate the agency's own employees suspected of being spies for the Soviet Union. While working there, he became familiar with the case of two American defectors: William Martin and Bernon Mitchell. In 1960, these two men defected to the Soviet Union, saying that they opposed U.S. policy on spy flights over enemy countries.

Martin and Mitchell had gotten advance word that Peloquin and other NSA investigators were snooping around. That prompted panic: the two men had long been selling information about the NSA's code-breaking abilities to the Soviet Union, and getting caught could mean spending the rest of their lives in federal prison. They decided to make a dash for freedom, taking planes to Mexico City, then Cuba, and finally Moscow. All they left behind was an anti-American manifesto in a safe-deposit box at a bank.

But Peloquin says the NSA wasn't nearly as close to discovering the truth as Martin and Mitchell thought. It was investigating the two men, but not for spying. The investigators were instead trying to figure out if Martin and Mitchell were gay. This was a time when even a suspicion of homosexuality created doubts about a person's loyalty to the government—and could end a career. Peloquin says the NSA had no idea the two men were active spies for the Soviet Union. But rumors of their sexual orientation had prompted the NSA's security people to start an internal investigation. If Martin and Mitchell had stayed, it is possible that they would have been

drummed out of the NSA for being homosexuals instead of locked up for being spies.

At about the same time, Robert Peloquin hopped to a new job. His supervisor had a contact at the Department of Justice, and Peloquin went to work at its internal security unit. From there, he jumped, again, to the Justice Department's Organized Crime and Racketeering section. This was the early 1960s, and John F. Kennedy had been elected president, naming his brother Robert as the attorney general of the United States. Bobby Kennedy was fascinated by the organized crime section, and Peloquin became Bobby Kennedy's boy. Peloquin would spend most of the next decade tracking down high-level Mafia figures and putting them behind bars.

At one point, while Peloquin was in New Orleans on an investigation, Kennedy called to see how it was going. The phone rang, and a voice with a New England accent asked, "Is this Bob Peloquin? This is Bobby Kennedy and I just wanted to see how you're doing."

Not believing that the attorney general would call such a low-level investigator, Peloquin suspected that one of the other investigators was having fun with him.

"Sprizzo, cut that shit out," he said.

"No, this really is Bobby Kennedy," came the reply. Peloquin leaned back in his chair and saw that the man he suspected of playing the joke, John Sprizzo, was in the next room—and he wasn't on the telephone. Peloquin was horrified. But Kennedy didn't mind. The Kennedys invited the young criminal division investigators, FBI agents, and others involved in the fight against the Mafia to Hickory Hill, the family estate in suburban Virginia. On one evening, a nervous Peloquin sternly warned his wife not to bring up certain topics in front of the boss. "Don't embarrass me," he told her. As he and Peggy settled their buffet dinners on their knees, though, Peloquin himself mishandled a piece of roast beef, sending it skittering onto the floor. That attracted the Kennedys' enormous

dog—a Newfoundland called Brumus—who came lumbering across the room, scattering tables and chairs. All eyes turned to the hapless Peloquin. Peggy leaned over and whispered, "Don't embarrass me." Her husband has never forgotten the lesson.

At the Justice Department, Peloquin learned another lesson he'd never forget: how to combine forces. While he was there, the department came up with an innovative structure for going after the mob. Using strike forces, the government pooled senior-level people from every agency that had a hand in the fight: the IRS, the bureau of narcotics, the FBI, the border patrol, and more. Each strike force would take a particular organized crime family and devote all its disparate resources toward taking that family down.

Peloquin headed up the first organized crime task force, and set his team on the Magaddino crime family in Buffalo, New York. Working with the Canadian Mounted Police, they broke up this long-reigning Mafia family, sending nine of its members to prison. Soon, the Department of Justice deployed similar organized crime strike forces across the country.

At the time, the Mafia was making inroads into all types of businesses. With a foothold in Las Vegas gambling, mob bosses were now poised to go big-time: into the National Football League (NFL). For owners of professional teams, the prospect of the Mafia influencing players to throw games or referees to make bad calls was a nightmare. Millions of dollars in future profits depended on the fans' belief that the game was honest. The football commissioner, Pete Rozelle, knew that the league had to develop some defense. He brought in Peloquin's boss, and Peloquin tagged along, jumping to a cushy job as associate counsel at the NFL.

The new team put together an innovative solution to the problem. Fixing football games was illegal, and so was gambling on them. But in order to weed out illegal attempts to fix the games, Peloquin's security team cultivated sources in the illegal gambling world.

"The last guy in the world who wants to see a fixed football game is a bookie, because if he's not in on it, he's going to get taken

badly," Peloquin reasoned. He saw the irony of illegal gamblers working to protect honest games, but still, the bookies became his best source of intelligence about the Mafia's attempts to fix games. If an unusual amount of money flooded in on bets on one team, Peloquin heard about it from his bookie informants and checked it out.

Before long, Peloquin and his boss Bill Hundley—who had been born in Brooklyn and had worked at the Department of Justice as an anti-Mafia fighter*—began to get restless. They'd both been commuting to New York during the week and living in Washington on weekends. They both had large families (each had six children). And both thought they could make even more money selling their services to clients beyond the NFL.

Once again, a powerful senior player stepped in to boost Peloquin's career: Pete Rozelle agreed to set Peloquin and Hundley up in a law firm of their own in Washington. After all, he was already paying their hotel bills and dining and travel expenses. The two men were getting expensive. Rozelle put up the first six months of their office rent and provided cash to hire a secretary and pay the phone bill; and the two men started their own law practice, with the high-profile NFL as their premier client. Soon they added others. *Life* magazine signed on for help with a series of articles it was doing on the Mafia. Each time *Life* published an article on a Mafia family in a given city, lawsuits would be filed, alleging that the magazine had libeled people not connected to the Mafia. It was Hundley and Peloquin's job to prove that *Life* had been right, and get the lawsuits thrown out of court. Leaning on their contacts inside the Department of Justice, they succeeded.

One morning, a former contact at the Justice Department called Peloquin. Could they meet at the office? Someone was there whom Peloquin should know.

---

*Hundley went on to an illustrious career in legal defense. When he died in 2006, his obituary in the *New York Times* noted that he'd represented President Richard Nixon; Attorney General John N. Mitchell, at Mitchell's Watergate trial; Tongsun Park, a South Korean accused of bribing congressmen; and Vernon Jordan.

The man was James Crosby, the owner of the Mary Carter Paint Company. He'd just purchased Hog Island, in the Bahamas, and was in the process of developing it as a resort and renaming it Paradise Island—a better draw for the tourists he hoped would flock to it. Crosby was maneuvering in local Bahamian politics to get a gambling license for Paradise Island, but he was terrified of getting into the gaming business, which was rife with gangsters and hoodlums. Crosby wanted Hundley and Peloquin to make sure his new employees weren't connected to the mob. "I didn't know diddly-shit about gambling," Peloquin recalls. But he knew the mob. And he got the job.

He hired a staff to work on the project, bringing in several of his old pals who had retired from the organized crime strike force, including an imposing former director of enforcement at the U.S. Bureau of Customs. This man, who had entered Peloquin's circle as the senior representative from customs to the Justice Department's organized crime task force, relocated to Paradise Island full-time and used his government contacts to screen new hires at the resort, determining if they had Mafia connections or any other criminal connections.

That technique became a hallmark of Peloquin's later career: charging clients fees to run background checks on people, and then using former work connections to dip into government files to make the checks. It was a great business model. And the U.S. taxpayer never knew that government money was paying for agents to run background checks on behalf of millionaire owners of Caribbean resorts.

Peloquin spent much of the rest of his career charging private clients for access to their own government's enormous security files. "We capitalized on private industry," he recalls. "But we depended on the government to give us the poop."

As long as secrecy was protected, it was a lucrative business. Asked what outsiders should make of his techniques, Peloquin replies, "I'm not that hung up on invasion of privacy, but a lot of people are. It depends on how you look at it. If you're in business,

there's nowhere for you to turn to find out what the hell is going on. What do you do?" Peloquin says he has no qualms about the private spy industry that he helped to invent: "I think it's a legitimate thing. I don't lose any sleep over it, that's for sure."

The new industry—charging companies for access to secret information for which the government had already charged them via taxes—took off after the first Resorts International casino in the Bahamas opened in 1970. The casino magnate Crosby was impressed by Peloquin's work, and, ever the entrepreneur, he had an idea. Why not spin off the investigative effort into a stand-alone company? With Crosby's financial backing, Peloquin formed International Intelligence, Inc., or Intertel, hiring former colleagues right out of the anti-Mafia strike forces of the Department of Justice. He opened offices at Seventeenth and H Streets NW, across the street from the tony Metropolitan Club of Washington, where he and his colleagues soon became regulars. Intertel was just three blocks away from the White House, and a short walk from the Department of Justice. The place felt almost like an outpost of the federal government. Situated among so many sober gray government buildings, it was a secret spy service for the private sector.

In 1978, a former CIA agent turned author, George O'Toole, described Intertel in his book *The Private Sector*:

> The men who run Intertel are not simply ex-cops embarked on a second career in midlife. You'll find no tell-tale bulge beneath the shoulders of their tailored, three-piece business suits, and their slim attaché cases are more likely to contain pages of computer printouts than brass knuckles or handcuffs. Their clients are not retail merchants or jealous spouses, but giant international enterprises that do business under the crazy-quilt pattern formed by the laws of a dozen nations.[1]

Before long, Intertel's staff included a cofounder, the former FBI agent John O'Connell; a former IRS investigator, William Kolar;

and a former director of investigations at the National Security Agency, David Belisle. O'Toole called it "the greatest collection of recycled brass ever assembled in the private sector."

Peloquin believed in the power of connections. Along with the others, he hired Herbert Hoover's only nephew—since Hoover never married, his nephew was in many ways his heir. "That brought in a lot of business," Peloquin says. "When you can say, 'I'll have Hoover's nephew look into it for you,' it's surprising."

JUST THREE MONTHS after opening the doors of the new company in 1970, Peloquin got a call from Chester Davis, the general counsel for Howard Hughes.* Davis reported that Hughes had decided to force out his long-serving loyal consultant, Robert Maheu.

Actually, Davis and another of Hughes's lieutenants, Bill Gay, were waging a power struggle against Maheu, who they felt had come to exert too much control over Hughes and his sprawling business interests, which included not only Trans World Airlines but Hollywood productions and Las Vegas casinos, among others. The increasingly paranoid Hughes had dropped almost entirely out of sight, living in his apartment atop the Desert Inn with the windows curtained against the sunlight, and communicating only through scrawled notes. Most of the people working for Hughes had never seen him in person.

Hughes now had long, scraggly hair, and he refused to trim his fingernails and toenails, which had grown into curled yellow claws. He was taking a staggering quantity of painkilling drugs, feeding an addiction that had begun when he broke his back in an airplane crash in 1946. Hughes had brought his struggling XF-11 reconnaissance airplane down in a crowded residential area in Beverly

---

*It was a small world: Chester Davis had been referred to Peloquin by a personal friend of President Nixon, the Florida banker Charles G. "Bebe" Rebozo. In later years, Rebozo would come under congressional scrutiny for allegedly passing along a $100,000 contribution from Howard Hughes to the Nixon campaign.

Hills. Thanks to the quick thinking of a passing Marine Corps sergeant who pulled him from the wreckage, Hughes survived. But after he began taking the painkilling drugs, he was never quite the same.* For Maheu, Davis, and Gay, control over Hughes meant domination of one of the biggest corporate empires in America, and millions of dollars in potential income for themselves.

Gay and Davis may have sensed an opportunity in the power vacuum created by Hughes's mental instability. For years, Maheu had served as an outside consultant to Hughes from his perch at his investigative agency in Washington, D.C., Robert A. Maheu and Associates. He'd become Hughes's go-to man for sensitive missions of all kinds, including compiling dossiers on the relationships between powerful figures in foreign governments, surveillance and investigation of Hughes's own executives, hiring actors who looked like Hughes to use as doubles in schemes to throw off process servers in court cases, and overseeing the distribution of political campaign contributions.[2] Hughes knew that Maheu had been a contractor for the CIA since the early 1950s, and that his firm was a front for some of the CIA's most covert activities. For a power-hungry paranoiac like Hughes, Maheu was a handy man to have around.

But most of all, Hughes valued Maheu because he knew the veteran spy's deepest secret—that in 1960 and 1961, Maheu had served as the CIA's point of contact with the underworld tough Johnny Roselli and the Mafia boss Sam Giancana in its failed plot to assassinate the Cuban leader Fidel Castro on the eve of the disastrous Bay of Pigs invasion. In August 1960, Maheu flew to Los Angeles to meet with Roselli at the Brown Derby restaurant. Surrounded by Hollywood executives and actors, the two discussed the murder of Castro.

---

*Peloquin recalls that one of his duties at Intertel was to deliver a monthly check for hundreds of dollars—a significant amount of money in those days—to William Durkin, the marine sergeant who had pulled Hughes from the burning wreckage. Peloquin's account of a generous lifetime reward contradicts the account of Durkin's family, who maintained that he never took money from Hughes. Durkin died in 2006.

At first, Roselli was incredulous. "Me? You want me to get in-volved with Uncle Sam?" he asked. "The feds are tailing me wher-ever I go. They go to my shirt-maker to see if I'm buying things with cash. They go to my tailor to see if I'm using cash there. They're always trying to get something on me. Bob, are you sure you have the right guy?"[3]

Maheu assured Roselli that the offer from the CIA was real. And he explained the conditions: no one could ever know that the government had worked with the Mafia to kill Castro. Maheu told Roselli that if the matter ever became public, he'd deny it. If Roselli accepted, he would be on his own. The mobster hesitated and then agreed. The CIA and the mob were officially business partners.

At a meeting in 1961 at Miami's Fontainbleau Hotel, Maheu's CIA controller handed him a white envelope containing several poison pills. The plan called for Maheu to pass the pills to the Mafia figures, who would use their connections from the prerevo-lutionary days of the Cuban casino business to pass the pills to someone in Castro's entourage to slip into the dictator's drink.

The problem was that all the time Maheu was dealing with the Mafia on behalf of the CIA, agents from the FBI were tailing both him and the mobsters. After all, the FBI had been trying to prove its case against the mob for years, and had detailed surveillance under way on the very men Maheu was meeting. The FBI wanted to know: *why was a veteran agent and known CIA contact suddenly palling around with the mob?*

One night, during a dinner meeting with Roselli, Maheu spot-ted two FBI tails in the restaurant. After Roselli left to go to the men's room, Maheu cornered the men and pulled them into the kitchen, trying to get them off the case. Roselli hadn't noticed them, but if he did spot the federal agents spying on his dinner meeting, he might get too spooked to go through with the plot against Castro. Back in his hotel room, Maheu called the CIA from the hotel phone—which he knew would be tapped by the FBI—and let the FBI's agents listen in on the conversation, just so they

could figure out what was going on, and why they ought to leave Roselli alone for the time being.*[4]

Maheu said later that he never got the "go-signal" from the CIA, even though there were reports from the Mafia that they were ready to deploy their end of the assassination plot. When the Bay of Pigs invasion ended in disaster, Maheu walked away from the mess. He said he was never again involved in the agency's attempts to kill Castro.†

Hughes knew this dark tale because he was trying to get Maheu to come to Los Angeles to work for him at the same time Maheu was in Florida plotting with the Mafia. Maheu, eager to curry favor with his most lucrative client, stepped out into the street and called Hughes back on a pay phone, saying that he couldn't come to work that day because he was in Miami working on a secret CIA plot to kill Castro. Hughes, though, wouldn't be put off, and talked Maheu into flying to Los Angeles to work on his project for a day or two. Hughes was impressed by Maheu's involvement in the scheme—unsuccessful though it was—and spent much of the next decade figuring out how to use Maheu's CIA relationship to his own advantage. Hughes, too, was connected to the CIA, and many of his companies served as fronts for CIA operations over the years.

But by 1970, Hughes's relationship with Maheu had begun to crumble. Hughes's paranoia and his increasing insanity had

---

*Roselli was killed in a Mafia hit in Miami in 1976. He had just testified about the plot against Castro before a Senate committee, and reportedly had not asked permission of the mob bosses beforehand. He was seventy years old. "They got him aboard a yacht and a hit man appeared out of nowhere, plugging his nose and mouth," Maheu wrote in his autobiography. "He was pretty weak, so it didn't take long for him to suffocate. Then, they decided to cut him into pieces. They stuck his foot in his mouth, wrapped his legs around his head, and then sank him in a steel drum." Sam Giancana had been killed a year earlier, just before he could testify before the Senate on the attempted assassination of Castro.

†But he remained an active participant in other CIA operations. Over the years, Maheu told Senate investigators, he allowed his firm to serve as cover employment for CIA officers on missions around the world. Maheu paid out salaries and expenses, sometimes for men he'd never met. "I mean, all they had to do was carry the credit cards and credentials and claim that they worked for Robert A. Maheu and Associates," he said. The CIA reimbursed Maheu for the cost of the cover agents.

something to do with this, but Maheu and Hughes also had disagreements over important issues. For one thing, Hughes wanted to intertwine his operations ever more deeply with the CIA, and Maheu resisted the idea. In 1975, in top-secret testimony before a Senate committee investigating wrongdoing by the CIA, Maheu told investigators of Hughes's plan.

"From time to time during conversations with Mr. Hughes, he would beg of me to try to help him set up a huge, the way he described it, a huge covert operation involving one of his companies," Maheu said.

"Why," asked a Senate investigator, "did he want you to set up a large covert operation under one of his companies?"

"His answer to the very same question when I put it to him," replied Maheu, "was that he wanted to be put in a position that if he ever became involved in any serious problem with the U.S. government, that they could not afford to prosecute him."

Maheu said he "categorically refused" to help Hughes set up the plan.

In 1968, Maheu said, Hughes asked him for help with an even more ruthless plot: to extend the Vietnam War. Two years earlier Hughes had begun selling a light observation helicopter, the OH-6A Cayuse, for which the army placed an initial order of 1,468 units.[5] It was a lucrative project, and Hughes was afraid the Vietnam War might wind down before he could make up some earlier financial losses. Peace would be bad for business.

"He was fearful that the Vietnam War would come to an end," Maheu told the Senate investigators, "and asked me if I would help him to conceive some plan whereby the Vietnam War would be extended."

Maheu added, "And I frankly told him to go to hell."[6]

It's possible, of course, that Maheu's description of Hughes's machinations is the self-serving account of a fired contractor; but whatever the truth, it was clear that Maheu and Hughes were growing apart.

It was bad timing for a rift. Hughes's insanity made him

vulnerable to a palace coup, as Maheu later told the journalist Jim Hougan. "The old man was a perfect target, isolated like that," Maheu said. "Whoever controlled the palace guard, the Mormon mafia [most of the half dozen aides who had physical access to Hughes were Mormons], controlled him. And he knew it. He didn't trust them, whatever anyone else may say. Howard and I knew they were manipulating him." Despite all the years he spent as Howard Hughes's consigliere, Robert Maheu never once laid eyes on Hughes. His only contact with Hughes was by telephone or through a series of scrawled notes passed between the two men by personal aides loyal to Bill Gay. Gay's total control of information going into and out of Hughes's office gave him the upper hand in the power struggle against Maheu. By this point, Hughes knew only what Gay allowed him to know.

When Gay and Davis teamed up to push Maheu out, they turned to Intertel to do the deed. For Peloquin, it was a huge boost for his tiny company. And the Hughes organization paid well: "Hughes was a wonderful client," Peloquin recalls. "We'd send a bill in on Monday, and on Thursday, that check would come right back. . . . I didn't have any money problems at all," he says, waving his arm in the direction of the soybean field. "That's why I've got this farm."*

Under pressure from Gay and Davis, Hughes fired Maheu. But now the challenge was to get Hughes out of Las Vegas, where Maheu might still have influence over him. Intertel made a logistical plan for moving Hughes. But on the night before Thanksgiving, Davis and Gay decided that the move needed to happen instantly—perhaps to take advantage of Maheu's decision to take a Thanksgiving vacation. Intertel junked its elaborate plan and sent a few agents whom it could scrape together on short notice to Las Vegas. There, Intertel men stood guard as Hughes's assistants carried the thin,

---

*In the winter, the Peloquins spend time at their condo in Plantation, Florida, situated just off the Lago Mar Country Club. And Peloquin still goes to Paradise Island sometimes. "I know people there who can get me a reservation," he says with a laugh.

sickly Hughes in a chair down the back stairs of the Desert Inn.

While the escape was in progress, Peloquin took up a position in the lobby, waiting to see if the operation would set off an alarm that would summon Maheu. He knew that if Maheu arrived on the scene, there wasn't much he could do other than stall for time. Even though it was Maheu's job to provide security for the hotel, he never discovered that Hughes was being slipped out the back door. The Intertel operation was so thorough that it was days before Maheu would know what had happened to Hughes. And although journalists through the years have wondered whether or not Hughes himself was aware of the move, since he was frequently delirious with drugs and paranoid fantasies, Peloquin says he was awake and aware that he was being moved to the Caribbean.

Outside the hotel, the Intertel team bundled Hughes into a waiting car and made a dash for nearby McCarran Airport. One of Hughes's planes was waiting on the airstrip. The team whisked him to the Bahamas and installed him in a new private lair on the ninth floor of the Britannia Beach Hotel on Paradise Island, where he would live for years, protected—at great cost—by Intertel's armed guards, closed-circuit television cameras, and bug sweepers.

The next day, Thanksgiving Day 1970, Maheu was enjoying a rare day off at his chalet on Charleston Peak, Nevada, to which he'd flown in some friends on a helicopter owned by the Hughes company. In his autobiography, *Next to Hughes*, Maheu recalled the scene. He was poised over a thirty-five-pound turkey, carving knife in hand, when the phone rang. Jack Hooper, the head of security for Hughes's holdings in Nevada, was on the line. He said just four words: "The Man is gone."

"What the hell do you mean, the Man is gone?" I asked none too calmly.

Everyone was seated at the table just a few feet away from me. I was trying like hell not to yell. It wasn't easy.[7]

Devastated by the palace coup, and suspicious that Hughes had been kidnapped by Intertel on behalf of Gay and Davis, Maheu hired his own team of private detectives to find out if Hughes was still in control of his company or if agents from Intertel had taken it over.

A team of eight agents working for Maheu traveled to the Bahamas, but they couldn't make any headway. Intertel deployed its own counterintelligence measures against them. By one account, they used bugs, phone taps, mail intercepts, and other tricks of the spy trade to keep Maheu's men from finding out anything about Hughes. (Peloquin says his firm never tapped phones or engaged in illegal conduct, and always thought it was important to obey the law.)

Maheu's spies set up shop on the eighth floor of the hotel, drilling a hole in the ceiling to slip a microphone into Hughes's quarters. But Intertel was waiting for that predictable move, and called the local police, who raided the room and arrested Maheu's team. Peloquin intervened with the Bahamian police force to have the men released without charges, so long as they would head straight back to the United States. The spooks returned home, defeated.

LIFE IN THE Bahamas was grand. Peloquin lived in style and rubbed shoulders with the rich and famous. In the late 1970s, Crosby called: the shah of Iran had just been deposed in the Iranian revolution, and President Jimmy Carter didn't want him to come into the United States. Could Peloquin help? Peloquin worked out the logistics with the government of the Bahamas, and got the shah admitted to that Caribbean country, where he stayed in Crosby's home. Peloquin recalls spending long hours playing tennis with the shah and his teenage son and heir apparent, Reza Pahlavi.

But the shah's Bahamian idyll didn't last long. Peloquin got a call from the office of Prime Minister Lynden Oscar Pindling of the Bahamas, who had gone out of his way to admit the shah into

the country. Pindling wanted to meet the shah, and Peloquin said he'd arrange it.

"The liaison guy from the state department was a perfect jerk," Peloquin recalls. The department wouldn't allow the shah to meet with the prime minister. Why? "The State Department guy said, 'I don't think the shah would be interested in meeting with a Negro prime minister.'" Peloquin knew that was nonsense. He didn't know if the shah was a racist or not, but he did know that the shah—who was dependent on American help—would meet with anyone the United States told him to. The State Department was throwing up roadblocks that didn't need to be there. The Bahamian prime minister, who had been the first black premier of the British colony, was offended by the crude rejection. "Two days later, they expelled the shah from the Bahamas," Peloquin says.

Back in Washington, Intertel's business was taking off, and a parade of prominent citizens with odd problems began marching through the doors. One visitor, Henry Ford, the grandson of the legendary automaker, sent Peloquin's secretary into a frenzy of preparations, shining the wooden office doors in anticipation of the great man's arrival. Ford was opening a casino on the Caribbean island of Saint Martin. He told Peloquin that he'd asked the head of the FBI, J. Edgar Hoover, for advice, and Hoover had recommended Intertel. Intertel men were soon running background checks on every one of Ford's new casino employees, making sure that no one with known Mafia ties was hired.

On another occasion the Washington super-lawyer Edward Bennett Williams walked into the Intertel office on Seventeenth Street with two clients in tow: the publisher of the *Washington Post*, Katherine Graham, and its editor, Ben Bradlee. They were in the middle of the high-stakes drama of Watergate, breaking story after story about corruption at the White House. They worried that Nixon's men were bugging their offices. Peloquin dispatched a team to sweep Graham and Bradlee's offices, finding no evidence of eavesdropping.

From the early 1970s on, Howard Hughes came to depend ever

more on Intertel. When Clifford Irving announced that he had cowritten an autobiography of Hughes to be published by McGraw-Hill, Intertel got the case. Irving was a fraud: Hughes had never granted permission for an autobiography. And he certainly had not received compensation for selling his life story, as the publishing house was claiming. Irving's interviews, documents, and anecdotes were either made up or lifted from other media accounts of Hughes's colorful life.*

"Chester Davis said, 'this is pure bullshit,'" Peloquin recalls. "The Hughes people were up in arms about it, because Hughes himself was up in arms about it. The author was a wacko."

Allegations that the book was a fake erupted in the media in January 1972. The Hughes organization called a meeting in a hotel conference room in Hollywood with seven reporters who had known Howard Hughes in the days before he'd become a hermit. Peloquin recalls that the reporters quizzed Hughes over a phone line especially piped in for the remote press conference. *Do you know this guy?* they asked. Hughes denied it.

For the moment, Hughes was as charming as ever. "I only wish I was still in the movie business," the disembodied voice said over the phone line. "Because I don't remember any script as wild or as stretching the imagination as this yarn has turned out to be."[8]

But that wasn't enough to derail the book. Hughes needed definitive proof.

To prove the book was a hoax, Peloquin set up a meeting with his former colleagues at the criminal division of the Department of Justice. He told officials there that Hughes had no intention of paying any taxes on the hundreds of thousands of dollars in income he had supposedly earned from McGraw-Hill. Peloquin's strategy was simple. He wanted to provoke an IRS audit. The government would find that Hughes had never collected a cent from the publishing house.

---

*This story made for great Hollywood fare: in 2007 it became a movie, *The Hoax*, starring Richard Gere as Irving.

But before the federal government could roll into action, Peloquin got an even better opportunity. An executive at McGraw-Hill went on the *Today* show to hold up three checks the company had made out to "H. Hughes," as payment for his life story. The checks had been cashed, and McGraw-Hill viewed them as proof of its agreement with Hughes. Chester Davis filmed the appearance, enlarged the image, and made out the names of the Swiss banks that had cashed the checks.

Davis called Peloquin: "Get your ass over to Switzerland and find out what the scoop is."

Peloquin took the next plane to Zurich. There, he began to reap the rewards of his shrewd hiring spree. He turned to Vadja Kalombatovic, a veteran of the FBI whose father had defected to the United States from Yugoslavia. Kalombatovic spoke perhaps a dozen languages, and—more important—he'd developed contacts in nearly every police force in Europe during his time as the FBI's legal attaché in France, Spain, and Italy.*

Now an executive at Intertel, Kalombatovic called a contact in Swiss law enforcement, and the Swiss dispatched a police sergeant to meet Peloquin at his hotel in Zurich. "I told him my problem," Peloquin recalls. "'We have to get into that bank to find out what is really going on.'" Who had been cashing the checks made out to "H. Hughes"? Once again, Intertel would profit from government sleuthing. The Swiss police sergeant told Peloquin to stay put.

He returned four hours later, proclaiming in slightly mangled English, "I have solved your Hughes."

As Intertel suspected, the person who'd cashed the checks wasn't Howard Hughes at all; it was a woman going by the name of "Helga Hughes." The police sergeant took Peloquin to the bank and

*Vadja Kalombatovic had one other connection useful to Intertel. During World War II, he'd served in the army as a corporal. The sergeant he reported to was Henry Kissinger, later to become Nixon's secretary of state. When the two men ran into each other in the deep-carpeted confines of Washington's elite Metropolitan Club, they'd embrace like brothers. The relationship was yet another vector into the federal government for Intertel.

introduced him to the private banker who had dealt with the supposed Helga Hughes. On a hunch, Peloquin showed the banker a picture of Clifford Irving's wife, Edith Sommer Irving, whose looks and long blond hair were reminiscent of the young Jane Fonda. The banker replied, "Yes, she has dyed her hair black, but that's the woman."

It was the smoking gun that Howard Hughes had been searching for. Clifford Irving and his wife had been in on the scam together, concocting the memoir on their own and duping McGraw-Hill into buying it. They had collected hundreds of thousands of dollars in the hoax.

By the end of January, Clifford Irving's story was falling apart, and he'd soon confess the fraud. Both Irvings wound up going to jail.

Hughes was delighted. "That made me, as far as Hughes was concerned," says Peloquin.

IN GRATITUDE, HUGHES—WHO almost never met with anyone— wanted to greet Peloquin in person. On Christmas Day, Peloquin got a call at home from Hughes's office. Hughes had decided to fly from Canada to London. He was in the air already, but he hadn't bothered to bring his passport or any papers at all. He'd need help in a few hours when he landed in London. What could Peloquin do to smooth his entry into England?

Again, Peloquin tapped Intertel's connections. On his board of directors sat Sir Ranulph Bacon, a former head of Scotland Yard.* Peloquin, in a panic, reached him by phone.

---

*The interests that intertwined Sir Ranulph and Peloquin are almost incomprehensibly complex. O'Toole writes that while Peloquin was still at the Department of Justice, he was already in contact with Crosby, of Paradise Island. (By Peloquin's account, they met only after he had left Justice.) And according to O'Toole, Peloquin began an investigation at the department of alleged corruption among Bahamian gamblers—who also posed a threat to Crosby's interests on the island. A Royal Commission of Inquiry was also formed to look into allegations of corruption among Crosby's competitors. That commission was chaired by Bacon and received direct cooperation from Peloquin. It succeeded in driving away several potential competitors to Crosby. Later, Peloquin invited Bacon to join his board of directors at Intertel.

"Ranulph, we've got to get Howard into London," he said.

About a half an hour later, Bacon called back: "He'll be fine." Hughes was warmly received in the United Kingdom.

That minor triumph set up Peloquin's only face-to-face meeting with Hughes. Peloquin got a call from Hughes's office ordering him to report to London immediately. He went to Washington's National Airport, where he was met by a Hughes airplane and crew. Peloquin would be the only passenger. The aircrew set up a bed so he could get some rest during the overnight flight. Before he knew it, he was landing at Heathrow Airport. Hughes was ensconced in an expensive hotel near Buckingham Palace, and hovering nearby was the ever-present Bill Gay. "Howard would like to meet you," he said.

Peloquin was prepared for the worst. Stories of Hughes's physical appearance were grim. Worse, Hughes had suffered another injury in England. Peloquin says Hughes—now nearing seventy, and in poor mental and physical health—had looked up an old British flying buddy, who offered to take him on one more flight over England. Hughes went along, possibly taking the controls of his friend's airplane for several minutes. The flight was uneventful. But climbing out of the plane proved too challenging for Hughes, who fell, breaking his hip.

He refused to be taken to a hospital, so English doctors tried to set the hip in his hotel room. The operation wasn't successful, and Hughes was in a lot of pain. He would be dead three years later.

Peloquin was, therefore, surprised to find a likable, lucid man in the hotel suite. "He wasn't that odd," Peloquin says. "His hair was reasonably long, but he talked sensibly."

Hughes, who had a notorious germ phobia, didn't shake hands, which made for an uncomfortable moment. But still, he didn't wear Kleenex boxes on his feet, as some reports had described. Hughes suffered from gut-wrenching constipation because of the drug cocktail he consumed daily, and Peloquin says he spent a large part of each day on the toilet. As awful as that sounds, Hughes continued to innovate: he developed a toilet seat for himself based on the

design of the military's McClellan horse saddle, which had a hole in the crotch area.* Later, suffering from bedsores, Hughes designed himself a new mattress that helped alleviate the lesions.

In April 1976 Intertel landed one last secret mission on behalf of the mad billionaire. Hughes was staying in Acapulco's Princess Hotel when he reached the end of his life. Naked, emaciated, and covered with bedsores, he lay dying. Gay and his other confidants decided to fly him back to the United States, but they said he died during the flight. For Hughes, it was the end of years of misery. But for his aides, who hoped to continue to run the Hughes empire, it was a nightmare. The first problem they faced was that Mexican authorities arrested the entire Hughes retinue in Acapulco. Mexican doctors had been appalled at Hughes's condition, and suspected neglect—benign or otherwise.

Once again, Gay called Peloquin with an emergency request: get to Mexico and spring the Hughes entourage from prison. Peloquin and a former member of the Arizona border patrol took flights to Mexico.

"Bob, have you got any money?" the man from the border patrol asked Peloquin when they arrived.

"I've got a couple of thousand."

"Give it to me."

Peloquin handed over the cash. (When dealing with Hughes, Peloquin was accustomed to carrying huge amounts of hard currency.)

The border patrolman disappeared up a back alley, Peloquin says. "A couple of hours later, he came back to the hotel with the Hughes aides, and they were free. That's Mexico." Bribing Mexican law enforcement officers was apparently one of Intertel's services—at least for the firm's best client.

Now the Intertel men faced another quandary. Hughes's rooms

---

*During the Thanksgiving eve escape from the Desert Inn in Las Vegas, one of Hughes's aides had the unpleasant duty of toting that saddle-shaped toilet seat down the stairs to load into the getaway car.

were loaded with his billionaire's drugs, legal and illegal, stacked in box after box filled with small glass bottles. The aides were afraid they'd be arrested again, on narcotics charges. The border patrol man left the hotel room. He came back with a truck, and Hughes's people loaded all the drugs into the back. He and Peloquin drove out into the Mexican desert, where the border patrolman had somehow secured a bulldozer. They watched as the drugs were dumped on the desert floor and crushed under the treads of the bulldozer.

"I think the fish in the bay got pretty high that night," Peloquin says with a chuckle.

Intertel's men spent the following months searching everywhere for Hughes's will. But it was never found—if one had ever existed at all. Eventually, Hughes's cousins in Texas, whom he had barely known, inherited his money.

AS ALL-CONSUMING AS he could be, Hughes wasn't Intertel's only client. Among others, there was the telecommunications giant ITT, and in 1972 the Intertel team played a tangential role in a Washington scandal known as the "Dita Beard affair."

That year, the muckraking newspaper columnist Jack Anderson revealed a memo written by ITT's Washington lobbyist Dita Beard. It appeared to link the company's pledge of $400,000 to sponsor the upcoming Republican national convention and a favorable resolution of an important antitrust case against ITT by the Department of Justice. Washington exploded—had the White House sold out for campaign cash? Everyone involved went into damage-control mode.[9] ITT decided to argue that the memo was a forgery and turned to Intertel's document experts to analyze it. The experts concluded that the memo probably had been written on a typewriter from Beard's office—and if so, it was probably genuine. But they also concluded that it would be almost impossible to prove that the document had been typed by Beard. This constituted enough deniability for ITT to go ahead with the claim

of forgery. If the memo couldn't be proved to be genuine, the accusation that it was a forgery couldn't be disproved, either.

Jack Anderson reported later that Intertel had also tried to dig up dirt on him, with an eye toward throwing him off the scent. But, as Anderson wrote in his memoir, Intertel couldn't find any damaging gossip to use against him.[10] Perhaps that's because Anderson was a Mormon who didn't smoke, drink, curse, or even drink coffee. (Peloquin denies that Intertel ever went after Anderson, saying, "I wasn't that wacky that I wanted to get written up by Jack Anderson.")

The existence of an intelligence firm for hire, connected to the Kennedys, terrified the Nixon administration. A confidential memo within the Nixon White House noted: "We should be particularly concerned about the new and rapidly growing Intertel organization. . . . Should this Kennedy-mafia dominated intelligence 'gun for hire' be turned against us in '72, we would, indeed, have a dangerous and formidable foe."[11]

Indeed, some journalists have long suspected that the Watergate burglars broke into Democratic Party headquarters on June 17, 1972, because of Intertel. The theory is that the burglars worried that Intertel had given the Democrats details of illicit payments from Howard Hughes to Nixon's associates. Thus, the break-in was designed to find out what the Democratic National Committee (DNC) knew about the Hughes connection.

For his part, Peloquin says that Intertel was never a spy agency for the Kennedys, although he acknowledges that Republicans feared it might be. He says that Intertel's Washington offices were broken into at one point, and the burglars attempted to drill holes in the safes that contained the firm's secret documents. The safes proved too strong for the drills, and the burglars left with nothing. Peloquin is convinced that the burglars had been sent by the White House. "They were supposedly fearful that we had info that Hughes had put Nixon on his payroll," Peloquin recalls. Ironically, Intertel didn't have the proof the burglars might have been after. Peloquin

says that he had his suspicions, but never proved that Nixon took bribes from Howard Hughes. "There probably was some payment made to Nixon or Nixon's brother. But I had no evidence of that."

Intertel maintained a much lower profile through the 1980s and early 1990s, but it maintained a roster of high-paying corporate clients. One former vice president of the firm recalls working on cases in the 1980s for McDonald's, Kraft Foods, Mars, and the Clorox Company.

Intertel worked on the famous Tylenol tampering case of 1982, serving as the central point of contact for all law enforcement officials who wanted access to Johnson and Johnson, the company that made Tylenol. But Intertel didn't do any investigating on that case, which was never solved. To this day, no one knows who killed seven people in the Chicago area by lacing Tylenol capsules with cyanide.

Intertel never grew large. At its peak it had something on the order of fifty employees scattered around the world. But those people had special skills. Jim Healy, who had served a long time at the FBI and who worked for Intertel from 1984 to 1994, says his colleagues at Intertel were almost all veterans of the government, including CIA officers, IRS investigators, and customs agents.

Intertel developed a new system of high-resolution closed-circuit television cameras for its casino customers. Intertel installed them to help casino security forces monitor the action at gaming tables. Were employees pilfering cash? Were players cheating? The cameras could tell. "The quality of the pictures was excellent," recalls Healy. "You could look at the customers and tell if they had real freckles or fake freckles."

In 1994, Intertel was bought out—ironically—by the Pinkerton detective agency. By that time, Pinkerton had become a security firm, providing armed guards to patrol factories and warehouses. But the executives there saw the growing market for corporate investigative services and wanted to get back into the business their company had invented. They acquired Intertel, operating it for a

time as an independently branded firm, but ultimately subsuming it into their own larger company.

Aside from Intertel, Peloquin served as an executive vice president of Resorts International. And when Crosby died in 1986, the company was sold to the New York real estate magnate Donald Trump. Peloquin thus became perhaps the only man in the world who has done business in person with both Howard Hughes and Donald Trump. But his new situation didn't go well. Peloquin and Trump butted heads. "Trump would say, 'You guys are scumbags.' And then he'd look up and say, 'Hey, Bob, have you seen my new boat?' We'd talk about that. And then we went back to being scumbags again."

Reflecting on the differences between the two men, Peloquin says, "Hughes was weird—an addict. I don't think Trump was on drugs. I think he was born on drugs. He's such an egocentric person."

INTERTEL BEGAN TO run out of steam because of retirements among its core employees; but another firm, begun in the 1970s, would far surpass it, and ultimately emerge as the twentieth century's heir to the Pinkerton legacy: Kroll.

In 1972, a former assistant district attorney in Manhattan, Jules Kroll, founded a small consulting firm—Kroll Associates—to work with corporate purchasing departments. It would grow to be much more than that: a nearly 4,000-person corporate investigative and intelligence juggernaut that would employ veterans of the FBI and CIA transitioning back into private-sector service. In the coming decades, Kroll would play a key role in the development of the modern intelligence firm—and Wall Street's gradual embrace of intelligence techniques.

In many cases, up-and-coming firms such as Kroll would turn to a well-connected network of former FBI agents for help in the spadework of their day-to-day investigations. There is even a quiet

but effective guidebook to the network of the top private detectives in the country. Once a year, a small company in Dallas publishes a spiral-bound paperback directory, the *Trapline*. This publication lists every retired FBI agent in the country who works in the private investigations business, giving names, telephone numbers, and addresses. The veteran agents pay to be included in the book, and they are listed by region and by specialty—including such esoteric skills as "electronic countermeasures," "hostage negotiations," and "psychological profiling."

The 326-page *Trapline* is distributed only to the several hundred FBI veterans it actually lists. It is not sold to outsiders by mail or in bookstores. The information in it is not available on the Internet. For security reasons, most FBI veterans won't give or sell copies of the directory to outsiders.*

The publication is put out every year by Trapline, Inc., which is led by Jim Abbott, a thirty-two-year veteran of the FBI, long retired. Abbott named his directory after an old FBI tool called a "trap line," a telephone technology used to capture a caller's phone number even if the caller is trying to conceal it. He is proud of being the central node in a vast network of FBI veterans.

On the phone, Abbott is polite and gracious, but he refuses to send a copy of the *Trapline* to a reporter. Later in the conversation, though, Abbott consults his own copy of the *Trapline* to rattle off the names and phone numbers of retired FBI agents who might be helpful in the research for this book. Connecting people who have problems with people who solve them is what Abbott does.

For its exclusive readership, the *Trapline* gives a one-man private investigative shop the national—and global—reach of Kroll or any of the other large investigative firms. Thomas Bara, an investigator with the Bara Hutton Group in Lavallette, New Jersey, retired from the FBI in 2000, at age fifty, after putting in twenty-eight

---

*A person listed in the directory lent a copy of the 2007 edition of *Trapline* to the author—on the condition that it be quickly returned. It was.

years at the bureau. His career included hunting fugitives, surveillance, organized crime enforcement, SWAT teamwork, and counterintelligence. "I joined counterintelligence because I figured out that spies eat at better restaurants than mobsters do," he says with a laugh. "My picture's on the wall at The Palm."

When he formed his private investigative firm, Bara was careful to make sure it was listed in *Trapline*, but nowhere else. His listing includes the alphabet-soup codes for an array of skills: GIM (General Investigative Matters), MVA (Motor Vehicle Accident Investigations), OC (Organized Crime), PH (Photography), PP (Personal Protection) PSS (Physical Security Surveys), SC (Security Consultant), and SU (Surveillances). "If I get a call from somebody from *Trapline*, I know I'm going to get paid," Bara says. "And I know it's not a bullshit case. If I advertised out there, I'd be getting calls from people who line their walls with aluminum foil."

As a result, he says, a steady stream of reliable business rolls in. Bara won't reveal details, but says he worked on a surveillance project for a pharmaceutical company recently. The company's head of security is a retired FBI agent, and got Bara's name from *Trapline*. For years, Bara says, he worked as a subcontractor for General Electric, where the head of security was another retired FBI man. The *Trapline* is a bit like an institutionalized old-boy network for retired G-men. Each member is able to trust it because Abbott promises to remove the listings of any private investigator who is not in good standing with the rest of the group. In the preface to the *Trapline*, Abbott notes:

In the event three or more documented complaints against a listee are brought to the publisher's attention, wherein the facts appear to impact adversely upon the reputation, business practices, and/or financial well being of the other listees, the publisher reserves the right to delete the designated party's listing.

In other words, *Trapline* polices itself.

When the cold war ended with the collapse of the Soviet Union in 1991, thousands of government-trained veterans of the nation's intelligence services flooded into the private sector, beginning a profound change in the way companies related to the world around them. In contrast to the operatives of the Pinkerton era, though, the new generation of corporate spies would be deployed by one company—or financial firm—against another, beginning with the corporate takeover wars of the 1980s. The new intelligence operatives didn't track down train robbers; they chased down hard-to-find witnesses for corporate lawsuits. They didn't spy on counterfeiters; they spied on corporate directors. But the tactics were still intelligence and investigation, and the goal was still the same: profit.

By the first years of the twenty-first century, a globalizing economy and the rise of large pools of private capital called hedge funds would create a market for corporate spying. The tactics, techniques, and technologies that had been developed by government intelligence services would now be for sale in the private market. The price would be high. So would the risk—and the drama.

Thug Busters

Like Robert Peloquin, Jules Kroll spent part of the 1960s socializing at Robert F. Kennedy's Virginia estate, Hickory Hill. Kroll was working his way through Georgetown law school as a staff aide to Kennedy in the Senate, where Kennedy served after his term as attorney general ended in 1964. Kroll was just twenty-three and a recent graduate of Cornell when he went to work for the newly elected senator from New York. He remembers that even the legislative assistants—generally twentysomethings near the bottom of the Senate's food chain—didn't have much time for him.

Kroll—along with dozens of other volunteers—had the job of grinding through a pile of more than 150,000 letters to Kennedy that had remained unanswered since his campaign for the Senate in 1964. Kroll and the other staffers organized the letters by topic, and cranked out responses to each one. When he was not writing letters, Kroll served as a general office gofer.

The work was not exciting, but it came with one unusual perk: on weekends, Kennedy would open his Hickory Hill estate for the staff, even though the senator and his wife, Ethel, were typically away at the family compound in Hyannis Port, Massachusetts. The people hanging out at Hickory Hill were ruled by staff aides in their early thirties—they were the only "grown-ups" around—and

for Kroll and the other junior aides, Hickory Hill offered the perfect social swirl: a time to relax, pursue romances, and make contacts that would last a lifetime.

For those lucky enough to be invited to the official parties
with the Kennedys themselves, almost anything seemed possible.
Dogs, ponies, rabbits, and other animals belonging to the Kennedys' eleven children roamed the grounds. Guests might include
the Beatle John Lennon, the actress Judy Garland, and the dancer
Rudolf Nureyev, along with other celebrities, politicians, and military officers. Washington's grandees engaged in raucous drinking
and dramatic escapades on the rolling lawn, on the tennis court,
and in the pool area. The historian Arthur Schlesinger, Jr., wrote
that at one party, Ethel Kennedy's chair slipped off the edge of a
poolside platform and she tumbled into the water along with it. As
he was standing on the edge of the pool deciding whether or not to
dive in after the senator's wife, Schlesinger recalled, Lee Udall, the
wife of the secretary of the interior, pushed him—fully clothed—
into the pool, for the rescue.[1] Dunking high-powered political
people in the pool became a regular cocktail-hour prank.

It was as a junior observer of this milieu that Jules Kroll got an
education in politics and business. An idealistic liberal inspired by
Kennedy, he determined that he'd go into public service himself.
And he also decided that he did not want to go into business, the
way his father, Herman Kroll, did, opening up a small company
called Book Printers, Inc. Kroll thought printing was a miserable
business, and he wanted nothing to do with it.

After doing a short stint in the Coast Guard and joining the
Coast Guard reserves, Kroll passed the New York bar exam in 1967
and went to work as an assistant district attorney in Manhattan.
But soon Kroll's father became ill with a grueling staphylococcus
infection that caused large carbuncles to erupt all over his body.
Herman Kroll was out of commission while he battled the infection, which doctors later found had been contracted during a visit
to the dentist. So Jules returned to the family printing business. In

the 1960s, the printing business was awash in corruption and under the heavy hand of the Mafia. Kroll found printers scratching for ways to chisel a little more cash for themselves. Kickbacks, sweetheart deals, and intimidation tactics were everywhere.

"For an idealistic kid, it was a pretty demoralizing experience," Kroll says. He was desperate to get out, and began plotting a way to get back into politics. His father recovered from his long-drawn-out illness, and the family wound down the company in 1971. That same year, Jules Kroll made a move to escape from business. He became a candidate for the New York City Council in Queens, where he ran up against the local Democratic political machine. These pols didn't have much use for a thirty-year-old outsider, and they crushed Kroll's campaign. He lost the election. Now unemployed, he went broke, and his car was repossessed.

For Kroll, politics was over, and so was his chance to become another Robert Kennedy. He went back into business, starting up J. Kroll Associates in 1972. In the new company he would build on lessons he had learned in the printing business and in the DA's office. Corruption was strangling the printing industry, inflating costs, and creating massive waste. Kroll would develop a business helping companies to do an end run around their own purchasing departments, which often chose the highest bidder—not the lowest bidder or the best supplier—after accepting food, clothes, trips, and even cash from eager vendors. Kroll knew he could knock prices down by running an honest purchasing effort for the companies. He signed up his first client, Cadence Industries, which owned Marvel Comics, published several catalogs, and ran a direct mail business. Cadence would be Kroll's only client for his first year, but it was a global company, and the fee it paid was enough to feed his family. Most important, Cadence gave him space to work—inside the company's own headquarters on Lexington Avenue in Manhattan.

After lowering costs for Cadence, Kroll began to develop new clients, focusing in each case on increasing transparency, creating

a competitive bidding process, and sending a message to employees that fraud wouldn't be tolerated. There was so much corruption in the industry that the methods were bound to work. Kroll couldn't miss.

It was a heady time. Society was changing—shedding old ways of doing things—and Kroll found himself at the intersection of powerful trends in America. "The chances of a business like ours being successful at any other time are probably de minimis," Kroll says. "But Watergate changed things." In the aftermath of the scandals surrounding President Richard Nixon, people at all levels of society were reevaluating corruption. After Woodward and Bernstein, crusading young reformers were in vogue. On top of that, the late 1970s brought malaise, oil shocks, and economic slowdown. The fat profit margins of an earlier era—margins that could more than account for waste and abuse in the system—were gone. And the industry reform that Kroll was selling was seen not as the naive concept of an outsider, but as a sensible business strategy for a new era of belt-tightening.

By 1978, Kroll had about thirty employees, new offices, and new opportunities for his growing company. He signed a joint venture agreement with a publishing house to put together a text for corporate readers: *Crimes against Business: A Practical Guide to the Prevention and Detection of Business Crime*. Kroll hired experts to write think pieces on each aspect of the problem that he'd seen: commercial bribery, theft of intellectual property, antitrust violations, and so on. The project put Kroll in touch with the leading thinkers in his field, and gave him time to organize his own thoughts on fighting corporate crime. The work led to an intellectual framework for the company he would build. Kroll concluded that the nation was about to enter a prolonged period of self-examination, and issues such as transparency and accountability would be more important in America's future than they had been in its past. He wanted to put himself at the center of the emerging trend.

Kroll's big break came in the form of a European playboy and

millionaire, Sir James Goldsmith, known as "Jimmy." Goldsmith
was a corporate raider with a taste for yachts and high living, and
the heir to a family fortune that traced its roots back to sixteenth-
century Germany. Goldsmith had already acquired a slew of companies around the world, including the British foods company
Bovril, the corporate parent of the French weekly newsmagazine
L'Express, and the American supermarket chain Grand Union. He
was eyeing other American targets for takeover. He settled on Diamond International, a paper company whose executives vowed to
fight any such attempt. It promised to be a bruising battle, especially since Goldsmith liked to brag about his tough tactics. "When
I fight, I fight with a knife," he once said.[2]

Diamond International decided to fight back against this swash-
buckling global raider, and its law firm hired Kroll to take a look
at Goldsmith's corporate holdings. Goldsmith was proposing a
stock acquisition, and Diamond's lawyers wanted to know what his
worldwide holdings were. They sent Kroll on a mission to find and
evaluate the companies Goldsmith controlled. Kroll looked at everything Goldsmith owned, questioning the way he accounted for
his profits, the character of his business partners, and the accuracy
of his official documents. "We were looking for chinks in their
armor," Kroll recalls.

The goal was to identify some weakness in Goldsmith's corporate holdings, to demonstrate that the stock he was offering was
not worth what he said. In the end, though, all Kroll could do was
delay the inevitable. Goldsmith succeeded in buying out Diamond
International, but Kroll was pleased with his own work. He felt
the efforts of his investigators had succeeded in buying time for
Diamond, turning what might have been a two-month process into
a two-year pitched battle. Kroll believed that the long fight had
generated a higher sales price for his client.

Kroll learned that there was money to be made in corporate
takeovers, win or lose. But he still wanted his first victory. He was
brought into another takeover fight: the chairman of Sharon Steel

Corporation, Victor Posner, raided Foremost-McKesson, a conglomerate that ran food, liquor, dairy, and pharmaceutical businesses. These were regulated industries, overseen by government bureaucrats. Foremost-McKesson's executives reasoned that Posner, who had already developed a reputation as a brash corporate raider, wouldn't fit the government's idea of the type of executive who should run a drug company. The battle, which had been brewing since 1976, turned ugly: Foremost and Posner threw allegations of mismanagement and improper conduct back and forth. To gain an edge, Foremost hired Kroll, giving his firm a mandate to find out what it could about Posner's dealings. Any dirt the investigation uncovered could be used to push back against the takeover bid.

Kroll and his team went to work. They scoured Posner's acquisition of Sharon Steel, and searched for sources who could describe how Posner ran his businesses. Kroll's men knew what Woodward and Bernstein had discovered a few years earlier: investigators must follow the money. And the best way to follow that trail is often disgruntled former employees. They often know where the trail leads, and they have a motive to reveal secrets.

Working their sources, Kroll's team stumbled across an interesting transaction. In 1975, Posner had donated twenty-two acres of land to Miami Christian College as a charitable gift and had taken a $1.7 million tax deduction. But the land wasn't worth anywhere near that amount. In fact, the school went on to sell it for just over $500,000 several years later. This transaction looked like tax fraud, and it was a juicy find. Kroll's team turned the evidence they'd discovered over to the IRS. Later, they found evidence that Posner's reported corporate earnings were suspect. They turned that information over to the SEC. Kroll's team also questioned lavish expenses at Sharon Steel that seemed to have little to do with running the company. Each new disclosure was a blow to Posner. He caved in, and by May 1981 he had sold his entire stake of the company's stock back to Foremost-McKesson for $42 per share. Posner didn't leave the deal empty-handed: he reaped about

$65 million from the transaction, which more than doubled his investment from several years before. Still, Foremost-McKesson was free.

In 1983, Posner and a colleague were indicted in the Southern District of Florida for their roles in the tax scam. Posner fought the charges for years, but he pleaded no contest in 1987. He was forced to donate $3 million to homeless causes and was assigned 5,000 hours of community service, including serving meals in a Miami shelter.[3] Posner's legal troubles would go from bad to worse. Soon he was entangled with the infamous Wall Street swindlers Ivan Boesky and Michael Milken. Jules Kroll had defeated one of the era's greatest corporate raiders. He was building a reputation for success just as the corporate takeover boom of the 1980s was set to begin.

JULES KROLL NOW had a vision for the future. Almost on cue, opportunity presented itself. The investment house Drexel Burnham Lambert underwent a damaging episode. The firm had taken the lead in underwriting a $25 million debt offering for a charter airline company, Flight Transportation, in 1982. Just a few weeks later, the FBI announced that Flight Transportation was a sham company—an airline without airplanes. Law enforcement officers rounded up the top executives. That Drexel had missed this obvious scam was embarrassing to its chief executive officer, Fred Joseph. He vowed that Drexel would never again be taken by surprise by such criminality. "Fred Joseph was appalled," Kroll remembers. "He said, 'we're going to check out everyone we underwrite in a way that has never been done before.'" Kroll got the contract to do the spadework. It was his firm's entrée into high-level Wall Street wheeling and dealing, and it was an opening to a huge new market.

"That's when 'Kroll' became a generic name on Wall Street," he says. From then on, firms on the verge of a huge transaction

would hire Kroll to dig into the backgrounds of the people sitting on the other end of the conference table. Solomon Smith Barney hired Kroll. Other big names followed. Fred Joseph made Kroll, setting up a firm that began with one man to become a business earning hundreds of millions of dollars a year. And Joseph wasn't shy about trumpeting his new investigative firm in the press, telling one reporter, "Kroll signals red flags, like the time we were told a company used underworld connections to solve some labor problems. We decided not to do the financing."[4]

But there was one problem: Fred Joseph's firm, Drexel Burnham Lambert, was increasingly dependent on the junk bond trader Michael Milken, who was based in Los Angeles. And in all the time Kroll worked for Fred Joseph and Drexel, its veteran law enforcement sleuths never figured out that their big client was running what amounted to, in many respects, a criminal enterprise based on insider trading in the junk bond market. Milken turned out to be one of Wall Street's worst crooks. Kroll didn't catch him, or even have a clue that fraud on such a vast scale was going on inside the prized client's office. It was all the more embarrassing because Drexel had hired Kroll to do internal investigations of people the firm's top executives suspected of insider trading. Those were limited, narrowly defined investigations. Drexel didn't hire Kroll for a systemic analysis of its own business. For the most part, Drexel hired Kroll's detectives to look out, not to look in. Kroll would continue to work for Drexel until the day the firm went bankrupt in February 1990.

To this day, Jules Kroll has a difficult time reconciling the two sides of his most important client. Fred Joseph presided over one of the most spectacular corruption implosions on Wall Street during the 1980s, and he was barred from ever serving as a CEO on Wall Street again. Drexel pleaded guilty to six felony charges and paid $650 million in fines in 1988. But Kroll sees only the good side of his old friend: "Fred is a very dear personal friend of mine," he says. "Fred Joseph is a very, very, straight shooter." In Kroll's eyes,

Joseph was simply another victim of Milken's scheming. "Fred was riding a tiger, and Michael Milken was a genius."

The late 1980s were a boom time for Jules Kroll, and his firm continued to expand its services. Kroll sent an undercover operative into the mailroom of the Wall Street law firm Davis Polk and Wardwell to help investigate a cocaine dealer suspected of selling drugs to employees. Kroll conducted a search of an advertising agency's offices to find files that went missing when several key employees departed to start up a competing firm. Kroll helped the magazine *Business Week* implement new internal security procedures when it became clear that someone was trading stocks mentioned in its weekly column "Inside Wall Street" before the issues hit the newsstands.

All along, Kroll was concerned about appearances. For years, he had resisted using the terms "investigation" or "detective." Those were low-rent labels, associated with toughs who wore fedoras and trench coats and hung around in dark alleys. Kroll had higher ambitions. He wanted to be seen as a social and professional peer of lawyers and accountants. Unlike Robert Dolan Peloquin and the corporate spies at Intertel, Kroll had high corporate aspirations. His was not a company that would be content to work for mad billionaires and sleazy casino operators. Although he made it into some of America's most exclusive corporate boardrooms, Kroll was never quite able to shake off the private-eye image. "No matter what we do," he complained, "people want to put a fedora and a trench coat on us."

In a way, though, Kroll himself reinforced the image—if unconsciously. A big man, with a bald head and, in the 1980s, ever-present suspenders and cigar, he was in many ways the physical embodiment of Dashiell Hammett's hard-boiled detectives of an earlier era. And when the *New York Times* came calling in 1985, Kroll embraced the chance to let the wider world know he had arrived. The *Times* reporter Fred R. Bleakley interviewed Kroll for a profile, "Wall Street's Private Eye," which ran on March 4, 1985.

Bleakley detailed Kroll's history, methods, and growing popularity on Wall Street:

> Mr. Kroll relies on a team of 50 full-time professionals who include a bevy of former FBI and law enforcement officers, business executives, lawyers, Ph.D.'s skilled in research and several former investigative reporters. In addition to a research library of business directories and electronic data banks, the firm has on call more than 300 detective agencies, specialized industry consultants, accountants and lawyers in the United States and around the world. One of these "subcontractors," he said, is the former Israeli Ambassador to Mexico who was chief of police in Tel Aviv at one time.

The article was accompanied by a picture of Kroll, with suspenders and cigar, looking every inch the private detective of legend. His reputation was made. One of his rivals says the publication of the article in the *Times* marked the beginning of a new era in the investigative business. Corporate investigators would now be seen as respectable players in the business community, on par with the lawyers and accountants that Jules Kroll hoped to match. Clients poured in his door. Before long, Kroll had detailed files on players across Wall Street. Like Pinkerton's 100 years before, Kroll's files became so valuable that access to the information in them was often reason enough for companies to hire his firm. Kroll had reinvented an industry, and dozens of competitors would spring up to imitate him.

One other large investigative firm was gathering steam at the time, too: Investigative Group International, which was based in Washington, D.C., and was headed by a former Watergate investigator, Terry Lenzner. Lenzner had started his firm in 1984, and before long he had abandoned the old Pinkerton code of conduct, becoming ever more deeply involved in political spying. That move

would make Lenzner the keeper of the most sensitive secrets of President Bill Clinton, and earn him the enmity of Republicans, many in the press, and some civil libertarians.

BUT EVEN AS a wider industry began to become aware of the opportunities in the new investigative business Kroll was perfecting, Kroll himself was focusing on ever larger targets. His next big break arrived in 1985, when an old friend called with a request. The friend was Stephen Solarz, a congressman from New York who chaired the House Foreign Affairs Subcommittee on Asia and the Pacific. Solarz had campaigned for Kroll during his unsuccessful political race in 1971, and the two men had stayed in touch as Solarz's career prospered. Solarz was now in touch with a group of Philippine expatriates living in the United States. They were horrified by the way Ferdinand Marcos was running their home country. These expatriates had been doing some investigating of their own, tracking down assets that they said Marcos had stolen from the people of the Philippines for his personal use. Solarz wanted Kroll to look into it. How much money did Marcos have, really, and where was it?

Kroll turned his team loose on the project, and he agreed not to charge Congress for his services. The case was significant: owing to Kroll's reputation and personal friendship with the congressman, his firm was now getting a call that otherwise could have gone to any number of federal investigative agencies. Kroll was sticking his nose into the government's tent.

Kroll focused on four buildings in New York City owned secretly by Marcos through American cutouts: 200 Madison Avenue, the Herald Center at Herald Square, the Crown Building at 730 Fifth Avenue, and 40 Wall Street. All told, the properties were worth as much as $300 million. At first, the American property managers would not acknowledge having anything to do with the Marcos family. But Solarz was armed with Kroll's evidence, and he

hauled them before his congressional subcommittee in May 1986. They confessed to the connection in a dramatic hearing, detailing meetings with Marcos at resorts to discuss business deals, and even to a dinner in 1981 at Sign of the Dove restaurant in New York—a dinner during which Imelda Marcos, who would become infamous for the astounding number of shoes she collected, showed them her Swiss bank account statement to verify her personal fortune of $120 million.

"Solarz was the hero of the day," Kroll says. But Kroll benefited from the spectacle, too. Kroll was now a global force, perceived as able to stand up to dictators and win. Soon Kroll would be drawn into other high-profile global asset searches. The firm worked for the Russian Republic, trying to track assets that were pilfered and taken out of the country after the breakup of the Soviet Union; made efforts to find the fortune of the brutal Haitian dictator Jean-Claude "Baby Doc" Duvalier; and, most famously, undertook a globe-spanning search for Saddam Hussein's billions after the first Gulf War.

Just two months after the Iraqi dictator Saddam Hussein invaded Kuwait in 1990, the Kuwaiti government decided it needed help as it mounted an intelligence effort against him. *How much money did Hussein have? Where was it hidden?* To find out, the Kuwaitis hired Kroll.

The investigators unraveled much of a convoluted international shell game used by Hussein and his family to hide assets: some stolen from the Iraqi people and others filched through an elaborate system of kickbacks for government contracts. Kroll told *60 Minutes* that Saddam and his family had pocketed 5 percent of Iraq's $200 billion in oil sales over the previous ten years. The investigation, reporters noted, relied on interviews with Iraqi expatriates and searches of global media accounts. It turned up embarrassing Iraqi connections with several western companies. One of the most revealing money trails Kroll followed was that of Barzan al-Takriti,

who was a half brother of Hussein and at one point had headed Iraq's feared security police force. In 1979, Barzan set up a company, Montana Management, Inc., which he registered in Panama. Two years later, the company began buying stock in Hachette, a French publishing company that owned several American magazines, including *Car and Driver*. By the eve of the first Gulf War, the Iraqi ownership stake had grown to include nearly 9 percent of the company. Whenever they were asked, lawyers for Montana declined to reveal the owners of the company, arguing that such details weren't required public information under French law. But once the true ownership was revealed, *Newsweek* magazine speculated that the French stock could simply be an investment. After all, a stake so small would hardly give Hussein editorial control over the editorial content of Hachette's array of magazines. But *Newsweek* also offered another, tantalizing, possible explanation for Saddam's interest in Hachette:

> Others have noted the coincidence that Hachette is controlled by Jean-Luc Lagardère, who also controls the French arms company, Matra. Some have speculated that Iraq thought it could influence Matra's arms sales to Iraq through Hachette holdings. Hachette denies knowing of a Saddam connection, and is prepared to buy back the stake if hidden ties emerge.[5]

Newsweek, impressed by Kroll's revelations, dubbed the firm the "thug busters."

Those thug busters were again walking the beat in early 1992, when Russia's newly empowered leader Boris Yeltsin hired Kroll to track down the billions of dollars' worth of national assets that had gone missing after the collapse of communism. The Russians estimated that they'd lost between $6 billion and $8 billion in 1991, as communist apparatchiks siphoned money out of the imploding

Soviet empire into personal bank accounts around the world. The
Russians wanted the money back, and they decided Kroll was the
man for the job.[6]

Kroll assigned fifteen agents to the Russian project, including a former intelligence agent for the U.S. Treasury Department
and the CIA's former station chief in Kuwait. The firm reportedly
billed $1,500 per agent per day. The Russians paid cash. "We're
going to be visiting and seeking records from Russia's major suppliers," Kroll told the *New York Times* that year, "particularly in
the food area and in oil-field equipment. And we'll also be looking at major foreign importers, again mostly of commodities. Outside Russia, commodities trading is highly computerized; records
exist."[7] The record trail led Kroll to exotic locales like Cyprus and
Monte Carlo, where many of the Russian assets had been hidden.

But Kroll ran into roadblock after roadblock. Among the most
frustrating problems was that the Russian government assigned
several former Russian intelligence officers to work alongside Kroll
on the investigation. None of these officers would give Kroll their
real names. They made it clear that they didn't like and didn't trust
Kroll. The Americans concluded that the Russian officers were
there not to help investigate the communists' money laundering
but to block the investigation from the inside. "We were interested
in uncovering information, and they were interested in obfuscat-
ing," Kroll says. "It didn't make for a good arrangement."

Russian politics made the situation worse. Yeltsin's government
was investigating money laundering that Kroll concluded in many
cases had been undertaken by Russian intelligence leaders. But to
stay in power, Yeltsin's fragile democratic government depended
on the former Soviet intelligence apparatus. Within six months,
the investigation became untenable, and Kroll ended its work on
the case. The firm turned over some of its leads to the Kremlin,
but the American investigators were never sure what became of the
information they passed along.

Although the former Russian officials were clearly uncom-

fortable with American investigators trolling through their finances, both the Kuwaiti and the Russian investigations dovetailed with the intelligence interests of the United States. America had already gone to war against Saddam Hussein once, and would do so again in the next decade. American officials had every incentive to learn how Hussein financed his regime, and where its weak points might be. It was the same in Russia: the CIA had been in a clandestine battle with the Soviet Union. As that nation dissolved, the CIA needed to keep watch on how the power and money centers were fragmenting. At the same time, Kroll was becoming closer and closer to U.S. intelligence, by hiring a number of prominent veteran CIA officers.

All that raises an important question: how much did Kroll work with American intelligence? Much like Pinkerton's more than a century earlier, Kroll's operatives were now conducting intelligence operations that benefited Washington in a time of crisis. Since the interests were so aligned, some observers began to wonder where Kroll ended and the U.S. intelligence community began. Indeed, one corporate intelligence professional with a long history in the industry has a pet theory about Kroll. It wasn't Kroll's efforts that helped U.S. intelligence, this person argues; it was U.S. intelligence that helped Kroll. The professional says that the accomplishments claimed by Kroll—tracing assets through a complicated series of international financial shells—can't be done by the private sector. But the global wiretapping abilities of the National Security Agency and the CIA's ability to track international banking transactions are just the types of tools that would have been invaluable in tracking global financial assets. Perhaps Kroll was secretly helped by American officials who wanted the information to become public, and wanted their own fingerprints kept far away from the disclosure. "What they're claiming to have done just isn't possible," the professional says. "There's no way they can do that without some intelligence help."

Was Kroll used as a front by an American intelligence

community that didn't want to reveal the extent of its own capabilities? Kroll wouldn't like the word "front," but he acknowledges that his investigators routinely sought out the help of intelligence agencies—foreign and domestic. "We would frequently approach the relevant intelligence agencies to see if it was in their interest to cooperate with us," says Kroll. "More frequently, we received that cooperation from foreign intelligence services than we did from U.S. intelligence."

Kroll is wary of getting into specifics, but he offers one example in which his firm was hired by a foreign government to investigate a former head of state. Kroll asked the government to put out the word publicly that his firm was on the case. Private intelligence operatives have a long tradition: they always talk to "walk-ins," or people who seek them out to deliver information. Most of those leads come up empty, because the walk-ins are ill informed, or even crazy, but sometimes the key evidence in a case walks in the front door. That's what happened to Kroll during the investigation of the head of state. Soon after word got out that Kroll was on the case, the firm got a feeler from a law firm in a foreign country. The law firm had detailed information on the case, and offered it to Kroll's team. The information was an intelligence bonanza: corrupt contracts, dollar amounts of bribes, and details of financial transactions. "We had reason to believe that it came from an intelligence agency," Kroll says. Kroll concluded that the law firm was just a cutout for an intelligence agency to pass along the documents.

But Kroll minimizes his firm's intelligence connections: "For the most part, intelligence services are a one-way street. They will take what you want to give them, but there's very little coming back the other way."

BY THE STANDARDS of its industry, Kroll has done a remarkable job of knowing where the legal and ethical lines begin and end. But the firm has had its share of improprieties, scandals, and controversy.

According to one account, as early as 1985, the firm decided to investigate the sex life of Ivan Boesky.[8] That invasion of privacy wasn't going to uncover anything at all to do with Boesky's alleged insider trading, but uncovering any of Boesky's sex secrets may have given Kroll's client, Drexel, valuable leverage over the disgraced arbitrageur.*

In another case, in 1989, Kroll and one of his star operatives clashed with congressional staffers in a dramatic showdown that threatened to destroy the entire company. The confrontation began with the House Energy and Commerce Committee's Subcommittee on Oversight and Investigation, then headed by the formidable Representative John D. Dingell, who was famous for using his investigative authority to dig into the dealings of companies across the country. The congressman had built up a staff of tenacious investigators that many corporate representatives in Washington viewed instead as ferocious inquisitors. The congressional team was known for firing off "Dingell-grams" to targeted companies, demanding information, documents, and sometimes personal appearances by executives on Capitol Hill.

At the time, Dingell's staffers had focused on Drexel Burnham Lambert, which had recently agreed to plead guilty to securities charges and pay a $650 million fine. They focused on a sideshow to the main saga, a $2.25 billion class-action lawsuit filed by an attorney in California, William Bertain, against Drexel and another defendant. Kroll was working for Drexel as usual, and its investigators were scrambling to figure out what was going on with the lawsuit. Kroll's John Gibbons led the West Coast piece of the investigation. Gibbons was a veteran of the U.S. Department of Justice; he had spent a long time there and had risen to serve as chief of the Criminal Division for the Northern District of California. He was a religious family man, who had devoted his life

---

*Kroll says he doesn't remember looking into Boesky's sex life: "We investigated Ivan Boesky on several occasions, but I don't remember any one occasion in which his sexuality was an issue," he said.

to law enforcement. But Gibbons's integrity was on the line when Bertain claimed that Gibbons had lied about who he was working for in the investigation. Bertain alleged that Gibbons said he was working for the congressional staff—not Kroll—in conversations. What's more, Bertain said he had tape-recorded Gibbons making the false statements.

This was a dangerous moment for Kroll. Dingell was bearing down and the press was lapping up the allegations that a Kroll operative had impersonated a congressional investigator. Corporate clients would flee the firm at the first sign of scandal. "It was pretty scary," Kroll says. "I saw that my life's work could have gone up in smoke." He relocated to Washington, D.C., to lead the fight against the accusations, setting up camp in the Mayflower Hotel.* This time, though, Kroll saw an opportunity in the growing scandal: in California, it is illegal to tape a conversation if both parties haven't agreed to it; therefore, the recording that Bertain made of Gibson might itself be illegal. That gave Kroll a way to fight back against the charges.

The drama came to a head in the congressional hearing room. Some members of Congress turned their attention to Bertain, asking him whether his recording was legal or not. Bertain dropped a bombshell: he said he had been told to make the possibly illegal tape by one of Dingell's own employees, the subcommittee's staffer Brian McTigue. What's more, he argued that the staff member's request made the recording legal, since it cloaked Bertain in the legal immunity of the House of Representatives. This was an astonishing claim, and a legal stretch. Bertain was arguing that a staff aide on Capitol Hill had deputized him as an investigator, allowing him to break California law.

When it was Gibbons's turn to testify, he refused to speak,

---

*It was an ironic choice because the Mayflower Hotel had itself been the scene of so much corporate wiretapping in earlier decades.

saying that he and his lawyers hadn't been given enough notice of the existence of a tape to prepare a response. Jules Kroll had a growing sense of unease. A congressional hearing is a freewheeling affair, buffeted by political agendas, subject to media scrutiny, and played out under rules that give enormous discretion to the committee chairman. Kroll felt lost. This was more like a Star Chamber than a public hearing.

Despite Gibbons's refusal to testify, it was Dingell who was now on the defensive. Had a staff aide really promised immunity to Bertain? Was that even legal? Behind the scenes, the committee members were in an uproar, demanding answers. Dingell's position got worse when the tape of Gibbons's conversation was played in the hearing room. It was far from clear that Gibbons had misrepresented himself. At one point on the tape, Bertain asked if Gibbons was working for Congress, and Gibbons replied "Well, not directly." This wasn't a slam-dunk case of misrepresentation.

Now Dingell was on the defensive. Had a rogue staffer on his committee made promises of dubious legality? And was the smoking-gun evidence as hot as it was said to be? Dingell saw his position weakening, and he decided to act to prevent any more damage. He removed McTigue from his job and canceled the remainder of the hearings into the Kroll matter. He apologized to the other members of Congress on the committee, and issued a statement exonerating Gibbons. "One conclusion I'm able to draw from your testimony is that you were acting in good faith," Dingell said to Gibbons. "I do not believe that any further inquiry into your conduct is warranted."

For Kroll it was as close to a total victory as the firm was likely to get. Jules Kroll dismantled his command center at the Mayflower Hotel and returned to New York. He's still angry about the incident. Dingell's accusations, he says, were "an outrageous thing to do. These were trumped-up charges." In the end, he says, Kroll's investigators were told that Dingell's staffers had hoped the whole

incident would pressure Kroll to turn over the material it had gathered in its files about Ivan Boesky. But no pressure was necessary, he insists. "We would have given it to them."

If anything, Gibbons remains even angrier than Kroll about the way Congress treated him: "Dingell, as far as I'm concerned, is an evil bastard," Gibbons says. Told that the aging Dingell gets around Capitol Hill today in a wheelchair, Gibbons responds, "Good. And I hope he's in pain, too."

Gibbons remained with Kroll until 1991, when he left to start his own company, which is now known as Spectrum OSO Asia and conducts due-diligence investigations on behalf of banks, insurance companies, and hedge funds. Gibbons became part of an enormous diaspora of talent from Kroll, as investigators inculcated in Kroll's techniques and business culture began to leave the firm to form competing outfits of their own. There are dozens of firms around the world that have roots in Kroll's offices. By the time Jules Kroll retired from the firm that bears his name in 2008, he had become the Johnny Appleseed of corporate intelligence firms.

The year 2009, though, began for Kroll as grimly as it did for many in the private intelligence business. The economic crash of 2008 caused business of every kind to slow down, hitting private investigators hard as a result. But even worse for Kroll than the sour economy was the embarrassing disclosure that the company had been working for Allen Stanford, who was accused of running a $7 billion Ponzi scheme and whose empire, the Stanford Financial Group, stretched from Texas to the Caribbean island of Antigua. Writing in the magazine *Vanity Fair*, Bryan Burrough revealed that Stanford hired Kroll to cement his reputation with potential investors. One former FBI agent told Burrough, "Kroll was essentially running a propaganda campaign in defense of Stanford's good name. They beat on me many times: 'Hey, you got this all wrong, he's not a money-launderer, he's a great guy, leave him alone.'"[9]

It was a blow to the reputation for independence that Kroll had

carefully crafted over the previous decades. Worse, this publicity was followed by news, first reported in the industry newsletter *Intelligence Online*, that Kroll was facing a lawsuit as a result of its work for the shadowy Caribbean financier.[10] A client—the Foundation for Electrical Construction, Inc.—sued Kroll for gross negligence in the U.S. district court in Florida. The client alleged that it hired Kroll to investigate the Stanford International bank in Antigua and warn of any red flags or concerns about Stanford's business practices. According to the lawsuit, Kroll completely missed Stanford's alleged fraud, despite giving assurances of a thorough investigation. And the suit says Kroll never informed its new client that the Kroll official who signed the contract was himself a former consultant to Stanford. That, said the suit, was a conflict of interest Kroll should have disclosed. As a result of Kroll's "gross negligence," the foundation said, it lost more than $6 million in investments with Stanford.

For its part, Kroll denies any wrongdoing and says it was hired only to do limited due diligence on a contract that paid the relatively modest sum of $15,000. "Kroll's report made clear in its very last sentence that 'given the nature of the bank and the fact that it is less stringently regulated, it is inherently a greater risk,'" says a spokesman for the company. "Kroll did not make any recommendations regarding [the client's] investment. Kroll takes very seriously its responsibilities to its clients and upholds the highest standards of integrity in its work."

Still, Kroll's ties to Allen Stanford show the deep and hidden web of connections underlying the global private intelligence industry. Somehow, a firm that had paid so much attention to its public image in its formative years wound up working for a man known in the media as the "pirate of the Caribbean."

The Chocolate War

The town of Vevey, Switzerland, is tucked between the Swiss Alps and the blue water of Lake Geneva. Famous for panoramic views of mountains and lake waters stretching to the nearby French border, the lakeside community is suffused with literary history—Henry James set his novel *Daisy Miller* here, and the writers Victor Hugo, Jean-Jacques Rousseau, and Fyodor Dostoyevsky all called the village home at times. Today it is best known for a company that was founded here in 1866: Nestlé, the $100 billion global chocolate and food conglomerate.

Lake Geneva's shoreline forms one border of Nestlé's corporate compound. The office complex, which is topped by the white cross of the Swiss national flag and shaped like a double-headed letter Y, has views of the soaring mountains, the lake, and the picturesque town nearby.

On March 4, 1998, there was a hint of an early spring rain in the cloudy skies over Vevey. Inside the enormous compound, Nestlé's chairman, Dr. Helmut Maucher, read a fax that had just come in from his fiercest corporate rival, the billionaire American candy titan Forrest E. Mars, Jr. To understand the fax, you need to know something about the competition between Nestlé and Mars. Certain corporate rivalries go beyond mere market share and quarterly

results: the competing companies are locked in a struggle that's more a grudge match than business as usual. That's the way it was with Nestlé and Mars. Any market share gained by either one of the giants seemed to come out of the hide of the other. The rivalry spanned the globe, encompassing—among other products—packaged meals, pet food, and, most of all, chocolate candy.

That afternoon's fax came at a delicate time for Nestlé. It had just announced a planned $1 billion takeover of the Spillers pet food business from a British company, Dalgety.[1] The huge deal would give Nestlé a boost in the pet food sector, adding well-known British brands such as Choosy cat food and Bonzo dog food, which would make excellent complements to Nestlé's existing Friskies pet food business. Along with the brands would come thirteen pet food factories, located throughout Europe.

Maucher, a German, was then seventy-one years old. His high forehead was topped by a curl of wispy graying hair, giving him a look of classic, restrained European business elegance. Earlier in the day, he'd had an angry telephone conversation with Forrest Mars's brother, John, who was a billionaire in his own right and formed the other half of the third generation of family members to run the Mars company. During their talk, Maucher hotly voiced his concerns about Mars: The Americans were encouraging the Food and Drug Administration (FDA) in Washington to take action against new Nestlé products. They were gathering information on Nestlé and its activities. Worst of all, they had "declared war" against Nestlé, Maucher charged. He demanded to know whether or not Mars would move to block the billion-dollar acquisition of Spillers. It was a reasonable question: the deal was a direct threat to Mars's own pet food brands: Whiskas for cats and Pedigree for dogs.

In his two-page faxed reply, Forrest Mars said he and his brother were "flabbergasted by your statements of this morning." He tried to allay Maucher's concerns one by one. Most important, Mars signaled that he would not try to block the pet food deal: "We have no

intentions of objecting to that via any of the legalities that you must go through. We will, of course, answer any questions that we are legally required to do, but do not intend to object to this merger."

Of Maucher's complaint regarding the FDA, Mars wrote: "Again, I reiterate that we did not cause you problems with the FDA." On the issue of gathering information: "We do collect information and read various reports available to us, not only about Nestlé, but all our major competitors. When a major competitor does something significant that changes the competitive scene, we immediately review all worldwide information, as I am sure you do with us and your other competitors. There seems to us to be nothing illegal or uncompetitive about this as all of it is published information and various amounts [of it] are obviously hearsay." Most important, he insisted, Mars had never "declared war" on Nestlé.

As he put the fax down, Maucher must have known that much of what Forrest Mars had written was a lie. Maucher was no fool. He had fought his way up the corporate ranks for decades, rising to become the first non-Swiss executive to head Nestlé. The year before, he'd given up the title of chief executive officer, but he still clung to the role of chairman of the board. He knew that for the past several months Mars had been secretly stirring up trouble for Nestlé at the FDA—and that these efforts had succeeded in shutting down production of a profitable new chocolate product. He would have known that Mars's competitive intelligence efforts went well beyond reading published information. And whether or not Forrest Mars—comfortable in his office in a Virginia suburb just outside Washington, D.C.—wanted to acknowledge it or not, Maucher knew that Mars and Nestlé *were* at war.

The chocolate war had already been raging for months.

How Maucher probably came to know all that information about Mars is the most intriguing part of the story. Even as he vociferously objected to Mars's alleged information gathering, Maucher's company had deployed its own intelligence assets in the chocolate war. It was one of the most sophisticated efforts of its

time, bringing together veterans of the Secret Service, the CIA, and American law enforcement to obtain copies of internal Mars documents, place Mars executives under surveillance, and unmask the identities of Mars's own secret operatives.

To understand this story, we have to leave the placid Swiss lake behind and travel thousands of miles to another body of water— Chesapeake Bay—and to another town: Easton, Maryland, which today holds some of the last remaining secrets of that war.

EASTON IS SITUATED on Maryland's Eastern Shore, an enormous peninsula that separates Chesapeake Bay from the Atlantic Ocean. About a ninety-minute drive from Washington, D.C., the Eastern Shore is an elegant weekend getaway for the capital's moneyed elite. Former vice president Dick Cheney and former secretary of defense Donald Rumsfeld both own multimillion-dollar properties in the small Eastern Shore town of Saint Michaels. Many other Washington insiders—politicians, agency heads, lawyers, and lobbyists—spend weekends in the small waterfront towns that dot the pastoral Eastern Shore landscape.

Though connected to the mainland by the 4.3-mile Chesapeake Bay Bridge, the Eastern Shore is still its own world. Indeed, the Maryland portions of this landmass have tried to secede from the state on several occasions. Long cut off from the outside world, the region thrived on agriculture and fishing. Oysters, crabs, and corn dominated the economy for hundreds of years. Today, tourism, sailing, and real estate speculation are included in the economic mix, but many parts of the area remain remarkably unchanged since the nineteenth century.

In short, this is a strange place to find the remnants of a once successful and secretive international corporate spying operation. But here they are. Beckett Brown International was a spy firm begun in the early 1990s by a small group of veterans of the Secret Service. The firm's clients included the multibillion-dollar Carlyle

Group, the Gallo wine company, Wal-Mart, and the cosmetics company Mary Kay. And over time, it spied on Greenpeace and other environmental activists, gun-control groups, and companies large and small.

There are dozens of firms like Beckett Brown around the world, but their activities are typically shrouded in secrecy. They tend to bind their employees to ironclad nondisclosure agreements, hide their work through a convoluted series of contractors and subcontractors, and argue that their activities are subject to attorney-client privilege. Documents revealing their operations rarely surface in public, even when they're involved in contentious court proceedings. But Beckett Brown is different. Because the founders of this firm eventually became bitter professional and personal rivals, the company collapsed. The corporate wreckage contains a treasure trove of documents that offer a rare glimpse inside a spy firm in action.

Crossing into the Eastern Shore from Washington over the Bay Bridge, a visitor travels down Route 50, passing the Kent Narrows and the town of Wye Mills before entering Easton. Along the side of the road, past an Applebee's but not as far as the Denny's, sits a rental facility called Bay Tree Storage. Inside one of its metal-lined storage units, in cardboard boxes precariously stacked from floor to ceiling, are the last remaining business records of Beckett Brown International.

Sitting next to those boxes, sorting documents by hand, is John Dodd, the man who put up most of the money to launch Beckett Brown in 1995. Dressed in a faded blue striped polo shirt, jeans, and a Florida Gators 2006 National Champions baseball cap, Dodd perches on a folding chair alongside a card table. He opens a worn briefcase to reach for documents, tapes, and supporting evidence. Dodd launches into a long tale, explaining how a company he partly owned deployed undercover operatives into gun-control groups, spied on Greenpeace, and gathered intelligence on Mars, all without his knowledge.

Even as he lays out the details of years of diving in Dumpsters,

intercepting phone records, conducting physical surveillance, and engaging in other spy tactics, Dodd insists he was appalled when he found out what had been going on at his company.

In 1994, Dodd had been enjoying the resort atmosphere of Chesapeake Bay, and spending some of his time in the bars of Easton. His family had sold its regional beer distributorship for millions of dollars several years earlier, and Dodd hadn't needed to work full-time since then.

In Easton, he met Richard Beckett, a local businessman who ran a small executive search firm, helping corporate clients find and place executives in high-level jobs. Beckett, as it turned out, was friendly with several law enforcement officers, current and former Secret Service agents, and a veteran officer of the Maryland state police.

Over beers, Beckett told Dodd that he'd come up with a plan for an exciting new business. Using their skills and connections from the Secret Service, the Maryland police, and the corporate world, the group would form a security company to provide protective services for executives at several of America's largest companies.

All they needed, he said, was an investor.

John Dodd was hardly a wheeler-dealer. He was just a guy who'd inherited a beer company, sold it, and grown rich; and he didn't know the first thing about running a security business. Still, he was intrigued. He was also impressed by Beckett's team members when he met them several weeks later. The men took Dodd to see the Secret Service headquarters building in Washington. They introduced him to Daniel D'Aniello, a founding partner of the $80 billion private equity firm Carlyle Group. At a meeting at the firm's spacious offices on Pennsylvania Avenue, D'Aniello sang Beckett's praises: *This is a great idea. I might even invest in this company myself.* In the elevator as he was leaving,

Dodd spotted the former secretary of defense and former CIA deputy director Frank Carlucci—now a partner at Carlyle. Dodd was starstruck.

At Easton's Sidetrack Saloon and McGarvey's Saloon and Oyster Bar in nearby Annapolis, the group pulled together a detailed business plan for the new company. Opportunities were everywhere for a company staffed by veterans of the Secret Service and the Maryland state police—Steve Forbes's presidential campaign, then in its infancy, was a prime prospect as a client for protective services. And CSX Corporation, the railroad giant, might need help reviewing its security plans for its enormous real estate holdings.

But they had to act fast. One member, Joe Masonis, was under pressure to tell the Secret Service whether he'd be staying or going. The opportunities could go to another firm.

Under that time pressure, Dodd agreed to put up $120,000 in start-up funding, and the company was officially started as Beckett Brown International* in August 1995. His total investment in the firm, he says, would eventually grow to about $700,000.

By the spring of 1996, the new company had begun to get traction. Beckett Brown hooked up with Nichols Dezenhall, a little-known Washington public relations firm that began to feed it business. The PR outfit specialized in crisis communications, the delicate art of helping companies in the midst of various corporate disasters: scandals, lawsuits, environmental catastrophes, and the like. As a result, this firm was in close contact with companies whose executives were desperate for solutions. At the same time, Beckett Brown began adding big-name intelligence veterans to its ranks. It hired Vincent Cannistraro, a former chief of the CIA's

---

*The "Brown" in the name was a reference to the lawyer who helped draw up the papers for the incorporation.

Counterterrorism Center, as a consultant.* It also added David Bresett, a former chief of the Secret Service's foreign intelligence branch, who had been a key liaison officer with the CIA while he was in government service. But it was the relationship with Nichols Dezenhall that kept Beckett Brown afloat as it struggled through its first year.

Nichols Dezenhall, having just landed its own first big project for Nestlé, put Beckett Brown to work for this lucrative client: Nestlé wanted all the information it could get on Mars.

The assignment wouldn't be easy. Even though Mars is a global giant that produces well-known products such as Snickers and M&Ms, it has a secretive corporate culture and remains privately held by the reclusive founders, the Mars family. There's no sign outside the company's headquarters building at 6885 Elm Street in McLean, Virginia. All a passerby sees is what looks like a brick two-story suburban office building. The parking lot is unremarkable, and there's no indication on the front door that you're entering the offices of a global conglomerate; there are just white letters on tinted glass: "No Soliciting." (Even the Central Intelligence Agency, which is situated two miles down the road, has a prominent sign visible to street traffic.) The e-mail addresses of Mars employees are cloaked, too. If you are e-mailing an executive at the company, you don't send the message to name@mars.com; you send it to an address ending with the suffix @effem.com. That makes it much harder for outsiders to figure out how to get in touch with key Mars personnel.†

Penetrating this secrecy meant going beyond the typical competitive intelligence techniques. After all, as a private company,

---

*Today, Cannistraro says he worked on only a few projects for the firm, and he thinks Beckett Brown wanted to hire him to use his name to generate business.

†The odd suffix "effem" is derived from the pronunciation of F. M., the initials of company founder Frank Mars.

Mars produced no detailed filings with the Securities and Exchange Commission, and left almost no other paper trail for the public to peruse.

BECKETT BROWN HAD arrived on the scene just in time to become Nestlé's own private intelligence agency in the chocolate war.

In late 1997, the candy giants were battling over a new product: Nestlé Magic, a two-inch chocolate candy ball encasing a plastic shell that in turn held a small Disney-themed toy. Nestlé planned to market the candy for children as young as age three. Given that age group, Nestlé knew safety would be a concern. What's more, the FDA had already warned Nestlé that the new product ran afoul of a decades-old law banning combinations of food and toys.

But Nestlé's executives were satisfied that they'd tested the candy sufficiently, and they argued that the Consumer Product Safety Commission had signed off on it. They thought their disagreement with the FDA was a minor technical point, nothing that would stop the rollout of Nestlé Magic. They signed a deal with Whetstone Candy, a family-run manufacturing company based in Florida, to set up an assembly line for the new chocolates. The deal called for Nestlé to spend up to $6 million to construct a new building at the facility in Florida, and Whetstone hired as many as 125 employees to operate new machines to turn out the chocolate balls.

Nestlé began selling the candy in July 1997, sending marketing material to retailers with the tagline "The power of Nestlé. The excitement of Disney." The product was an immediate success, moving swiftly off the shelves. The Disney tie-in was sure to be a winner. The toys inside the candy were based on the hugely popular animated film *The Lion King* and included such characters as Simba the lion and his sidekicks Timon and Pumbaa. There were also figurines of other characters from great Disney films: Cruella de Vil from *The 101 Dalmatians*, the genie from *Aladdin*,

and more.* Nestlé also knew that children four to twelve years old have an astonishing amount of purchasing power in the economy. The company calculated that parents of children in that age group spent about $3 billion every year. The Nestlé team predicted that Magic would soon be generating $1 billion in annual sales. "There was an obsession with Magic," recalls one person who was involved. The chocolate pros knew how powerful the new rollout could be: "Whoever gets the toy-chocolate combination right, they've got the holy grail."

But almost immediately, Nestlé came under a wave of assault from critics across the country. Complaints about the candy with a toy inside were being heard at federal agencies, on Capitol Hill, and in the offices of consumer groups. Even the Centers for Disease Control and the state attorneys general in Minnesota and Connecticut registered alarm. To Nestlé's embattled executives, it looked like a coordinated attack. But they weren't sure where it was coming from. In a 1997 memo stamped "Confidential," a top officer at Nestlé summed up the few facts the company had: "We are aware that an individual (or individuals) are attempting to create questions about the safety of Nestlé Magic (i.e., that its marketing is illegal and/or presents a choking hazard for young children)."

Nestlé and its consultants decided to winnow down the list of potential suspects in the attacks, and consider the evidence before them. There were complaints about children who had choked, but Nestlé's team couldn't identify a single actual child who'd been harmed by the product. Science-minded Nestlé executives spent an inordinate amount of time examining and reexamining the product. They inserted the little plastic toys every which way into a plastic cylinder known as a "choke tube"—a device designed to mimic the opening of a small child's throat. If any object fits entirely within the cylinder, the U.S. Consumer Product Safety

---

*Nestlé Magic had such appeal that the toys are still available for sale on eBay—and have appreciated nicely in value. A box of twelve of the cheap plastic toys was offered for sale on eBay recently for $45, plus $8.75 for shipping.

Commission considers it a potential choking hazard for kids. None of the Disney toys fit inside the choke tube, although the little Timon figure caused some worry. Still, Nestlé had designed the figurine to have overly large feet—feet that conveniently poked just over the lip of the choke tube. Nestlé concluded that its product was safe. Also, it still couldn't find any kids who had been harmed.

To the veteran crisis experts at Nichols Dezenhall, the fact that no children had actually choked suggested that the campaign against Magic wasn't prompted by one group often behind such publicity: trial lawyers. After all, if trial lawyers planned to sue for huge damages, they'd need plaintiffs. Without any actual children in evidence, that wasn't happening. There was only one other possibility: the attack was coming from competitors.

In the candy business, a victory for one company often comes at a direct cost to another. Suddenly, Nestlé Magic was making the Mars market share disappear. Nestlé suspected that Mars was behind the sudden flurry of complaints about the new candy. Perhaps Mars was using friendly consumer groups to start an ostensibly grassroots campaign against Nestlé. Mars reminded some people at Nestlé of the dark paranoia of the Nixon White House. Surely the secretive company was capable of orchestrating a dirty-tricks campaign?

Nestlé needed to know for sure, and quickly. It wasn't clear that all the attacks were coming from Mars, but the charges were starting to sting:

- A letter to the deputy commissioner of the FDA called the candy "extremely dangerous."
- An anonymous fax to columnists and food writers across the country called the idea of toys inside candy a "crazy gimmick," and complained that "this lunacy proposed by Nestlé to the FDA today should be loudly branded a bad idea by anyone who loves children."
- And—going right to the top, or almost—someone sent a

letter to Vice President Al Gore's fax number at the White
House, urging a ban on Nestlé Magic.

The chocolate war was raging in Washington. Soon, even
odder things began to occur. In late 1997, a mysterious stranger
stopped by the offices of the activist group US PIRG, which issues
an annual report on toy safety. The mystery man chatted with the
receptionist at the front desk—and left behind a package that included damning information about Nestlé Magic.

Over the next several months, the man continued to send packages
to US PIRG, encouraging the group to take a stand on the issue.
When the people at Nestlé found out about this anonymous source,
they nicknamed him Deep Chocolate—a reference to the most
famous secret source of all, Watergate's Deep Throat.

Anxious to unmask Deep Chocolate, and eager to hear any information its allies could gather about him, Nestlé put out the word: Help
us expose Deep Chocolate. One afternoon a lobbyist from Nestlé's
law firm, Hogan and Hartson, came to the offices of US PIRG for a
meeting on an unrelated subject. She started asking questions about
the mysterious stranger, and sent her impressions to other executives
in a high-priority e-mail headed "Deep Chocolate Strikes Again":

> I met with Ed Mierzwinski, with US PIRG, today on an-
> other matter. At the conclusion of that meeting, I asked if he
> had been contacted by Deep Chocolate recently.

If Mierzwinski knew the true identity of the spy, he wasn't going
to reveal it to a corporate lobbyist. The e-mail continued:

> Ed said he couldn't remember whether the most recent
> package had been mailed or delivered by Deep Chocolate. A
> staffer with Ed reminded me that Deep Chocolate had de-
> livered the first package in person and had chatted with the
> person at the front desk. However, the staffer became a little

nervous when I asked him what Deep Chocolate looked like or how he sounded. Clearly, he didn't want US PIRG to be the one that gives the guy away.

Mierzwinski did offer the lobbyist one clue: "Ed told me that he believes Deep Chocolate is being paid by or in league with Mars, probably working through a public relations firm," she wrote. But who was he?

To unravel the mystery, Nestlé hired Kroll Associates, which investigated Mars's Washington team, gathering background information, addresses, media clips, and in some cases Social Security numbers and children's names. They researched the lobbying firms involved, pulled the records of campaign contributions from key officials, and noted which people involved in Mars's effort had gone to the same schools, which ones were old family friends, and which were former colleagues.

Kroll's investigator was James Bucknam. He had retired the year before from government service as a senior adviser to the FBI's director Louis Freeh. At 11 A.M. on September 30, 1997, Bucknam sent a thirty-two-page fax to Christine Pfeiffer, a senior counsel in Nestlé's legal department, laying out a strategy for Nestlé to fight back against the maneuvers by Mars:

> The general theme for the response should be that Mars will do anything to stop Nestlé Magic. The reason is that Mars does not have a product that it can put on store shelves this year; thus, pending entry of its own product on the American market, Mars cannot afford for Magic to be sold unabated. In other words, this matter involves corporate greed and market share, not child safety.[2]

Kroll also noted that Nestlé should underscore the political connection: Mars was using a "cadre of Democratic Party operatives" in Washington to make its case.

But it was too late. The FDA had granted a damning interview to the *New York Times* about Nestlé Magic, including one comment that made it all but impossible for the Nestlé company to continue to market the product: "This product is illegal under our act," William Hubbard, the associate commissioner for policy of the FDA, declared to the *Times* reporter.[3] That was the end. Nestlé surrendered. In a defensive-sounding press release issued on October 1, the company said, "Nestlé Magic meets all Consumer Product Safety Commission (CPSC) safety standards; however, due to an unresolved technical, legal question related to food/toy combination products, Nestlé has agreed to voluntarily withdraw the product." Frank Arthofer, president of Nestlé's Confections Division, conceded that the company faced "an unfavorable environment to market the product."[4]

Losing a skirmish in the ongoing battle with Mars was a blow to Nestlé's pride—as well as its bottom line. Nestlé had put enormous resources and effort into Magic. Now all this input had vanished. Hank Whetstone, who ran the company in Florida that was churning out the candies, got the word to shut down the assembly line on the same day the Nestlé press release went out. He walked over to his brand-new building, told the 125 workers that they were fired, and turned off the main power switch for the machines. "It made me so sick," he says.

Whetstone says that Nestlé officials told him they'd lost $30 million on Magic. The hole in their balance sheet was a far cry from the dreams of billions that had nourished the Magic project from the outset. Soon, the manufacturer in Florida would find himself in a protracted legal battle with Nestlé over who had to pay the costs of the new manufacturing facility, now sitting idle. Nestlé's hired spies would find their way to his facility, too, this time eager to learn whether Nestlé's former subcontractor was using the factory that Nestlé had built to produce candy for the enemy: Mars.

The "chocolate war" was about to see a new offensive. Nestlé continued to pour in resources. It needed better intelligence to

unravel what had happened in the defeat of Magic. Nestlé wanted to know the players, the techniques, and the time line of the effort. After all, Nestlé suspected that other battles were looming.

Now Nestlé turned to Beckett Brown, which set up elaborate surveillance on a small consulting firm, the Hawthorn Group in Alexandria, Virginia. This firm is almost entirely unknown outside public relations circles. But it has a close association with Mars, and James Kiss, the chairman of Hawthorn's advisory board, is an elder statesman of the public relations business. He has earned the rare privilege of being allowed to cite his work for the highly secretive Mars in his marketing material.

Beckett Brown decided to target Richard Swigart, a consultant with Hawthorn who seemed to be deeply involved in its strategic work for Mars. Could Swigart have been Deep Chocolate? Beckett Brown knew that Swigart was an important figure: when the former Secret Service men at Beckett Brown drew up an organization chart of the Mars team, Swigart was shown working closely with Edward Stegemann, the general counsel of Mars, who was said to be one of the few close personal friends of the reclusive Mars brothers.

Finding Swigart's home address—3119 Circle Hill Road in Alexandria—was easy. With that information, Beckett Brown found his home phone number. And it wasn't much harder to find out who Swigart was talking to. Beckett Brown hired a small private investigative agency in New York to gain access to Swigart's home phone records. That firm, Science Security Associates, Inc.,* submitted

---

*Watergate buffs may recognize the name Science Security Associates. In the months leading up to the infamous break-in, a New Zealander working for Science Security, James Woolston-Smith, learned of the plans being drawn up by the Committee to Reelect the President (CREEP). The veteran CIA officer George O'Toole described what happened next in his 1978 book *The Private Sector*: Woolston-Smith passed the word to a former client, William Haddad, who in turn alerted the Democratic Party chairman, Larry O'Brien. The information passed to the Democrats even included the names of James McCord and G. Gordon Liddy. "It seems incredible," wrote O'Toole, "but nearly two months before the arrest of McCord and the four Cubans inside the Watergate offices of the DNC, the Democrats had been fully briefed on the CREEP operational plans to bug them." It never became clear how Woolston-Smith had gotten his intelligence.

a detailed handwritten account of telephone calls from Swigart's home phone number listed on the AT&T phone bills Swigart received in the mail in January 1998, and November and December 1997. The report listed about eighty long-distance and credit-card calls, and included notations about who was listed as the owner of each of the extensions Swigart dialed. Science Security billed Beckett Brown $1,250 for this intelligence.

Beckett Brown also wanted to know about Swigart's financial situation, and somehow gained access to records from his bank indicating that he had an account balance in January 1998. But there was nothing dramatic to be found there, either: Swigart had a modest balance of $14,410. The spies followed Swigart's movements, issuing reports that read more like foreign agents' intelligence dossiers than corporate e-mails: "Swigart appears to be working from home. He sets up a weekly schedule that rarely includes the Hawthorn Group." And they had no hesitation about delving into his personal life, even noting the name and occupation of a woman he was dating at the time.

Nothing in the record shows that Beckett Brown came to any conclusions about whether or not Swigart had been Deep Chocolate. And it is not clear that Nestlé ever solved the mystery. But both must have known they were getting close: Richard Swigart was Deep Chocolate.

Working as a subcontractor for Hawthorn Group, which in turn was working for Mars, Swigart was one of the leaders of the covert effort against Nestlé Magic. As part of his campaign, Swigart reached out to consumer groups, government agencies, and the media, making the case that Magic was dangerous and noncompliant with the FDA's rules. And even though Swigart had spent a career as a corporate consultant working against consumer groups like US PIRG, he needed to work with his old enemies on this operation. He dropped off packets of information against Magic at the offices of various consumer groups.

Next, Nestlé's hired spies turned their attention to Patton

Boggs, a prominent law and lobbying firm in Washington that worked for Mars. The lawyers had pressed the case against Magic at the FDA, arguing that Magic violated a decades-old law against embedding toys inside food products. Beckett Brown identified the individual attorney within the large firm to investigate: a young lawyer, Daniel Kracov, who specialized in matters before the FDA. Working closely with Mars, Kracov had done what he could to nudge the FDA to take action against Nestlé.

The operatives accessed the billing records for Kracov's private phone at the M Street offices of Patton Boggs, jotting down the details of fifteen calls, noting which numbers were called most frequently and which states Kracov dialed in each case. Pinning down Kracov's faxes proved more difficult. His fax line, as it turned out, was shared by a number of lawyers in the office. There was just no way to tell who Kracov had been sending his faxes to—any one of the attorneys in the office could have been using the same machine. The spies were temporarily flummoxed.

They moved on to a phone number at Mars itself, pulling phone records there that showed a Mars executive calling the White House twice on January 15, 1998. *What could that call have been about?* They needed to dig. Soon, Beckett Brown learned that executives at Mars were planning a company retreat in February to the Eastern Shore sailing town of Saint Michaels, Maryland. It was Beckett Brown's own home base, and this would be a perfect chance to gather intelligence to fill in the gaps in the information obtained so far. Beckett Brown deployed agents to Saint Michaels. They needed to know where the Mars executives would be staying. There are only a few hotels in Saint Michaels, but getting the right one would be crucial. The Beckett Brown team cased the Mars headquarters in Virginia, noting the placement of surveillance cameras and other security measures. They called the local waste management company to find out when trash was collected each week. And despite Mars's reputation for nearly obsessive security, they found penetrating its complex easy. They headed straight

for the rear of the Mars headquarters building, and into an area where decorative hedges hid the company's Dumpsters from view. There, they swiped bags of Mars office trash, switching them with bags of old trash they brought along as replacements. They had to make sure no well-intentioned Mars maintenance people noticed that the bags were vanishing before trash day.

In time, they began to bring old Mars trash back to the Mars Dumpsters, replacing the fresh bags with older material they had already scoured for clues. Most of the time, they also hired an off-duty police officer to join them for their raids. That way, the Beckett Brown team would have somebody to run interference on their behalf if they were spotted and questioned by the local cops. Although the legal issues surrounding "Dumpster diving" can be murky, and often depend on where garbage is situated and how it is secured, the Beckett Brown men operated on the assumption that everything they did was legal, since people discarding trash for public collection have abandoned the presumption of privacy for material. Still, they knew the police might be suspicious—or might not buy their legal reasoning—and they thought it was worth the investment to have a police officer on hand, and on the payroll. Beckett Brown gathered trash for months at Mars headquarters, bringing the discarded bags back to their own office, where they sifted through the material.

Dumpster diving is one of the oldest tricks of the corporate-espionage trade. The term itself invokes images of private eyes rummaging through banana peels, desperately digging up dirt on a target. And that's partly correct. But Dumpster diving is a time-tested technique, and it's a lot more common than most business-people think. Amid all the detritus of a modern corporate office are documents that can be invaluable to corporate spies trying to re-create the activities going on inside a company: e-mail print-outs, billing records, used calendars, and the like.

As the Beckett Brown team spent hours plowing through the trash at the Mars headquarters office, they found documents

covered with food, coffee grounds, and other foul-smelling waste. On one occasion, they found a pair of soiled underpants. Someone at Mars had a terrible case of diarrhea, and had simply thrown the dirty underpants into the garbage. Still, Beckett Brown's spies pressed on. They found shredded documents—Mars had some security measures—but found that Mars staffers invariably threw all the shreds of a document into the same wastebasket. The pieces migrated around inside the bag as it was jostled out of the building and into the Dumpster, but they were all still in one place. Beckett Brown set about painstakingly re-creating each document. They developed a list of code words to look for as they read through the reams and reams of papers that they discovered in the trash bags. They created a smaller pile of papers that included the words "Nestlé," "Magic," "choking," "attack," and "go after," or the names of any of the top executives of either company.

And then they hit pay dirt. Deep in the trash, they found a guest room contract signed by a Mars executive, Bob Cargo, for ten rooms at the Saint Michaels Harbour Inn and Marina on Harbor Road for Thursday to Saturday, February 19–21, 1998. The contract called for access to the hotel's meeting room, along with audiovisual equipment. It stipulated that Mars would be charged a rate of $95 per day for the rooms.

Now Beckett Brown had all the information needed to mount an intelligence-gathering operation as well-paid operatives in the chocolate war. And they were opening a crucial new front in the long battle between the two companies: pet food.

That winter, Nestlé announced its agreement to buy the Spillers pet food business from Dalgety, PLC, for $1.16 billion.[5] After the debacle with Nestlé Magic, Nestlé knew it would have to be alert for any response by Mars to this encroachment. Fortunately, the corporate retreat in Saint Michaels would fall just two weeks after the announcement about Spillers.

Beckett Brown dispatched Tim Ward, a former officer in the Maryland state police, and Mike Mika, a former Secret Service

officer, along with a few other agents, to the hotel. The Saint Michaels Harbour Inn is a classic resort hotel: situated on a picturesque finger of the Chesapeake Bay, it features dozens of sailboat slips in its own marina, and balcony views of the Chesapeake Bay Maritime Museum just across the water. February, though, was off-season, when barren trees and chilly breezes keep tourists away. The influx of Mars executives and corporate spies from Beckett Brown would provide a noticeable boost to the hotel's monthly revenue.

Ward and Mika were among the best men Beckett Brown had to offer. Ward was one of the founding members of the firm, and Mika was a veteran of the Secret Service's Counter Assault Team, with which he traveled the world in the course of missions to protect presidents and vice presidents. For a veteran agent like Mika, it was a simple matter of checking into the hotel, dropping his belongings in Room 209, and stepping downstairs to the restaurant, Windows on the Water, for dinner.

The Beckett Brown team knew that the Mars executives would unwind after their meetings each day at the small hotel bar and then adjourn to the restaurant. Each day the spies positioned team members inside the bar, sitting two to a table and trying to look as if they were attending some other business conference. They positioned themselves in the room so that wherever the Mars executives sat, they'd be within earshot of the Beckett Brown men. From their years in the Secret Service, the men were skilled in the difficult art of maintaining a quiet, meaningless conversation while straining to overhear every word said at the next table. It worked. The Mars executives didn't notice they were being observed. From their perspective, they had walked into an already half-filled bar. They barely cast a glance at the spies.

As the Mars team adjourned to the restaurant for dinner, the Beckett Brown men pre-positioned themselves at tables, again spreading out to cover as much territory as possible. But the dining room was too big for their small group to eavesdrop on every possible table, so they kept a two-man team waiting in the hallway. If the

Mars people sat at a table not covered by a Beckett Brown listening team, the backups would walk in and claim the next table. Each night, they rotated the positions of their team members, with some in the bar, some in the restaurant, and some playing the backup role in the hallway. They didn't worry too much about being recognized. Since the Eastern Shore plays host to so many corporate retreats, Mars executives would expect to see the same faces among their fellow guests over the course of a weekend. Nothing at all would appear out of the ordinary. On his first night in residence, the expense report shows, Mike Mika spent $184.24 on his meal at the hotel's restaurant. But it was in every sense a working dinner.

In a report to the client, Beckett Brown noted that its operatives had overheard some important conversations during dinner at the restaurant that evening. Mars executives, while choosing from the menu's pan-seared rockfish, lump crab cakes, and veal sweetbreads, didn't notice the spies at the nearby table. And they talked frankly about how the sales of Mars's Milky Way bars in Europe had been "adversely affected" by Nestlé Magic. The executives worried that the small plastic toy included inside the Nestlé Magic candies could become a collector's item. It could have turned into a fad like "Tickle Me Elmo," they grumbled, becoming the must-have children's gift of the year.

The Mars executives were exulting in their victory over Nestlé, unaware that a team of eavesdropping spies surrounded them at that very moment.

Each day, the Beckett Brown team paid members of the hotel's janitorial staff to leave the trash collected from the Mars executives' rooms off to the side of the Dumpster behind the hotel. They collected that trash, too, bringing it back to the Beckett Brown offices for analysis. One team member noted that the janitors did not look at all surprised when they were offered a bribe of about $20 to leave the trash for the snoopers to collect later. He wondered if the janitorial team took bribes like that often.

Pulling together the phone records, hotel surveillance, and

documents from the trash, Beckett Brown began to develop a torrent of intelligence on developments within Mars. But much of it was haphazard information, each data point seemingly unrelated to the others. The hardest part wouldn't be gathering the information; it would be making sense of the hundreds of disparate pieces of information the spies gathered about their adversary. In the first few months of the year, Beckett Brown noted the following pieces of information in briefing reports prepared for their client:

- "Mars will donate $100K to the Moscow Tretyakov Gallery. Approved by Forrest Mars."*
- "The Mars Hackettown plant has switched to using Canadian dairy products at a savings of $85/tonne."
- "Mars may be developing a peanut butter plant in Mexico using Nicaraguan and Mexican peanuts."
- "Due to a redesign of the British 2 pound coin, Mars' product dispensing machines in the UK have been rendered unusable."
- "Patton Boggs—Paid $2,597,916.70 for period ending 8-20-97."

One challenge that confronts any intelligence operation is how to separate the important information from the enormous volume of information churned out by any global company every day. Beckett Brown didn't distinguish between the pieces of information. It passed them all along to the Dezenhall P.R. firm. Executives there would decide what was important, and what needed to be sent along to Nestlé.

It turned out that Beckett Brown had also pulled out of the

*Forrest Mars, the reclusive billionaire son of the company's founder Frank Mars, was a famous figure in the industry for having invented M&Ms and the Mars bar. He died in 1999. This item probably refers to his son, Forrest, Jr., who was by that time in active control of the company, along with his brother. Tretyakov is Russia's national gallery of fine art. At the time, Mars was becoming increasingly concerned with business opportunities in the former Soviet Union.

Dumpster information vastly more important than the trivial details of day-to-day operations inside the rival chocolate company. The spies discovered that Forrest Mars had not been telling the entire truth in his dramatic fax to Nestlé's Dr. Helmut Maucher. Although Forrest Mars wrote that he would not object to the $1 billion deal with Spillers, the spies found that his company had secretly put together an elaborate plan to derail the acquisition. For Nestlé, the spying effort was the corporate equivalent of Ronald Reagan's famous line about the Soviet Union's arms control commitments: "Trust, but verify." They wanted to know whether Mars would keep its pledges. And they were willing to pay for the information.

Discovering this one document, Beckett Brown's spies figured, would be worth about $100,000 in fees for the firm. But they didn't plan to leak the documents all at once to their high-paying client. Instead, they'd string out the revelations, doling out nuggets of information every so often, to keep the client's interest up and to preserve the illusion that this information was difficult to gather—and thus worth the high fees. Holding back some of the details also gave Beckett Brown a backlog of information that it could save to give the client at some future point when other investigations weren't panning out.

As Nestlé discovered, Mars was mounting an operation very much like the operations companies around the world conduct when they calculate that it is easier to lobby governments to block their competitors than it is to compete in a free market. It was, of course, possible for Mars to undertake a free-market offensive against Nestlé, perhaps rolling out newer and better pet food products, or slashing prices on existing products. But that would require time and cost an enormous amount of money. It was far simpler and cheaper to manipulate European governments to think it was in their own interests to block Nestlé's aspirations. Getting government help can be vastly more rewarding than anything many companies can do in the private sector. That's one reason, for example, why they spend so much

money lobbying the U.S. Congress for earmarks—those special, targeted, spending provisions often stuck into legislation moving through the Capitol. In 2005, on average, companies received as much as $28 in earmark revenue for every single dollar they spent on lobbying expenses.[6] That's a much better rate of return than many could get producing and selling products.

In this case, Mars aimed its plan at the European legislators who would be in a position to keep Spillers out of Nestlé's hands. First, Mars planned to convince the countries of the European Economic Area (EEA) that the acquisition by Nestlé would be bad for consumers. The idea was to use Mars's Pedigree dog food division to pull together factual and historical information to highlight inaccuracies in the material that Nestlé submitted to European bureaucrats. "The information would highlight Nestlé's history of job cuts or consolidation after mergers," noted Beckett Brown.

Next, Mars would spur seemingly independent third parties to help thwart the conclusion of Nestlé and Dalgety's deal. Beckett Brown noted that the plan called for Mars lobbyists to provide European politicians with negative talking points and tabloid newspapers with negative headlines about the deal. "BBI has obtained a copy of this plan," the report noted helpfully.

"To a degree, Mars is willing to be criticized, albeit lightly, by their own third-party people," noted Beckett Brown. "For example, they will argue that a Pedigree/Nestlé duopoly would dominate pet-food markets within the EEA and would hurt suppliers and manufacturers as well as consumers." That was an important discovery, and Beckett Brown didn't lose the opportunity to emphasize the point in its report: "It could be significant that Mars is willing to suffer criticism over the Nestlé/Dalgety acquisition."

In the coming months, Beckett Brown would prowl ever deeper into the secrets of Mars. Through its contact at Science Security Associates, it continued to monitor phone calls going out of the Mars headquarters, tracing down the identities of people and firms that the Mars executives were calling.

But the internal security at Mars proved daunting. By spring, Science Security Associates sent a note asking for payment on an invoice relating to James Kiss of the Hawthorn Group and Ed Stegemann, the general counsel of Mars. The subcontractor explained (in mangled grammar) that he wasn't able to come up with all the phone records Ward wanted. "It appears that the 'security blocks' which are in place are such that my person can not overcome what is in place," he wrote. "If you get any other thoughts reference to this I might attempt for you do let me know." The firm submitted an invoice for $2,455 for the work already completed. "If you have any comments reference to the invoice do understand that the larger portion of it has been my expenses on this which, as you know, can run expensive," the note read.

Beckett Brown was becoming so closely involved with Nestlé's business that Nestlé asked Tim Ward to fill out a nondisclosure form. In the legalese typical of such documents, Nestlé wrote to Ward, "You will have access to information which is confidential and proprietary to Nestlé, including but not limited to plans and future activities of Nestlé, marketing plans and strategies, business plans and information, and new product developments. . . . Because of the highly competitive nature of the food industry, policies and procedures have been established by Nestlé to protect its Confidential Information." Ward signed the paper.*

It is worth pausing here to note just how strange all this was. After all, Nestlé was spending hundreds of thousands of dollars and deploying high-end crisis communicators, veteran Secret Service agents, and former law enforcement officials to find out what had happened to its new chocolate ball. But the chocolate industry has been secretive for generations. In fact, the famous children's book

---

*Asked in the fall of 2008 to comment about the relationship with Beckett Brown, Nestlé's spokeswoman Laurie MacDonald said Nestlé never paid any money directly to Beckett Brown. She declined to confirm Nestlé's hiring of Nichols Dezenhall, citing a company policy against discussing outside vendors. And she said she could not offer any comment on the tactics applied by Beckett Brown, "because we have absolutely zero working knowledge about them."

by Roald Dahl, *Charlie and the Chocolate Factory*, has scenes eerily reminiscent of what happened at Nestlé. At one point Grandpa Joe explains to the child protagonist, Charlie, that chocolate can be a duplicitous business:

> "You see, Charlie, not so very long ago there used to be thousands of people working in Mr. Willy Wonka's factory. Then one day, all of a sudden, Mr. Wonka had to ask *every single one of them* to leave, to go home, never to come back."
> "But why?" asked Charlie.
> "Because of spies."
> "Spies?"
> "Yes. All the other chocolate makers, you see, had begun to grow jealous of the wonderful candies that Mr. Wonka was making, and they started sending in spies to steal his secret recipes. The spies took jobs in the Wonka factory, pretending they were ordinary workers, and while they were there, each one of them found out exactly how a certain special thing was made."[7]

In this story, Willy Wonka resolves the problem of spies by hiring only the extremely loyal Oompa-Loompas to man his chocolate factory. Nestlé didn't have that luxury. It hired spies of its own.*

Now Beckett Brown was poised to gather information on a new target: Nestlé's own former manufacturer, Whetstone Candy Company. And in an ironic twist, Nestlé would run just the type of operation against its former subcontractor that, infuriatingly, Mars had run against Nestlé.

In the months after Nestlé recalled Magic, Whetstone continued

---

*Roald Dahl based much of his description of Wonka's chocolate factory on corporate espionage he observed in the business during his own childhood in England in the early twentieth century, according to Joël Glenn Brenner on Slate.com in 2005. Dahl also had personal experience as a spy: he was a covert operative for the British government in Washington during World War II.

to work on the concept of packaging a toy with a chocolate candy. The huge sales of Magic were clear evidence that the concept would be an enormous hit. After months of research, Whetstone developed a plan for a chocolate that could include a toy and still meet the FDA's safety requirements. Hank Whetstone patented the plan, and then flew to the Glendale, California, offices of Nestlé to pitch it to executives there.

"They didn't like it that I had the patents," Whetstone recalls. "They asked me why I hadn't come to them first." Nestlé didn't bite on the new idea; it told Whetstone that it wasn't interested in the chocolate-and-toy category anymore. It had lost too much money on Magic to sink any more investment dollars into another try.

Whetstone went ahead with plans to develop the chocolate himself, and his relationship with Nestlé became more and more strained. All along, he had other business with Nestlé, producing various chocolates for it at his three-building manufacturing facility in Saint Augustine, Florida. But in October, he recalls, Nestlé ended its last contract with his firm. Nestlé, he says, was worried that he might do a deal with Mars—and what was worse, that he might use the facility Nestlé had paid for to produce chocolates for its archrival.

Soon after Whetstone says his contract with Nestlé ended, Beckett Brown's records show that the corporate spies were sniffing around the manufacturing facility in Florida, trying to discover what it was producing, and for whom. Beckett Brown's team was executing a play from a well-worn playbook when, at 3:45 A.M. on November 17, a car rolled up Coke Road in Saint Augustine, pulling into the parking lot of the Riverside Centre shopping area. Behind the wheel was Larry Dyer, a local private investigator subcontracted by Beckett Brown. In a surveillance report he dutifully prepared the next day, Dyer noted that his parking space gave him a "direct line of vision" toward the chocolate plant.

Everything was quiet, until 5:04 A.M., when Dyer spotted a trash truck from a private hauling company, BFI Waste Systems,

pull into the manufacturing facility to collect the day's garbage. When the truck pulled out, Dyer pulled his car into traffic right behind it. He followed the truck for several blocks, pulling alongside it when it parked at a branch of Prosperity Bank.

> I exited my vehicle and approached the driver. The driver stated his name was Marc. I asked Marc for the garbage bags from Whetstones. He stated he had talked to his boss at BFI about giving us the bags of garbage. His boss told him if he did, he would be acting . . . on his own. The driver further stated he was afraid of losing his job. He refused to give me the bags. I asked him if we could work something out. He said no. Again he stated he was afraid it might somehow cause him to lose his job. He said to check with the other driver . . . because he might do it.

Dyer headed back to his office.

Somehow Beckett Brown was able to get materials from inside the Whetstone facility. And just as it had in the Mars case, Beckett Brown generated a torrent of information about this company.

- Beckett Brown obtained a document showing that Whetstone took delivery of a high-speed machine from Germany that made hollow candy. "Although the equipment was shipped by Aasted-Mikroverk (Denmark), the invoice indicates the customer is M&M Mars, Waco TX," noted a Beckett Brown briefing paper.
- The spies also obtained a copy of a customs document showing British Airways shipping plastic candy molds to Whetstone's plant.
- And most important, Beckett Brown was able to prove that Whetstone had hired Stephen Cogswell—a marketing whiz who had worked at Nestlé on the Magic project.

Taken together, this suggested that Whetstone was gearing up to introduce its own version of Nestlé's ill-fated Magic. If it could steer the new candy through the regulatory challenges in Washington, Whetstone would be in a position to steal market share from both Nestlé and Mars. Clearly, that would be unacceptable to Nestlé. Magic had been Nestlé's idea, after all. The thought of Whetstone cashing in on the millions of dollars Nestlé had missed out on must have been unbearable.

So Nestlé, ironically, began the same type of coordinated media, consumer, and regulatory attack against Whetstone that Mars had run against Nestlé just two years earlier. And now Nestlé would do some rent-seeking of its own, pushing the government to shut down the rival product. The old game of spy versus spy had now become spy versus spy versus spy. At that moment, private detectives, veteran Secret Service officers, high-powered PR executives, well-connected lobbyists, and international corporate titans were engaged in an international secret war over the fate of a two-inch chocolate ball. It would be hilarious if it weren't true.

"Two consumer groups ran to the FDA and the Consumer Product Safety Commission and attacked my product," Whetstone remembers. "I knew what was going on, because Mars had done it to Nestlé. There was no question about it." Whetstone became convinced that the spies were using Willy Wonka's tactics on him. He fought back, and was able to bring his product—a chocolate-covered plastic egg he called Megga Surprize—to market. It was now legal because Whetstone's hard work had paid off. He'd figured out how to create a toy-inside-chocolate combination that could pass government review. The safety commission concluded that even though the chocolates encased a rigid plastic egg that contained a paper toy, they weren't hazardous.

And then something unusual happened: Megga Surprize failed. Not because of a stealth political campaign or an elaborate spying operation, but for a much more mundane reason—the customers didn't like it. Whetstone says that in shaping his product like an

egg, he made a fundamental miscalculation. Retailers didn't want to buy egg-shaped chocolates unless it was Easter time. And when Easter rolled around, Megga Surprize was up against hundreds of other egg-shaped candies. Whetstone's product didn't stand out enough, orders were slow, and he gave up on Megga Surprize.

Disheartened by the flop, and by now having lost his lucrative manufacturing contracts with Mars *and* Nestlé in the collateral damage of the chocolate war, Whetstone decided to get out of the candy business altogether. He entered an industry he thought might be somewhat less cutthroat: commercial real estate.

"Life," Whetstone says, "is too short."

Corporate life was short for Beckett Brown, too. By late 1999, it began to splinter as rivalries among the founders developed into an all-out battle for control of the firm, which now had twenty-five employees. The key executives began fighting over cash flow, expenses, and allegations of unsavory activity. Back in Easton, Maryland, John Dodd, who had put up the money to start Beckett Brown, was hearing of all this and getting worried about his invest-ment. He describes himself as the ultimate passive investor, who was unaware of the business Beckett Brown had built, but happy to take the money as it flowed in. Dodd says that in the late 1990s he began to ask to see financial statements. Each time he asked, he says, Beckett Brown's management stalled. "It should have both-ered me more in hindsight," Dodd says now. "But they were saying, you know, 'We're doing great.'"

The meltdown began in August 1999, when Richard Beckett left the company that bore his name. The company changed its name to S2i for a while, but staff defections and ill will among the remaining employees drove it to near-collapse. One morning in 2000, John Dodd got a call from a staffer at the company's head-quarters who was loyal to him. "John, they're packing up boxes and shredding documents. You'd better get over here."

Dodd rushed to the office, stopped the shredding, and as legal owner of the company, took control of the remaining computers, office equipment, and boxes of documents. He's been mired in litigation of one sort or another since then, and he keeps the documents he secured that day in the storage unit in Easton. Dodd says he wasn't able to rescue everything, and he suspects that records of many of Beckett Brown's most sensitive activities were the first papers fed to the shredder.

Many of the key officers at Beckett Brown stayed in the corporate intelligence industry, setting up shops with similar business models, and staying close to the Chesapeake Bay area. Tim Ward, for example, today has his own security firm, Chesapeake Strategies. Joe Masonis works for another security firm, the Annapolis Group. And Richard Beckett runs yet another firm, Global Security Services.

As the legal wrangling over the fate of the company continued, Dodd read through the documents, piecing together what he could about what the company had been doing. He also began to contact the people and companies he saw as the victims of Beckett Brown's operations. Dodd says he called Mars to let officials there know about Nestlé's spying operation, and Mars sent a squadron of attorneys from the white-shoe law firm Williams and Connolly to the storage unit in Easton, where they spent several days reading and copying documents related to the corporate espionage against Mars. Dodd also reached out to others to let them know about what happened in each case. Finally, Dodd went to the press, inviting several reporters to the storage unit to dig into the Beckett Brown saga.

The clandestine operations carried out by Beckett Brown remained secret for almost a decade. But in the spring of 2008, the magazine *Mother Jones* disclosed some of the most elaborate episodes in the company's history.

The exclusive for *Mother Jones*, written by a veteran Washington investigative reporter, James Ridgeway, revealed Beckett Brown's extensive client list:

BBI engaged in "intelligence collection" for Allied Waste; it conducted background checks and performed due diligence for the Carlyle Group, the Washington-based investment firm; it provided "protective services" for the National Rifle Association; it handled "crisis management" for the Gallo wine company and for Pirelli; it made sure that the Louis Dreyfus Group, the commodities firm, was not being bugged; it engaged in "information collection" for Wal-Mart; it conducted background checks for Patricia Duff, a Democratic Party fundraiser then involved in a divorce with billionaire Ronald Perelman; and for Mary Kay, BBI mounted "surveillance," and vetted Gayle Gaston, a top executive at the cosmetics company (and mother of actress Robin Wright Penn), retaining an expert to conduct a psychological assessment of her. Also listed as clients in BBI records: Halliburton and Monsanto.[8]

A follow-up story detailing an extensive undercover infiltration operation generated national headlines because *Mother Jones* revealed that an operative connected to Beckett Brown, Mary Lou Sapone, had for years been posing as a gun-control advocate and had joined the boards of several important gun-control groups, even as she was secretly working for the National Rifle Association. Sapone was a multipurpose undercover agent. She also helped plant an operative inside an environmental group in Louisiana on behalf of a corporate client of Beckett Brown.[9]

These days, John Dodd is a sad figure. He's in his early sixties and no longer works, instead living off the remnants of his fortune. He spends most of his time poring over old documents and calling sources, attorneys, and anyone else he thinks might be able to help him get the word out about Beckett Brown. He complains that his first set of attorneys left him the loser in his fraud lawsuit against the other participants in the Beckett Brown fiasco. He says he lost

every penny of his initial start-up capital plus more than $1 million in legal fees in the years since the company's crack-up.

IN VEVEY, A Nestlé fax machine spit out another letter from Mars on March 6, 1998, two days after the sternly worded letter from Forrest Mars to Nestlé's chairman Helmut Maucher. This exchange took place one rung down the corporate ladder: Mars's general counsel Edward Stegemann was reaching out to his counterpart at Nestlé, Dr. Hans Peter Frick, in an effort to call a cease-fire in the chocolate war.

Nestlé's people were upset because a group of leftist consumer activists was about to hold a press conference on the danger of mixing toys with candy. Nestlé suspected once again that Mars was the real force behind the group. Stegemann explained that he had no idea how Nestlé could have come to that conclusion, and that Mars had been investigating the issue itself. "Mr. Maucher, and presumptively all of Nestlé, believe we are behind this press conference," Stegemann wrote. He then made an attempt at humor: "If only I were this clever I could demand a triple bonus from my owners." In fact, he insisted, Mars had been thinking Nestlé was putting up the press conference. "We began to get the sense that this was one of your Machiavellian ploys."

But even as he insisted that he didn't control the activist group, Stegemann told Frick that he had reached out to its leaders and asked them to postpone the embarrassing event. It seemed that Mars was making a peace overture by getting the consumer group to stand down. Now Mars expected the other side to stand down, too. Stegemann cautioned his counterpart at Nestlé against doing too much research to find out who was behind the group's activities. "I believe the more you and we thrash about trying to find out just what is behind this—and regrettably we really have been thrashing about—the greater the chance that it will become

a story and attract a hell of a lot more attention than it otherwise could," he wrote. "I believe," he declared, "that we should treat this as if we were making love to a porcupine—we can handle it, but very carefully and calculatedly."

There may well have been a temporary cease-fire that year. But the chocolate war continues to this day. Many of the combatants and battlefields have changed, but the tactics are familiar. In June 2008, for example, the Associated Press reported that the Swiss chapter of a left-leaning antiglobalization group called Attac had filed a legal complaint against Nestlé in a Swiss court. The document alleged that Nestlé had hired the intelligence company Securitas—the firm that bought Pinkerton—to plant a spy inside Attac. It was a move the Pinkertons had invented more than 100 years before. The operative allegedly attended meetings, the Associated Press noted, at which the group planned a book to be titled "Attac against the Nestlé Empire," criticizing the company's position on genetically modified organisms, water privatization, and trade unions.[10] Did Nestlé suspect that Mars, once again, was the secretive force behind an activist group's efforts?

It is difficult to tell for sure. Nestlé wouldn't say.

PART II

Techniques, Technologies, and Talent

Tactical Behavior Assessment

On August 2, 2005, a group of executives in Alameda, California, gathered around their telephones for a second-quarter "earnings call" with investors. As far as they knew, this call would be business as usual. Hong Liang Lu, the chairman and CEO of a company called UTStarcom, would walk through the numbers with a telephone audience of Wall Street investment bankers.[1]

With his slicked-back hair, rimless glasses, and wide smile, Lu projects an image of intelligence and competence. He began his call with a benign comment: "Thank you everyone, for joining us this afternoon. Q2 was a constructive quarter for UTStarcom."

Lu couldn't know that the phone call was also being patched into a room thousands of miles away where interrogators trained by the CIA would analyze each inflection in Lu's voice. The analysts were human lie detectors, working for Business Intelligence Advisors (BIA), a company with deep connections to the CIA. They were trying to find out whether Lu was telling the whole truth about UTStarcom's financial health. When they came to their conclusion, they'd report it to BIA's client, an enormous hedge fund. The secret intelligence they produced would help the hedge fund decide whether to buy or sell UTStarcom stock. If the intelligence analysts did their jobs, the hedge fund would be far ahead of the rest

of the market. The information they gleaned from this phone call could be worth millions of dollars.

Earnings calls are an important Wall Street ritual. They're a direct line from the corporate boardroom to the trading floor, allowing the company to put its best spin on the events of the quarter and give investors a sense of where it is headed in the three months to come. During the calls, analysts for top-of-the-line investment houses ask probing questions of senior management, enhancing their already intimate knowledge of the company's technical details. Earnings calls are capitalism in action, as information flows from the company to the markets, where it is used to calibrate the value of the company's stock. Generally, the calls are open to professional analysts and the media, but anybody can dial in.

For people trained in interrogation by the CIA, an earnings call is a bonanza of other indicators about the people speaking on the line. In this instance, the investment analysts were sharp, but BIA's analysts were about to make them look like amateurs.

The company Hong Liang Lu ran sells broadband, wireless, and handheld Internet equipment and technology around the world. It had generated more than $700 million in revenue that quarter, and although it was still losing money, that performance was good enough to bring it close to profitability. The company thought the results were positive, and the CEO seemed optimistic.

Investment analysts from Bank of America, Smith Barney, Deutsche Bank, and other Wall Street powerhouses were the official participants in UTStarcom's call. Using their own skills, they were trying to do the same thing that BIA's interrogators were trying to do. They had just gotten a look at the company's balance sheet for the second quarter, and were investigating signs of weakness or unexpected strength. They thought the company's numbers were good, but not great. On August 2 the stock price would drift down from $8.82 per share to close at $8.54. The analysts prepared their best questions to help them figure out where the price would go in coming days. *Would UTStarcom emerge as a hot*

stock in the third quarter? Or should investors sell shares and eat their losses before things got much worse?

Lu's opening remarks were laced with the complex jargon of the financial and technical worlds. (Only a truly determined analyst—or a spy—can penetrate a sentence like "We believe the new ASICS can take approximately 10 percent out of our cost of handsets and will bring our PAS handset gross margin back into the high teens in the next several quarters.") He then threw open the session to questions from the Wall Streeters.

One of them, Mike Ounjian, a keen-eyed analyst with Credit Suisse First Boston, jumped in to ask about the guidance the company was giving that day on what its third-quarter (Q3) performance was likely to be. "Just related to the Q3 guidance on the personal communications division," Ounjian asked, "how much of that business would you estimate being your own designs as opposed to, versus, resale?"

"Mike, this is Hong," said Lu. "We have, for the rest of the balance of the year; we're expected to have 0.5 million handsets. And out of that, we are going to probably for the second half of the year, from a run rate wise, we expect to ship a little bit more than 3 million handsets. So I'll probably say percentage of a number handsets we should be able to get some meaningful numbers. From a dollar amount, are still going to be relatively small because our handsets will be selling less than one half of what normal ASP's that we are selling."

"Right. Thank you."

BIA's analysts spotted a cluster of telltale indicators in what Lu said. First, Lu's remarks aren't always intelligible. And along with his garbled grammar, he offers a series of qualifiers: "we're *expected* to," "*probably*," "we *should* be able to." The interrogators' training told them such weasel words meant Lu might be trying to avoid offering a weak third-quarter prediction.

Ounjian then asked about potential problems he'd spotted with revenue recognition as a result of a backlog of products. Revenue recognition is the way companies record income. It can be done

either on a cash basis, with companies recording income only when the checks arrive in the mail; or on a more aggressive accrual basis, which means recording the revenue when it is earned, not when the money is in hand. Ounjian wanted to know what was causing the backlog, where in the world it was, and what kinds of delays were involved. All this could affect when the company would be able to record the revenues from the products involved. If the problems were serious, they could affect the company's financial results in the next quarter, and might cause the stock price to dip.

"Are there any issues related to recognizing revenues on these?" Ounjian asked.

The voice of Michael Sophie, then the company's interim chief financial officer, came over the phone line: "Yes, with the backlog, the vast majority of the wireless backlog is clearly PAS [an acronym for one of the company's products, Personal Access System]. I think you saw the announcement at the end of June where we announced on the PAS infrastructure orders in China. And again, it's just the timing of deployment and achieving final acceptance, we've also got some CDMA [an acronym for a type of mobile phone standard] to a lesser extent in the backlog. . . . But Q3 is clearly a little more handset oriented than we would typically run."

After analyzing the call, BIA's employees supplied a twenty-seven-page confidential report to their client, and they singled out Sophie's response to the question about revenue recognition for particular attention. They noted that Sophie qualified his response and referred back to another announcement from the end of June. BIA called that kind of conversational reference a "detour statement," and its analysts were convinced that Sophie was trying to minimize the delays. "Mr. Sophie avoids commenting on any issues related to revenue recognition, and his overall behavior indicates that revenue recognition problems cannot be ruled out." They recommended a presumptive and direct follow-up question for BIA's client to ask of executives at UTStarcom: "What issues are there related to revenue recognition?"

Overall, BIA's team rated the second-quarter conference call as a "medium high level of concern"—the same rating they'd given UTStarcom's call the quarter before. This time, though, the BIA team found more problems, which they listed in a box on the first page of their report: "Lacks Confidence," "Underlying Concern," "Avoids Providing Information."

In the report, BIA went through the call line by line, highlighting possible red flags throughout the transcript. The team offered asides about what they'd noticed and recommended more specific questions they thought might get to the root of the problem. In their conclusion, the BIA team said they'd found that the executives were worried about the timing of the company's profitability date and the issue of revenue recognition. The report says:

> Management's behavior indicates that they will post poor third quarter results, and it is also highly unlikely they will achieve profitability in the fourth quarter. In addition, during a response addressing backlog problems, management fails to comment on part of the analyst's question related to revenue recognition problems.

That kind of insight could help an investor make a decision to short a stock. Shorting is an investment maneuver in which firms borrow stock in a company and then sell it, betting that the price will go down and they can buy the stock back for less money before they have to give it back, pocketing the difference in price. If the price goes down, they make money. If it goes up, they lose. Basically, shorting is a bet against the company. Good short sellers look for unnoticed flaws in a company and exploit them for gains.

Because they're always trying to discover corporate dirty laundry, short sellers are particularly good clients for BIA—the techniques taught by the CIA are ideal for scrutinizing executives' forecasts of their company's prospects. Short sellers are hated in corporate boardrooms across the country. But BIA loves them.

BIA's client had no way of telling whether the deception analysis report was accurate or not. It was the client's job to take the report, combine it with other information known about UTStarcom, and make a bet for or against the company.

With the benefit of hindsight, though, we can go back and check the record to find out if BIA made the right call in 2005.

They nailed it.

Over the next month or so after the call of August 2, UTStarcom's stock price lost about $1 per share, a nice win for any short seller. But on October 6, 2005, the company released its third-quarter results, shocking NASDAQ traders with numbers that were below the guidance executives had offered during the conference call.[2] In October, UTStarcom said it expected total revenues of between $620 million and $640 million, compared with its previous target of $660 million to $680 million. The next morning, investors frantically sold their shares: more than 23 million transactions took place on October 7, 2005. A day after the third-quarter results were released, the stock was down roughly another $2, closing at $5.64.[3] It had been at $8.54 when the BIA team listened in on the conference call in August and flagged the potential problems with revenue recognition.

And what reason did UTStarcom give for its poor third-quarter performance? Revenue recognition. In a press release on October 6, UTStarcom said, "The Company attributes the revenue shortfall primarily to the delay in recognition of approximately $40 million in revenue."

What was much worse for the company was its announcement in the same press release that it was under investigation by the Securities and Exchange Commission (SEC), which it said was looking into "certain aspects of the company's financial disclosures during prior reporting periods." That was not the primary focus of the conference call.

Apparently, however, the SEC had suspicions of its own, concerning UTStarcom's past earnings reports. The SEC proceeding

was ultimately settled, with Lu paying a $100,000 civil penalty but admitting no wrongdoing.

IT WAS A PowerPoint presentation like many others in corporate America. It was held in 2006 in the bland conference room of SAC Capital Partners—one of the world's largest and most secretive hedge funds—on Cummings Point Road in Stamford, Connecticut, a stone's throw from the sailboat-speckled waters of Stamford harbor. Each attendee was given handouts emphasizing key points of the meeting.

But the session at the hedge fund's offices was like nothing the money managers in the room had ever seen before. The presenters that day included two women with backgrounds in intelligence. Patsy Boycan had spent twenty years with the CIA. She had specialized in polygraph, interviewing, and deception detection during her time at Langley, where she managed the CIA's crucial security clearance process. Kathleen Miritello had been a senior special operations officer at the CIA; she had more than twenty-five years of interrogation experience in military, law enforcement, and national security environments around the world.[4]

The women would put on a presentation that day that would dazzle the moneymen. In their intensity, they reminded one money manager of Clarice Starling, the no-nonsense FBI agent played by Jodie Foster in the movie *The Silence of the Lambs*: "You could tell they knew exactly what they were doing."

First, they promised that they'd teach the hedge fund managers the CIA's own foolproof techniques, crafted over decades of clandestine combat, to tell when someone's lying. Then they said they'd teach the money managers to make money—lots of money—by spotting lies. Of course, it would also cost lots of money to get the training. Sessions with this crew cost as much as $30,000 per day.

By the time of the meeting at SAC in 2006, Boycan and Miritello were no longer working for the CIA. They both had the title

"senior expert and instructor" with BIA. Since its founding in 2001, BIA has given its clients access to the same intelligence techniques the U.S. government uses and some of the same employees the government has hired.

BIA takes advantage of a little-known program inside the CIA that allows serving officers to moonlight in the private sector during their off hours and on weekends. A government official familiar with the plan explains it as an employee-retention effort by the CIA. In order to keep officers from decamping for the high-paying private sector, the CIA lets them earn money on the side. The official says that employees have to go through a detailed approval process before they're allowed to take on outside work. It's not clear whether companies other than BIA have hired serving CIA officers, and if so which ones, but some inside the CIA express surprise that the practice is allowed. Veterans familiar with the moonlighting say that it may be taking place only at BIA.

It's more than just a personnel matter. If, as the government official says, the moonlighting program is in place to keep serving officers from jumping to the private sector for higher pay— during a time of war, no less—it's an indication of the pressure that the rising private intelligence industry is placing on government. There's no way the federal pay scale can keep pace with the sums available at large corporations, hedge funds, and the like. Some keen observers of the intelligence community say the brain drain to the private sector is chipping away at U.S. national security, as people whose training was financed by the taxpayers quit the government to sell those skills to private businesses.

The presence of so many current and former CIA personnel on the payroll at BIA causes confusion as to whether the intelligence firm is actually an extension of the agency itself. As a result, BIA places a disclaimer in some of its corporate marketing materials to clarify that it is not, in fact, controlled by Langley.

. . . .

BIA WAS FOUNDED by a small group of CIA veterans, including Phil Houston, one of the CIA's top interrogators. According to a former CEO of the company, the founding group left the CIA with a feeling of disgust over the Bush administration's policy on torture after 9/11. The group of CIA veterans (some of whom had been with the CIA for more than 20 years) felt that the administration's so-called "enhanced interrogation techniques" betrayed everything they stood for as officers—not because torture was morally wrong, they told this former CEO, but because it produced bad intelligence. For a CIA officer who's proud of his work, there's nothing worse than an inferior product.

It seemed like a good time to start a private company designed to train law enforcement agencies in the CIA's state-of-the-art techniques of detecting deception—the science of telling when someone is lying. Using advanced techniques, psychological research, and years of trial and error, Houston had developed a system—in the private sector he called it "tactical behavior assessment" (TBA)—that he maintained was a nearly foolproof way to spot a liar. Unlike polygraph machines, the TBA technique allows examiners to work without hooking up their subject to a series of wires. The subject never knows he's being scrutinized.

Polygraph machines work by measuring a person's physical responses, such as heart rate, that indicate stress. Analysts using the machine need to sit with their subject for a long time. They have to establish a person's physiological baseline, so they begin with a "control" conversation about neutral topics, before they can begin grilling the subject. Conducting an interview and doing a thorough analysis of polygraph results can take hours.

TBA focuses on the verbal and nonverbal cues that people convey when they aren't telling the truth.[5] Psychologists familiar with the method say it works because human beings just aren't

hardwired to lie well. Holding two opposing ideas in your brain at the same time—as you have to do in order to tell a lie—causes a phenomenon they term "cognitive dissonance," which creates actual physical discomfort. And when people are uncomfortable, they squirm. They fidget ever so slightly, they pick lint off their clothes, they shift their bodily positions. Without even realizing it, they reach for ways to avoid the physical discomfort. They reach for every way to tell the literal truth while still misleading the questioner.

A CIA veteran trained in the TBA technique will begin any session by getting himself into what BIA calls "L squared mode," which means "look and listen." Agents look for the physical indicators of lying. They watch for a person shifting anchor points. If the person is leaning forward on one elbow, does he switch to the other one? If the person is seated, does he shift his center of gravity? Interrogators watch for grooming gestures such as adjusting clothes, hair, or eyeglasses. They look to see if the person picks at his fingernails or scratches himself. They watch for the person to clean his surroundings—does he straighten the paper clips on the table, or line up the pens? If he does, he could be lying.

To obtain verbal clues, agents listen for several kinds of statements. They'll listen for qualifying answers, phrases that begin with words like "honestly," "frankly," or "basically." Those are generally an indicator that the person is trying too hard to convince his audience of what he's saying, and they're a red flag for agents trained in TBA. The agents will be listening for detour phrases like "as I said before . . ." They'll want to hear if the person invokes religion—"I swear to God"—or attacks the questioner: "How dare you ask me something like that?" These can be unconscious tactics to avoid actually lying to the questioner.

Other red flags: Complaints—"How long is this going to take?" Selective memory—"To the best of my knowledge." Overly courteous responses—"Yes, sir." In each case, analysts trained by the

CIA see a pattern. And if they spot enough red flags, they know they've caught a liar.

The tricky part of TBA is that any one of these indicators alone doesn't mean much. Maybe the guy just has an itch and needs to scratch. That's why agents trained in TBA watch carefully. They're looking for clusters: indicators that come all at once. If the subject shifts his anchor points, grumbles about how long this is going to take, and then takes off his glasses while scratching his nose, he's probably a liar. BIA's trainers teach clients how to take short-hand notes as an interview progresses. They tell trainees to note down a number for each question asked in the interview, and then mark a dot next to that number for every indicator they spot during the answer. The advantage of this note-taking system is that you don't have to look down at your page very often, since you're only making dots, not writing down in words what the person says. You can keep your eyes off your notebook and on your subject.

And it doesn't take long to put all this together. Houston tells colleagues that the crucial instant comes within the first five seconds after a question is asked. That's when a person can't keep himself or herself from exhibiting the signs of a lie. BIA training, in fact, teaches agents to ignore any events that come more than ten seconds after a question. It's in the first moment that a liar reveals everything to a trained observer.

Once they spot a lie, agents shift into what they call "elicitation" mode, which is the art of getting someone to confess something even if it is against his own best interest. Mike Floyd, a veteran of the CIA and a colleague of Phil Houston, was known for his ex-tensive preparation before conducting an interview with a suspect. Typically, he'd bring in another expert to help with the interview, so one person could ask the questions and keep the conversation flowing while the other just focused on the suspect, watching for indicators of dishonesty.

They'd ask "bait" questions, such as, "Is there any reason why

we might find your fingerprints at the scene of the crime?" They'd phrase the touchiest questions in a neutral way. So they wouldn't ask, "Did you embezzle the money?" Instead they'd say something like, "Tell me what happened to the money." They'd ask "presumptive questions" in which they showed the suspect they already knew something about what happened. So they wouldn't say, "You're guilty, aren't you?" They'd ask something like, "Weren't you worried that the SEC might be able to trace the funds?" That question assumes that both the interviewer and the suspect know the suspect is the perpetrator, and this conversation is simply clearing up some small details.

That kind of questioning is based on the assumption that people want to confess their crimes. Somewhere deep in their souls, they can't stand holding on to a secret. And if they're questioned in a careful, nonconfrontational way, they'll spill everything.

BIA's training begins with an introduction to Phil Houston's techniques, followed by a series of videos of executives being interviewed on CNBC. The goal is to learn how to separate the truth tellers from the liars. Then come so-called red-letter drills, in which staff volunteers are organized into a team. One of the volunteers is told to steal a pre-placed red letter from an office. The "thief" and a group of innocent volunteers are brought into the conference room, where the trainees put their new skills into practice. They grill the volunteers to find which one is lying about the theft and is therefore guilty.

Trainees are taught how to position themselves in a room during an interview. Don't sit across a table from the subject; sit on the same side of the conference table. If you're sitting at a corner, push your chair back from the table until you can spot movements of the subject's legs.

One person familiar with the sessions says many of the students can spot the liar after just a day or two of training. But often, it is the students in the back of the room who identify the liar first, not the student designated to ask the questions. For a

beginner in these techniques, it can be tough to both quiz a suspect and watch for clusters of indicators.

At many of their stops, BIA trainers distribute laminated cards with deception-detection tips for trainees to remember after the session. The cards, headed "Tactical Behavior Assessment and Strategic Interviewing Pocket Guide," urge students to "Be in L2 Mode—Look and Listen." Over time, BIA's clients have included several hedge funds and investment banks.

PHIL HOUSTON WAS convinced that there was nothing anyone could do to defeat his system. That is, even if an agent was trained in the TBA method, and knew what another trained observer would be looking for, he still couldn't lie without getting caught. Houston and his colleagues from the CIA had tapped into something deep within the human psyche, and they knew it was powerful stuff. People trained in TBA often make terrible liars themselves. Once you're convinced that lying is always transparent, it becomes almost impossible for you to carry off a successful lie.[6]

Phil Houston and his colleagues thought that selling this timeless TBA training to law enforcement agencies across the country might be a good business. At first, it was. After 9/11, local police forces realized they needed to beef up their interrogation techniques on the front lines against terrorism. Police officers signed up for the training, and Houston and his colleagues traveled the country evangelizing about TBA. But although Houston is a brilliant interrogator, his colleagues say he's not a brilliant businessman. His company kept bleeding money. Police forces were late paying their bills. Houston and his colleagues were more interested in delivering the training than in following up on invoices.

Soon, the struggling little firm faced an impasse. It needed a buyer to inject business discipline and make it thrive. That's when Houston met Liam Donohue, a venture capitalist based in Boston who was then running an investment fund called Arcadia Partners.

TBA and the CIA's "elicitation" techniques captivated Donohue, and he saw a wide-open new market for them: corporate America.

Arcadia bought a large percentage of Houston's firm, and the CIA veterans retained a significant equity share in the reconstituted new company, which was now called Business Intelligence Advisors, or BIA. The acronym was a deliberate reference to the CIA.

Officers of BIA declined to be interviewed during the writing of the book. But the firm describes itself, succinctly, in a document distributed to clients and signed by its current president, Cheryl Cook:

> Business Intelligence Advisors Inc. (BIA) adapts techniques developed in the context of international intelligence gathering and national security to enhance high-value, high-risk decision making in the private sector. BIA's services are targeted to, and most valuable in, information driven processes, where the reliability of information can make a crucial difference in outcomes.
>
> BIA's employees and network of experts include the world's leading intelligence resources, with unparalleled expertise in strategic interviewing, intelligence gathering, risk assessment and security. BIA combines these resources with experienced analysts, consultants and project managers to ensure that resources are deployed to maximize return and business impact.[7]

Liam Donohue eventually became chairman of the board of the new company. Under his leadership it began to thrive. As an MBA from Dartmouth's famous Amos Tuck School of Business Administration, he brought in a series of managers who shared his background. He reoriented BIA from an enterprise primarily focused on law enforcement to a business focused on generating corporate clients. He hired a CEO, Don Carlson, who was a lawyer and had

been with the investment banking firm Goldman Sachs. By 2005, Carlson says, BIA was generating between $10 million and $11 million in annual revenue.

Donohue is extremely secretive about BIA, and the firm has opened up to the press about its services only once, for an astonishing article in *Barron's* by Jonathan R. Laing, "Is Your CEO Lying?"[8] The article laid out BIA's deception-detection techniques and set off a flurry of interest in CIA-style interrogation within the hedge fund community.

The CIA didn't invent these techniques. Although it spent years working on tactics based on the best information modern science has to offer, at most it was just reinventing something that had been developed more than 100 years ago by the first private eye, Allan Pinkerton. All the biographies of Pinkerton mention his ability to get criminals to confess. In the 1850s Pinkerton wrote that there was a reason for this astonishing success: "Criminals must eventually reveal their secrets," he noted. "And a detective must have the necessary experience and judgment of human nature to know the criminal in his weakest moment and force from him, through sympathy and confidence, the secret which devours him."

Allan Pinkerton and Phil Houston, separated by more than a century, came to remarkably similar conclusions about the human condition.

Pinkerton said that his technique was based on judgment of human nature, and that is also true of the TBA technique. Pinkerton noted that detectives should use "sympathy," which is what "elicitors" trained in TBA do as well. And Pinkerton talked about using "confidence," just as the CIA's elicitation method uses presumptive questions, in which the interrogator projects confidence that he already knows something crucial. Finally, Houston and Pinkerton agree on the most important point: the secret devours the criminal. Criminals all want to confess. The interrogator is just helping them along.

Pinkerton probably didn't invent deception detection or

elicitation, either. These may be among the things that smart, observant people invent for themselves. What's remarkable, actually, is that every generation produces people who think that the best way to get information out of someone is to beat it out. In the face of so much evidence that deception detection and elicitation work, there are still interrogators who don't want to be polite to a suspect. And usually, those are the interrogators who can't get a confession.

IN THE SUMMER of 2005, BIA was on a roll. On July 14 Phil Houston and Patsy Boycan led a BIA team listening in on a Southwest Airlines earnings call with investors. Southwest was coming off a boffo quarter in which it beat Wall Street's all-important expectations with an earnings spike of 42.9 percent over the same quarter the year before. BIA's interest in Southwest was prompted by a client, Ziff Brothers Investments, a private equity fund controlled by the three billionaire sons of William Ziff, Jr., who built the Ziff-Davis publishing empire. Ziff Brothers wanted to know whether or not Southwest could continue its excellent run into the next quarter. Did Southwest's executives believe their own rosy forecasts?

After a preamble, Southwest's CEO, Gary Kelly, and its chief financial officer, Laura Wright, began to take questions from analysts. The back-and-forth was cordial and warm. Many of the analysts had been covering the company for years, and had spoken with the management dozens of times. Some analysts interspersed their questions with a few words of congratulations for the great quarterly results. But BIA's spies on the call weren't into schmoozing. They didn't say a thing. They were in "L squared mode."

BIA's report on that call is not available, so it's difficult to say exactly what conclusions the analysts reached. But a look at the transcript of the conversation of July 14 reveals several moments that may have stood out for the BIA team.[9] First, J.P. Morgan's Securities analyst Jamie Baker asked a question about potential fare

increases—which could be deadly for a company like Southwest that makes its name as a discount airline.

"I know AMR [the company that owns American Airlines] put a $2 to $3 one-way increase into the majority of your markets yesterday, but would you characterize Southwest as still in the study period or have you definitively chosen not to match that?" Baker asked.

"Well, we haven't changed our fares," responded Kelly. "We want to be a leader, but we want to be the low fare leader."

"Mmm hmm."

"This is actually a perfect environment for us where all of our competitors are raising fares and it really helps us differentiate who we are," continued Kelly.

On the basis of his noncommittal response, "Mmm hmm," we can guess that Baker might have been skeptical about this point, too, but a trained TBA analyst might home in on specific phrases. Kelly responds to a direct question about raising fares in the present tense with information that's not an answer at all: "Well, we haven't changed our fares." He doesn't say what the company plans to do in the future, which is what Baker asked. BIA would call that a *nonanswer*.*

Kelly follows his nonanswer with what BIA calls a *protest statement*: He says, "We want to be the low-fare leader." Again, he doesn't answer the question, which was whether Southwest is still considering a fare increase. He describes what Southwest wants to be, not what it is going to do. Were the BIA team's pens scribbling furiously during this exchange?

Then, as a closer, Kelly adds what BIA would call a *qualifying answer*: "This is actually a perfect environment for us." By using the word "actually," was Kelly trying to persuade the listener of something that on its face wouldn't make any sense?

---

*The *Washington Post*'s reporting team of Bob Woodward and Carl Bernstein had a term of their own for this sort of response when they spotted it during their Watergate investigation in the 1970s. They called it a non-denial denial.

Was Kelly trying to duck the question about whether Southwest would have to raise its fares? Soon enough, it did just that: at the end of 2005, Southwest bragged in its annual report to shareholders that the company had raised fares only "modestly" throughout that year. The report noted that the average passenger fare increased from $88.57 in 2004 to $93.68 in 2005.[10]

Later in the earnings call, the trained BIA observers listening in might have concluded that the executives were uncomfortable with their own earnings predictions. Lehman Brothers' analyst Gary Chase tried to pin Kelly down, asking, "Can you just sort of help us think through why you think 15 percent is an achievable growth goal for next year?"

"Well, first of all, it's a goal," responded Kelly. He added several caveats about what it would take for the company to hit the number: the economy would need to remain healthy, competitors would need to remain predictable, and maybe some improvements in the Baltimore market would be needed.

Still, he said, "We are not conceding that we cannot improve our earnings next year by 15 percent. And we just want to make that very clear because there are already reports out there that are suggesting that our earnings are going to decline, and that is not acceptable to us."

But then he concludes on this tepid note: "At this point, it certainly looks to us like a reasonable goal." Notice Kelly's use of several qualifying phrases in a row: "at this point," "certainly looks to us," "reasonable goal." That's far from a full-throated endorsement of the company's own revenue projections.

Certain statements in the Southwest earnings call contrast with the positive buzz the company received that day. Even though the company has an excellent reputation and even then was receiving kudos for an innovative hedging strategy to blunt the impact of rising fuel costs, something was giving the executives discomfort about their future.

Sharp traders at Ziff Brothers could have used that information

in conjunction with everything else they knew about Southwest to form a picture of a company unable to keep up its earnings streak. In fact, an executive familiar with BIA says Ziff concluded from the call that Southwest's executives weren't confident they'd be able to repeat their earnings success in the next quarter. The source says Ziff shorted Southwest's stock, and in doing so, may have made a good deal of money. The positive glow from the healthy earnings report lasted only until July 18, when the stock peaked at around $14.75 per share before settling into a slump that would last for more than a month. By the end of August, the stock was trading at about $13.50 per share.

DESPITE THEIR SUCCESSES, not every client was as impressed by the BIA team's presentation or its tactics. That same summer of 2005, BIA's Don Carlson, who had been an attorney with Goldman Sachs, brought Phil Houston and Mike Floyd to meet with Goldman's own internal business intelligence division. The BIA team hoped to land Goldman Sachs as a client. For BIA, working with Goldman Sachs would be a gold mine: it had thousands of employees, so a contract for BIA's interrogation training alone could be hugely lucrative. In 2005, Goldman had more than $20 billion in revenue. The firm would have nearly unlimited budgets for research and investigations. Conceivably, this one client could double BIA's revenue as soon as it signed a contract.

A lot was on the line when Carlson, Houston, and Floyd strolled into the conference room at Goldman's headquarters at 85 Broad Street in lower Manhattan. They were used to being greeted deferentially. Even brash investment bankers are a bit intimidated by certified spies, particularly the CIA's legendary interrogators. But this time the BIA team met a harsh reception. Goldman's fourteen or so employees in the room asked question after question as the BIA team struggled to plow through its standard proposal. One Goldman employee at the meeting was Jeffrey Starr, who was

then on loan to Goldman's business intelligence team from an intelligence agency at the Department of Defense. As an expert on intelligence tactics, he began to rip up the BIA argument piece by piece.

Starr pushed his chair back from the table and began to grill BIA's presenters. *Are you saying that these indicators prove someone's a liar? Why wouldn't actions outside the five-second window be relevant? What if somebody's just combing his hair? How can you put your faith in this kind of stuff?* It was the roughest treatment Houston and Floyd had received. When they showed a short video to illustrate their point, Starr laid into them.

In the video, an investigator quizzes five people about a stolen laptop. The audience members at the training session are supposed to look for the indicators of deception and figure out who stole the laptop. Starr pounced on a flaw. The video featured actors, not real people. If the actors had been coached on what to do, they wouldn't be giving the indicators that real human beings would give—they'd be giving the indicators BIA told them to give. Starr was incensed. What good was this video? Why didn't they bring in a video of a real interrogation? BIA's team couldn't come up with a good answer for him. They felt as though they'd failed.

They hadn't. Ultimately, the weight of BIA's argument began to convince even the skeptical Starr. He saw some potential in what Houston and Floyd were offering. Goldman, despite the disastrous pitch meeting, soon became a client of BIA. Of course, not everyone within Goldman is bullish on BIA. Asked about BIA's intelligence techniques, Goldman's global head of communications, Lucas van Praag, mocks the capabilities of veterans of U.S. intelligence: "If these guys were really that good, and the techniques worked as well as they said they did, how come we're still in Iraq?"

Training in deception detection and eavesdropping on conference calls are just BIA's baseline service. Prices, and services, get more elaborate from there. For about $50,000 per day, a client company can hire a team of CIA-trained interrogators to come to

its offices and question subjects, typically when the company suspects some internal fraud or wrongdoing.

Perhaps BIA's most important—and least known—client is Cascade Investment, LLC, a small outfit in Kirkland, Washington, which is just across Lake Washington from downtown Seattle and easily accessible by boat via an adjacent marina.[11] In this bland suburban office park is one of the most powerful financial firms in the world, a firm that almost no one has heard of. Cascade isn't just any private equity firm. It's the personal private equity firm of one of the richest men in the world, Bill Gates. With just over $4 billion in assets under management, Cascade's year-end 2007 filing with the Securities and Exchange Commission (SEC) showed that it owns shares of assets as diverse as Coca-Cola, Pacific Ethanol, and, of course, Berkshire Hathaway, the successful company owned by Gates's friend and fellow billionaire, Warren Buffett.[12]

People familiar with Cascade say it uses BIA to help with due diligence. The old saying caveat emptor—let the buyer beware— was never more true than in the private equity industry, where money managers live in fear of investing $100 million in a company that turns out to be a lemon. Private equity investors need every scrap of information they can find to help them make a good decision. But BIA's due diligence for Bill Gates's team at Cascade goes beyond the information gathering you might find at lower levels of the financial stratosphere. For Gates's team, BIA's interrogators and investigators evaluate potential acquisitions.

Private equity firms such as Cascade often find themselves acquiring private companies. When you're buying a privately held company, you can be in the dark about what you're actually getting. People familiar with the relationship between them say that Cascade asked BIA to find answers to specific questions about companies that were potential acquisitions. For example, if a firm was founded by an entrepreneur, what is that person's family like? Is the CEO's son, who will inherit control of the company, a dysfunctional alcoholic? If so, the company might sell at a much lower

price, since there's no reliable successor to keep it going. Knowing even one piece of information could be worth millions.

In an acquisition of a private company, BIA's team will investigate all the top executives of the company under scrutiny. Who are their professional contacts? What are their families like? What kinds of pressures are they under? The BIA team will also fan out to cover the target company's customers, interviewing them about their transactions with the company. *Are you going to re-up your contract for next year? Are you going to spend more or less money with the target company next quarter?* The same with suppliers. A company needs certain raw materials to do business. BIA's team approaches suppliers to find out how much the target company has been buying. *What's the trend line? Is the company buying more now than ever before? And what about price—is there an increase coming that could damage the target company's profitability?* Every tidbit helps form an overall picture of the company, and what Cascade should be willing to pay to buy it.

Such due diligence, of course, could be done by young MBAs, or even college graduates with specific training in corporate analysis. You don't need veteran CIA spies to analyze a company. But having their expertise helps. The CIA experience can help BIA's team spot a supply chain vendor who's lying about whether he's planning to raise prices next quarter. Their elicitation techniques can help draw that vendor out about when the hike is coming and how much it might be.

The secret, whether it's a crime, intelligence, or the expected price of soybeans, devours the keeper.

BIA's team of research analysts was, for a time, led by Jim Roth, a veteran of the CIA. Roth's team offered investigative research, primarily to hedge fund clients. In one case, a hedge fund hired BIA to investigate a publicly traded home builder. The hedge fund investors had a hunch: the builder's company might not make its revenue projections for the quarter, as it didn't have enough land in the Los Angeles market to develop all the residences it was telling the market

it would build. But how to prove that? The fund managers called BIA, which put Roth and his CIA-trained agents on the case. Roth's team began working the phones. They called real estate agents in Los Angeles and asked about the local market. *Who is buying land? Is the home builder a big buyer? Which plots does it already own?* In each conversation, the BIA team used deception-detection techniques to spot dishonesty or uncertainty, and used their skills of elicitation to get the agents to reveal information about the market.

Roth's team also called local real estate speculators and large landowners to find out who was buying up property. They did research into hard-to-find public records to find out who was making new land purchases. They talked to competitors to see if the home builder was buying land through proxies to avoid detection. After making hundreds of calls and poring over scores of documents, Roth's team concluded that the hedge fund was right. The home builder didn't own nearly as much land in Los Angeles as it was saying it did. There was no way the company could make its earnings targets in coming years.

On the basis of Roth's written report and other information it had developed on its own, BIA's hedge fund client shorted the home builder's stock. In the case of the home builder, the client told people at BIA that it pocketed $20 million as a result. Compared with the tens of thousands it had spent on Jim Roth's work for BIA, that's a huge return on investment.

Jim Roth has since left BIA and recently was working at his own consulting firm, doing the same kind of work for hedge funds. He is secretive about his new operation, called the Langley Group, in a nod to the site of the CIA's headquarters. Roth's firm's Web site at www.thelangleygroup.net betrays no other hint of the intelligence background of its founder. The firm has an unlisted phone number. The Web site registration is privacy protected. E-mails sent to the address listed on the site bounce back.

That's OK, though. The well-networked hedge funds know how to get in touch.

. . . .

CLIENTS WHO HAVE BIA on a retainer of as much as $400,000 to $800,000 per year are entitled to another service: undercover operations. For its highest-paying clients, BIA sends its CIA-trained interrogators to investors' conferences or meetings under the guise of traditional business consultants or simply as unidentified "colleagues" traveling with a client.

On one occasion, a team of BIA's deception-detection experts traveled to Palo Alto, where they went with a client to an investors' conference sponsored by the investment bank Morgan Stanley. At these events, start-up companies make pitches to an audience packed with potential investors. The companies need money, and the investors are looking to pick winners that will generate returns on their capital. The executives who make presentations at these gatherings put the best spin on their companies—what they do, how they make money, and what their prospects are. Because the pressure is on to dazzle the moneymen in the room, the temptation to exaggerate or even lie is enormous. *Why not paper over that bad quarter? No need to bring up the big customer who just canceled his contract.* But the unflattering details are the ones that can make or break a wealthy investor's decision to place his money in a company. If the start-up company's executives are lying, investors need to know it immediately so they don't waste their time and money.

As they sat through the series of presentations by hopeful corporate executives, BIA's team of analysts watched all the presenters for signs of deception. Were they using red flag terms like "frankly" and "honestly"? What were their hands doing while they were presenting the financials? Did they rock on the balls of their feet as they detailed new customer acquisitions? Each time BIA spotted a cluster of telltale signs, one of its analysts would nod subtly to the client. Instantly, the client could home in on the touchiest issues for each company. If the executives were lying about material issues, BIA's client knew not to invest.

For the executives making presentations at a conference like Morgan Stanley's, it can be stressful enough to run through the financial details with the fate of the company on the line. Imagine how stressed they'd be if they knew that they were being scrutinized by the CIA's best human lie detectors. But they never knew.

Spies who've spent the best years of their careers grilling suspected members of Al Qaeda might not seem like people who'd be interested in spending their time in hotel conference rooms watching corporate suits sweat out a pitch meeting. But it's steady work, and safe. Also, it can pay much better than government work.

Generally, CIA officers work at the same government pay scale as employees of the Department of Transportation or the Department of Education. Known as the General Scale (GS), the system has fifteen grades of seniority, each of which is divided into ten "steps." In 2008, entry-level government employees made just over $17,000 per year. The most senior GS-15 employees earned $124,010.[13] Even for elite CIA leaders, pay tops out at around the highest level for the government's so-called Senior Executive Service (SES), $172,200 in 2008. The government allows minimal adjustments for cost of living in expensive areas of the country. CIA officers sometimes get hardship pay for particularly difficult work. And overseas, CIA officers also get one other nice perk: paid housing.

Although $124,000 sounds like a lot of money to most Americans, it is not much if we consider the amount of education, training, and valuable experience these people have. The private sector pays a lot better.

For relatively junior CIA officers making GS-10 to GS-12 wages of between $43,000 and $57,000 per year, a jump to business intelligence can be lucrative. One person familiar with the way CIA veterans are compensated in the private sector says CIA officers at the GS-10 to GS-12 levels can leap to $120,000 to $150,000 as a base salary, with the potential to rise well into the $200,000 range as they develop more corporate experience. Depending on when

in their career they make the move to the private sector, veterans of the CIA may also bring with them a generous government pension that pays them a percentage of their highest salary for the rest of their lives. Most people cannot resist the opportunity to double or triple their wages, and the CIA's veterans are no different.

Ironically, BIA is known as one of the stingier private-sector employers of CIA talent. Its former CEO Don Carlson recalls that CIA veterans at the firm topped out at roughly between $180,000 and $210,000 when he ran the operation in 2005. Not many of the CIA veterans there asked for or received equity in the firm, he recalls. For all their talent and training, Carlson says, "I think we dramatically underpaid people."

One way for employees of the CIA to bolster their earnings is to moonlight for corporate intelligence firms like BIA. CIA officers routinely ask their bosses for permission to work at BIA on the side to boost their government incomes. According to a government official knowledgeable about the practice, to apply for permission for outside work CIA employees must fill out a form stating who they're going to work for and what they're doing. Permission must be granted by a group of vetters that includes the CIA's ethics lawyers.

Indeed CIA employees must fill out a standard form to disclose any outside affiliations at all, whether it's a summer job or volunteering for a local Boy Scout troop. One of the considerations the CIA uses to decide whether or not to grant permission to moonlight is whether the work will interfere with the officer's responsibilities at the CIA. Permission is granted on a case-by-case basis.

The active-duty CIA part-timers became particularly helpful for BIA, says another person familiar with the firm, when the new crop of college graduates flooded into the big four accounting firms each year. BIA provides training in deception detection for all the firms, and the influx of new employees in the summers meant BIA, too, had to staff up. Typically, the firm did that by relying on moonlighting CIA officers who could train the new accountants in TBA and then return to the CIA. At one point before he arrived at

BIA, Carlson says, the firm had twelve to fifteen active-duty CIA officers employed part-time as analysts.

Still, BIA is careful to make a distinction between itself and the CIA. In a brochure distributed to clients, "Strategic Information Collection for Investors," BIA included this disclaimer on the first page: "This is to advise that Business Intelligence Advisors Inc.'s training is in no way connected to or endorsed by the United States government or any agency thereof, BIA's instructors are acting solely in their capacity as private citizens and not as representatives of any federal governmental agency."[14]

In later years, BIA began to bring in entry-level college graduates and train them in TBA. These young employees staffed a boiler room of sorts, where they listened in on corporate conference calls, pored over transcripts, and even looked at companies' press releases and SEC filings, in order to spot clusters of indicators of deception for BIA's many clients. At one point, BIA tried to develop a training program to teach corporate clients how to lie. "We wanted to be able to say, 'Here's how you can get away with it,'" recalls Carlson. But BIA ran up against the fundamental barrier of cognitive dissonance. It could never figure out how to coach a liar to conceal the telltale signs of his lies. BIA never sold training in how to lie.

BIA advises that there are also certain indicators that a person is telling the truth. Because the truth is less useful to an interrogator in the early stages of an interview, BIA training tells clients to ignore the truthful behavior; but the firm does provide a handy list of the things that reveal when someone is telling the truth: direct answers, spontaneous answers, attentive and interested behavior, and consistency.

The truth, it seems, is easier to tell than a lie.

The Eddie Murphy Strategy

Monday, March 5, 2007, dawned cool and clear in the Virginia countryside outside Washington. As Bobby Ferraro made his morning commute past the strip malls and open fields, he didn't see anything in the sky that hinted of a problem, or of the multi-million-dollar riddle he'd need to solve in just a few hours.

Ferraro is the director of satellite operations for GeoEye, a company in Dulles, Virginia, that flies spy satellites for government and corporate customers. Begun with the merger of two smaller companies just over a year earlier, in January 2006, GeoEye was heading into its busiest season yet. It had just renegotiated a government intelligence contract to provide images taken by the company's satellites.

That weekend, OrbView-3, one of GeoEye's satellites in low orbit, had been photographing the Earth's surface and beaming pictures to ground stations located around the world. From those points all over the globe, the images had been sent to GeoEye's nondescript headquarters building in Virginia, where they were stored in a raw data form called "level zero" on a bank of high-speed computers. As Bobby Ferraro steered into the parking lot of his office complex, made his way to his fifth-floor office, and settled into his morning routine, the pictures awaited processing by GeoEye's Monday-morning shift workers.

Ferraro left his regular 9 A.M. meeting and strode down the hall past the company's flight operations center, a dark room crammed with the computers that control the satellites. Michael Schmidt, the company's processing manager, walked up to him.

"We've got a problem with the images," Schmidt said.

The pictures taken by OrbView-3 over the weekend had been fine for a while. But then the images taken on Sunday went black. One minute, this 670-pound satellite had been sending down photos from over the Caspian Sea, and the next, nothing.

"Oh, no," murmured Ferraro. This could be bad.

At age forty-three, the normally cheerful Ferraro knew his way around satellites. He'd begun his career in the air force, and he had worked on research and development for the Strategic Defense Initiative, an effort in the 1980s to develop a missile system to protect the country from incoming Soviet ICBMs. Later, he'd worked at the command and control facility for the Global Positioning System (GPS).

Ferraro knew that any one of a number of problems could cause the images to turn out black. There could be a problem inside the GeoEye computers in Virginia, causing them to misread the data from the image files. There could be trouble with the transmission from the ground stations. There could be a glitch in the equipment that had initially received the pictures from the satellite.

Or, the problem could be with the satellite itself. This would mean that the multimillion-dollar machine was a total loss. There would be no way to get a repair crew to the satellite to fix even minor damage. The machine had been launched in 2003 and was supposed to last at least five years. Many satellites had lasted for a decade or more. It was far too soon for OrbView to conk out.

Ferraro walked down the hall to talk with the company's head of spacecraft engineering.

"We may need to get a tiger team together," Ferraro said.

Soon, GeoEye's offices were crawling with engineers, operations

specialists, and technical advisers from the vendors who had built OrbView-3 and its key components. Those included Orbital Sciences Corporation and Northrop Grumman. Collectively, they formed a "tiger team," of elite satellite mechanics to perform what they called "anomaly resolution." They'd work over every inch of the system, from the headquarters building up to the satellite, to find the problem.

The first steps were to notify the government, the client expecting to take delivery of that day's fresh images; and then to notify the company's licensing authority, the National Oceanic and Atmospheric Administration in suburban Silver Spring, Maryland, which granted GeoEye—a private-sector company—the right to operate a satellite in the first place. Calls also went out to the National Geospatial Intelligence Agency, and to GeoEye's customers around the world.

By the end of the day, GeoEye had a diagnosis. The problem was with the camera. And the camera was on the satellite, zipping around the edge of the Earth's atmosphere. It had been designed with "single string" components, so there were no backup systems on board. There was no way to fix it.

This was a serious blow to GeoEye, whose stock was traded on the NASDAQ exchange. Wall Street securities regulations meant the company was duty-bound to disclose the event to the investing public, as it did in an 8-K filing with the SEC on Thursday, March 8. The document said the company could control the satellite, but couldn't get pictures from it. GeoEye couldn't tell the markets whether the satellite could be fixed, or when its fate might be known. In the meantime, GeoEye would try to service its customers with an older satellite, IKONOS.

Investors were startled by the news, and GeoEye's stock fell sharply, dropping from $18.28 on Thursday to $16.25 by the time the markets closed at 4 P.M. Friday. It had been a lousy week for Bobby Ferraro, but such is life in the high-stakes satellite game.

Ferraro and his team spent much of the next month trying to think up a way to fix the camera. They worked on the problem over and over again until late April. Then they finally gave up.*

WHEN THE SATELLITE OrbView-3 went down, U.S. intelligence agencies weren't the only ones inconvenienced. GeoEye, which has more than 400 employees worldwide and generated more than $180 million in revenue in 2007, estimates that almost half of its business comes from the private sector. Companies use GeoEye's three satellites for all kinds of monitoring.

Oil companies can check on the status of their rigs in the Gulf of Mexico. Agricultural giants can generate false-color images of fields, in which red areas show healthy growth and yellowish areas show crops that need help. Developers can generate topographical maps of real estate they might want to buy. Google buys images for use in its popular satellite application GoogleEarth.

GeoEye also sells satellite images of the ocean to fishermen. The pictures identify heavy underwater concentrations of phytoplankton, where the fish will go to feed. Every day, GeoEye's technicians e-mail satellite maps of these places to ship captains on bridges of trawlers around the world. It's hardly sporting, but satellite images can save a ship's captain as much as 10 or 15 percent in fuel costs. Instead of wandering around the ocean hoping to bump into a rich school of fish, the captain steers directly for the best spots.

The commercial satellite industry is still small. GeoEye has only one American competitor: DigitalGlobe, which is based in the Colorado Rockies. DigitalGlobe flies a QuickBird spacecraft that was launched into orbit 450 kilometers above the surface of

---

*In September, GeoEye's insurance company, Willis Inspace, paid $40 million on the insurance policy for the satellite. By the summer of 2008, GeoEye had begun negotiations to donate the busted satellite to the University of Colorado. After all, everything on the satellite except the camera worked perfectly. Engineers at GeoEye figured that the aeronautics students at the university would get a kick out of being able to maneuver their own satellite.

the Earth in 2001 and captures 75 million square kilometers of imagery data each year.

Overseas, there are several more image providers, including the French company Spot Image, which boasts that its FORMOSAT-2 is the only high-resolution satellite that can take pictures of the same location each day—other satellite companies must wait days before the orbits of their spacecraft bring them around again to reshoot a given location.

But it is the American company GeoEye's newest satellite that demonstrates the astonishing overlap between government and corporate intelligence technology. It's not just that the private sector has access to the same types of satellite technology as U.S. spy agencies. In this case, companies will be using the *same satellite* as some of the nation's most sophisticated intelligence operatives.

GeoEye participates in a program called NextView run by the federal government's spy satellite operator, the National Geospatial-Intelligence Agency (NGA). The program is designed to allow the federal government to pick up much of the cost of developing the next generation of spy satellites, which cost millions to design, build, and launch. Under the NextView program, GeoEye developed a new satellite, and the NGA kicked in $237 million federal tax dollars to help build it. The contract allows GeoEye to use the satellite for its commercial clients, too.

Here's what GeoEye said in its May 2008 quarterly filing with the Securities and Exchange Commission (SEC): "The Company anticipates that NGA will account for approximately half of the satellites' imagery-taking capacity during this time, with the remaining capacity available to generate commercial sales, including sales to international ground station customers and municipal customers."[1]

The company launched the new satellite, GeoEye-1, from Vandenberg Air Force Base in California in late August 2008. Boeing rockets were used. Technicians from General Dynamics prepped the satellite. GeoEye-1 spends much of its time taking pictures for

the CIA and the Department of Defense, and the rest taking pictures for paying clients, which have included Wal-Mart, commodities traders, and commercial fishermen.

GeoEye's corporate spokesman is Mark Brender, an amiable former ABC News Pentagon producer. Sitting in a conference room at GeoEye's headquarters, he flashes a picture on a display screen of the first spy photo ever taken. It is a grainy image taken by the highly classified spy satellite Corona on August 18, 1960. You can barely make out an airstrip at a base called Mys Shmidta on the Far East coast of what was then the Soviet Union. A parking area is also visible, but that's about all.[2] Still, the image was revolutionary at the time. Military leaders could now see what the enemy was building, and where. Piecing together the observed activities, military officers could infer the Soviet Union's overall strategy. Brender flashes more images on the screen. Today's commercial satellites can see individual people walking on the ground. They can see cars well enough to pick out the make and model. They can see coral reefs underwater in the ocean.

"For forty or fifty years, the intelligence community kept their overhead intelligence capabilities highly secret," Brender says. "This technology was the family jewels of U.S and Soviet intelligence. It was developed in order for two cold war rivals to be able to watch each other very carefully."

The doctrine of the time, Brender points out, was called mutually assured destruction. Neither side wanted to attack first, because the other side had the ability to strike back with devastating consequences.

Now, though, the technology is in corporate hands. "Now we've moved into an era of mutually assured observation," Brender says. "Governments used this technology to better understand the capabilities of the enemy. There's no reason companies can't use this technology to better understand the capabilities of a competitor."

GeoEye plans to launch a fourth satellite in 2011. GeoEye's IKONOS satellite, launched in 1999, orbits the Earth from the

north pole to the south pole and back again every ninety-eight minutes—"It's moving fast," says Brender, about 17,000 miles per hour. That's about four miles every second. Because the Earth rotates underneath the satellites as they orbit at an altitude of more than 680 kilometers above its surface, each lap around the planet takes place a little farther to the east. As a result, GeoEye's satellites can see any spot on the planet once every three days.

The flagship spacecraft, GeoEye-1, is two stories tall; in orbit, this whole satellite can tilt, pivoting about fifty degrees in any direction to shoot specific targets as it whizzes by. It makes twelve or thirteen orbits each day. It maintains what's known as a "sun-synchronous" orbit: that is, it can pass over a given area at 10:30 A.M. local time every day. In a single pass, it can capture two images of the same target from different points in space, and so it has the ability to create three-dimensional pictures.* It will be able to capture images of up to 700,000 square kilometers per day, and more than 225 million square kilometers per year. It is expected to last for ten years, but as GeoEye found out with OrbView-3, this doesn't necessarily mean it will.

To download pictures from satellites in orbit, GeoEye maintains ground stations with satellite receivers in places as remote as Barrow, Alaska, and Tromso, Norway. It maintains an unmanned station at the Troll research station on the antarctic ice sheet. In this regard, GeoEye is better positioned than the U.S. government. As the result of international treaties, the military and intelligence agencies aren't allowed to build their own ground stations at the bottom of the world. But GeoEye can.

Despite its advanced capabilities, GeoEye doesn't know how its customers are using the images they buy. Brender says clients simply give GeoEye the location they're after, and the satellite snaps the

---

*The video game *Hawx*, released in September 2008 by Tom Clancy's production company, features fighter jet dogfights over cities around the world. The cities themselves were created for the game using GeoEye 3-D images. So when a player is fighting over Brazil, for example, he sees real images of Brazil beneath his jet.

picture. The provider doesn't know why the client wants the picture, or who the client is snooping on. All the company gets is the location. And that's all it needs: whether the client is spying on a competitor or looking at its own assets is irrelevant to GeoEye—the company gets paid either way. To GeoEye, every location is the same. "It's all Earth," says Brender with a shrug.

He points to a satellite image of a strip mine in West Virginia. The mining company has chopped off the entire top of a mountain, clearing hundreds of feet of earth to get at the precious coal beneath. A picture of the mine's progress would be somewhat helpful for the mining company, but the executives there already know how the dig is going—they walk the site every day.

The image would be truly helpful, Brender says, to the mining company's competitor. Mining bosses at a rival company don't have access to the site. "If you were the competitor to that mining company, you might be able to watch that mine to see how much progress they're making," says Brender. The competitor could figure out how much coal had been found, how much it would cost to recover the environmental damage done by the massive excavators, and how much profit would be generated. With a sufficiently knowledgeable observer, you might be able to get a pretty good sense of whether or not the mining company would hit Wall Street's estimates of its quarterly earnings.

ONE CLIENT OF GeoEye is Lanworth, a thirty-person firm in Itasca, Illinois, about forty minutes east of Chicago.* This company uses images from GeoEye and other satellite providers to beat the U.S. Department of Agriculture at its own game. To understand how, you need to know a bit about how the commodities market is closely linked with the government.

---

*Itasca is also about a thirty-minute drive from Allan Pinkerton's hometown, Dundee, Illinois.

Each week, the Department of Agriculture (USDA) releases several reports on the prospects for different types of farm products, such as soybeans, chicken, eggs, and farm-raised catfish. The reports detail prices, harvesting progress, inventory, and other information that goes into calculating the prices of commodities futures on Wall Street. (Commodities futures are simply contracts to buy or sell a given product.)

In a hilarious movie from 1983 starring Eddie Murphy and Dan Aykroyd, *Trading Places*, the climactic scene involved Murphy's and Aykroyd's characters intercepting a crop report on orange juice in an attempt to corner the futures market on Wall Street.*

Traders buy and sell futures all day long, without ever touching an actual farm product. Much like trading stocks, the game is all about predicting the future price of the contract. If you think it's going up, buy. If you think it's going down, sell. Or you can short a commodity, selling its futures contracts at a high price now, and then buying them back later when the price is low. You pocket the difference as profit. It's not easy: if you guess wrong and prices increase, you're on the hook.

In the movie, Aykroyd's character explains the drama: "One minute you're up half a million in soybeans and the next, boom, your kids don't go to college and they've repossessed your Bentley."[3] The movie's heroes get an advance look at the USDA crop report on oranges. With that information, they know which way the market will move and position themselves to make a fortune and wipe out their rivals.

In real life, people are trying to do something similar. They, too, want to be able to send their kids to college and buy a Bentley. Because the USDA crop reports are a key element in moving the commodities markets up and down, the ability to predict what's in the reports has become an enticing prospect. And now that satellite

---

*In real life, the USDA does put out a crop report on orange juice. It's titled *Orange Juice: World Markets and Trade*.

technology is available to anyone, the government doesn't have as much of an advantage in predicting crop yields as it used to.

Lanworth uses satellite data to put together reports on the prospects for various agricultural products. Using satellite imagery of the fields, weather data, and other information that the USDA forecasters themselves use, Lanworth works up predictions of what the government will say in its reports. The company sells those predictions to commodities traders desperate for any information on what the market might do next.

Lanworth's cofounder Shailu Verma says his customers include giant agricultural companies, real estate investment companies, hedge funds, and financial firms. "It's not our objective to steal USDA's thunder," Verma says. "But if we are good, we're generating the same information as the USDA, just a little bit earlier."

Lanworth reportedly charges $100,000 per year for its reports,[4] but the information those documents provide can be worth millions in the commodity markets. "Our customers are trying to figure out if there's a deviation between what Lanworth is telling them and what the market expects. If there is, that's a monetizing opportunity," says Verma. He, too, is a fan of the movie *Trading Places*: he calls Lanworth's business plan "the Eddie Murphy strategy."

Here's how it works in the real world.

In June 2008, Lanworth gathered all the data it could on the corn crop in the United States. Disastrous flooding in Iowa that month had caused more than $200 million in damage, and had thrown into question the size of the nation's corn crop for the entire year (since Iowa normally produces a large proportion of that crop). The USDA's annual report on crop acreage was due to be issued on Monday, June 30, at 8:30 A.M.

As the report was being prepared, the mid-June floods threw the government's counting process into disarray, and the diligent bureaucrats at USDA went back to reinterview 1,150 farmers to find out how much the floods had affected the crops. But while

the government was working its way through that tedious process, Lanworth's analysts were poring over images from satellites high overhead. The company uses relatively low-resolution Japanese, Indian, and U.S. government satellites, and calls in high-resolution, more expensive GeoEye and DigitalGlobe images for spot checks.

What Lanworth found was surprising. Despite the flooding, the corn crop appeared to be in good shape. Some areas that had been flooded weren't a total loss. And although the markets were bidding up the price of corn futures—traders expected corn prices to go up as supply went down after the flood—Verma and his team knew better. The price should come down from where it was, because the corn supply wasn't damaged as badly as most traders in the market assumed. Corn futures, which are contracts to purchase 5,000 bushels of corn, were trading at about $7.50. Verma and his team reported their findings to their clients, who made new bets in the market.

On Monday morning, right on schedule, the USDA put out its report. The first sentence of this press release was all most traders needed to know: "Despite the recent flooding in the Midwest, U.S. farmers expect to harvest nearly 79 million acres of corn," said the USDA release.[5] Prices began to fall. The government report meant that corn futures were overvalued, and traders rushed to dump them as fast as possible. Ultimately, corn futures dropped nearly $2 in value. But Verma's hedge fund clients were well positioned to profit from the fall. They didn't tell Verma exactly how much they earned—"These guys are very cagey," he says—but such a sharp price collapse could have been worth millions to a trader who made a big enough bet on it.

It turns out that Iowa is not the best place to use satellite technology, despite Lanworth's success there in 2008. After all, the state is readily accessible, and the USDA already does a rigorous job of reporting what's going on there. Satellite technology comes in most handy to measure crops overseas, where supply affects global prices but governments don't do as good a job reporting the details as the

USDA does. "In India, the question always is, How correct are the government estimates?" says Verma. "Are there political pressures that make them say one thing and do another?"

With a satellite, it doesn't matter what kind of pressure the local bureaucrats are under. Verma says Lanworth makes some of its most valuable predictions on crop yields in India, China, Kazakhstan, and Russia.

And the company is moving on to other sectors. Verma is looking at ways to help the insurance industry. He's held several meetings with investment banks hoping to use satellite surveillance to spy on Chinese factories. With a good enough picture, Verma says, his team could count the number of trucks going into or out of any factory in China, and get a good sense of that facility's production rates. Those rates will affect the costs of products in the United States and the stock prices of any number of companies around the world. Verma predicts that Lanworth will be selling such analyses soon.

IN MANY CASES though, companies aren't spying into foreign countries, or even looking at competitors. They're spying on themselves. Take Wal-Mart, the world's largest retailer. This company hired GeoEye's predecessor several years ago to take satellite pictures of its stores. Wal-Mart knew where its best-performing stores were, but it wanted to know why they were doing so well. What made these stores so profitable?

The satellite company took pictures of the locations and analyzed the images.

GeoEye recruits many of its employees from the military and intelligence agencies. Walking down the halls at any time, you can bump into veterans who were trained in the military in battle damage assessment (BDA). The same skills they used to decipher images of blown-up Iraqi military hardware can be used to interpret pictures of Wal-Mart's parking lots.

The satellite analysts looked to see what it was about the placement of the stores in their communities that made them successful.
What were the housing demographics? How close was the nearest
high school? What were the road patterns? They dug deeper. Did
the parking lots have room for trailers, where RV owners could
plug in and charge up their vehicles? Did the doors face north,
south, east, or west? How many entrances did the parking lot have?
Were there islands with trees in the parking lots, or were the lots
just large expanses of asphalt?

From the detailed analysis, Wal-Mart was able to create tem-
plates of success: a list of all the things that successful stores had in
common, such as the neighborhoods where they were located and
the configurations of their parking lots. And then the company
could make sure that all its new locations had as many of those
features as possible

For all its sophistication, this kind of analysis is not very
expensive.

Imagery from the company's extensive archive costs $7 per
square kilometer, with a minimum order of fifty square kilometers. That makes the minimum purchase price $350. At the top
end, accurate 3-D map images can cost as much as $30 per square
kilometer. A few thousand dollars will generate the highest-quality
images of any relatively large location in the world. A company
can also pay extra fees to keep the images it seeks out of GeoEye's
archive for several months, or indefinitely.

With a GeoEye satellite, companies can see objects the size of
home plate on a baseball diamond, and with GPS technology, they
can plot that object's location anywhere on the planet to within
nine feet. It's a spy's dream.

SPY SATELLITE TECHNOLOGY wasn't available at all to private individuals until 1972, when NASA launched the first civilian remote
sensing satellite, Landsat-1. The images that this satellite delivered

back were eighty-meter resolution, too rough for much commercial use. The technology remained largely in the hands of scientists and teachers.[6] Early on, the U.S. government established a key principle called "nondiscriminatory access." Landsat images would be available to anyone who requested them, for a price.[7]

In 1979, President Carter transferred authority over the Landsat program from NASA to the National Oceanic and Atmospheric Administration (NOAA) and pushed NOAA to help expand the civilian satellite market. But the corporate world was slow to realize the potential of the available satellite images, and Congress had to act again in 1984 to push satellite images into the private sector. The legislators did this by turning the entire Landsat program over to a private contractor, Earth Observation Satellite Company (EOSAT), a joint venture of RCA Corporation and Hughes Aircraft Company.

But the government didn't come through with expected federal subsidies, and the venture faltered. Without much federal cash flowing into the program, prices soared to a point where one image could cost $4,000 or more. Academics and many scientists were priced out of the market, and the number of orders dwindled. EOSAT limped along for the next several years as a cobbled-together public-private partnership. It had to go hat in hand to Congress for funds.

By the early 1990s Congress and the Pentagon had begun to panic. The French had launched two satellites of their own, which were selling more pictures than the Landsat program was. And in 1991 the Gulf War in Kuwait showed the Pentagon how helpful satellite imagery could be during a land war—planners began to realize that a thriving commercial satellite system could be a national security asset if another war broke out.

Congress weighed in with the Land Remote Sensing Policy Act of 1992, which shuttled the troubled Landsat program back into the purview of NASA and the Department of Defense, and streamlined the licensing process for potential corporate satellite

operators. That move, and the end of the cold war, helped lift the culture of secrecy from the satellite community. Companies began to issue optimistic predictions of the size of the future commercial market.

In early 1993, WorldView, Inc., became the first company licensed to operate a commercial land view satellite. WorldView's corporate descendant is DigitalGlobe, which is still going strong today. Since then, NOAA has issued seventeen licenses.[8] As the 1990s went on, advances in computing technology and the availability of broadband Internet access meant that a much wider audience had the means to access and process satellite images instantly. And in 2006, Google introduced its GoogleEarth application, bringing instant satellite images into the home of anyone in the world with an Internet connection.

But even as the government pushed for two decades to get satellite technology into the private sector, it placed restrictions on how far that technology could go. Today, companies like DigitalGlobe and GeoEye operate under several federal constraints.[9] First, image resolution is limited to 0.5 meter and higher. That means that the U.S. military and intelligence agencies still maintain an edge in picture clarity. By some accounts, American military satellites can see images as small as ten centimeters, but their true ability is classified.

The U.S. government also maintains what's known as "shutter control" over American satellite imaging companies. This means that at any time, for national security reasons, the feds can declare any part of the world off-limits for U.S. commercial satellites. This provision was written into federal law in the mid-1990s when defense experts began to worry about the implications of having such sophisticated spy technology available in the private sector. They were thinking of General Norman Schwartzkopf's famous "left hook" maneuver in the Gulf War, in which American armored units swept hundreds of kilometers to the west of the location where Iraqi forces were expecting them. Surprise meant

everything in such a situation. What if Saddam Hussein's forces could simply have downloaded satellite images of the American positions from the Internet? That would have been a disaster for Schwartzkopf's troops.

In the real world, though, such concerns have been swept aside by the astonishing pace of technology. Since shutter control was implemented, the United States has fought two wars, in Afghanistan and Iraq.

In 2001, as the Pentagon was drawing up plans for the battle against the Taliban in Afghanistan, planners wrestled with the issue of what to do about commercial satellites. If they used shutter control to block the Afghanistan region, they might face lawsuits from American media over freedom of information. Instead of hashing out the issues in court, the Pentagon decided to buy up the entire inventory of commercial satellite imagery of Afghanistan.* For GeoEye, that meant the entire inventory of IKONOS images of the region for three months.[10]

The military didn't need the IKONOS pictures—it has plenty of satellites of its own of far higher quality. It just wanted to keep the images out of private hands: otherwise, anyone with a few hundred dollars to spend might have been able to spy on preparations for the ground war against the Taliban. During the invasion, no images of Afghanistan were available to the public. But after the three-month period, many pictures taken at that time entered the public archive, and they can now be purchased commercially.

Just a year and a half later, when the United States laid its war plans for Iraq in early 2003, the government made a different decision. Figuring that by then there were so many satellite images available from foreign companies, the U.S. military didn't restrict American commercial satellite imagery at all. The genie was now

---

*Some people in the satellite community called this maneuver "checkbook shutter control," since it accomplished the same result as banning the images outright would have.

out of the bottle. From that point on, any military force invading any location in the world would have to assume that cheap and accurate satellite images would be available to its enemies. Today, anyone with a computer can do a Google Maps search, pull up a picture of downtown Baghdad's Green Zone, and admire the swimming pools and Blackhawk helicopters of the U.S. occupying force there.*

During the long coming-out period of commercial satellite imagery, private-sector companies recruited veterans of the U.S. military and intelligence agencies—these were the biggest pipeline of experienced satellite jockeys. So it is not surprising that GeoEye is linked to the CIA: the company's board of directors includes James M. Simon, Jr., a veteran of the CIA who served as the senior intelligence official for homeland security. Simon established and chaired the Homeland Security Intelligence Council after 9/11. Earlier in his career at the CIA, he was responsible for acquiring technology, overseeing budgets, and setting policy for the fourteen agencies that make up the intelligence community. He started his own intelligence consulting firm outside government in 2003.

SUCH CLOSE AFFILIATION with U.S. intelligence can scare away global customers, who fear that their own use of satellite imagery companies based in the United States will be monitored by American intelligence agencies.

In 1994, because of that fear, a group of American and Israeli entrepreneurs and defense veterans had an idea: why not start up an international satellite company which would be free from the perception that it was controlled by U.S. intelligence? There

---

*That's not just an issue for the military. Google's images are also disconcerting to advocates of privacy. Punch in almost any address in the United States, and you'll see a satellite picture of it. Do you want your old college boyfriend to be able to see your house? What about that angry guy you fired at work last year?

were plenty of clients around the globe that wanted to buy satellite imagery, but not necessarily have the CIA know what they were buying.

To avoid giving the company an American feel, these entrepreneurs incorporated their company in the Cayman Islands, naming it West Indian Space, Ltd. They moved its official registration to the Netherlands Antilles in 2000. That year, too, they gave the company its present name, ImageSat.

In the early days, the company focused on giving global clients confidence that they could conduct surveillance without the U.S. government knowing about it. Companies and national governments could snoop aggressively without having to worry that agents in Langley were looking at their pictures, too. To that end, the American investors were never allowed to own more than 50 percent of the company. (American ownership of more than 50 percent would subject it to the same licensing requirements as its fully American-owned competitors, GeoEye and DigitalGlobe.)

Here's how several company founders described the need for a non-American business plan in a court filing:

> ImageSat's competitors were (and still are) backed by the largest United States aerospace companies and the U.S. government. ImageSat's principal competitive advantage against its financially superior and technically more experienced competitors was its profile as an independent and robustly international company able to sell truly independent high-resolution satellite imaging capabilities to governmental customers worldwide, free from the unwanted influence of a politically motivated regulatory or licensing regime, such as that of the United States.[11]

The foreign clients were allowed to operate ImageSat's satellite from their own ground stations, control the pictures taken, and keep those pictures from ImageSat's other customers. The only

restrictions came from the Israeli government: the company would not be allowed to sell to any country or customer within a 2,500-mile radius of Israel's own ground station, and it would not be able to sell to the "rogue states" of Iran, North Korea, and Cuba. Clients began lining up for the service, and ImageSat sold satellite surveillance to countries including Venezuela, Angola, China, Taiwan, and India.

But soon, some shareholders grew disillusioned with Image-Sat's management. The group of dissident shareholders felt that the company was being brought under the control of the Israeli government—which, because of the historic ties between Israel and the United States, meant that American intelligence would be able to obtain the details of ImageSat's operations. In July 2007, they filed a lawsuit for up to $300 million in damages, alleging corporate malfeasance and arguing that the effective takeover was ruining the company's business prospects. Shareholders bringing the suit included American and Israeli businessmen, and companies registered in the Cayman Islands, Switzerland, and the British Virgin Islands.

Citing this international constellation of plaintiffs, and noting that most of the relevant action took place in Israel, Judge Denise Cote of the U.S. District Court dismissed the case a year later on jurisdictional grounds. Even so, allegations that the Israeli government may influence ImageSat could continue to scare off the company's international clientele.

It's no use pitching yourself as a non-American company if your customers think the U.S. government has access to your top executives. As we'll see in Chapter Nine, the business of corporate espionage has gone global. And not everyone in this business has America's best interests at heart.

Nick No-Name

The wiry former British special forces officer introduces himself only as Nick* and sits on the edge of his plush chair in the lounge bar at the Hilton London Green Park hotel. Nick is not tall—only about five feet, seven inches. He is dressed casually: long-sleeve black crew-neck shirt, dark jeans, and gray sneakers. "No voice recordings," he says, putting up one hand. "I just can't afford to have my voice on tape. And no company name either. Sorry."

Nick has a good reason to be cautious. Now in his early forties and just beginning to show specks of gray in his military-cut hair, he is one of the top corporate surveillance operatives in London, and thus in the world. He knows how far people will go to win in the corporate spying wars, and he knows that if he's identified, his lucrative career could be over.

Today London is the crossroads of western corporate executives, Russian oligarchs, oil-rich Middle Eastern sheikhs, and the troops of lawyers, aides, drivers, bodyguards, and bag carriers who hang around them. This neighborhood, Mayfair, may be the dead center of corporate spying. Mayfair exudes money. Bentleys and

---

*Although they have the same first name, this corporate spy and Nick Day, the CEO of Diligence, are not the same person.

BMWs cruise the streets. Billion-dollar hedge funds set up shop in elegant townhouses, many of which display small signs letting passersby know which kings and notable members of British royalty once lived on the premises. In spring and summer evenings, the neighborhood's pubs spill out into the streets, with expensively tailored young lawyers and financiers toasting one another's success. Buckingham Palace is just a short walk across the park from here.

Because the money is in Mayfair, the spies are here, too. Nick is sitting just a brief walk from several of the most important spy firms in the world, including Hakluyt, whose own townhouse headquarters and small brass nameplate understate its global reach, substantial fees, and world-class corporate connections.

Surveillance operatives hate talking to a reporter, even when they've done everything they can to ensure that their comments will never be matched with their identity. Nick No-Name says he's agreed to this interview only because it's been arranged by one of his most important clients, a man who thinks nothing of paying Nick as much as $30,000 to place some of the world's highest-powered corporate executives under surveillance. It's a good living: A top operator in London can earn as much as $200,000 per year.

"If my colleagues knew I was here talking to you," says Nick, "I wouldn't say I'd be ostracized, but they'd be upset. There's no good reason for a surveillance man to talk to a reporter. I've never done it before. Nothing good can come of it." Maybe his colleagues have *him* under surveillance right now? "No, I'm clean at the moment," Nick says matter-of-factly. "I've got a man in here."

Which of the people in the bar is Nick's "man?" There are two young women at a far table, looking over a map of London and comparing notes. There's a bespectacled, balding gentleman reading a newspaper over a late-afternoon lunch. And several waiters in maroon suits glide into and out of the room. Nothing seems at all out of the ordinary. But then just as Nick sits down at the table facing a window overlooking an interior courtyard, a workman puts

a large sheet over the window, blocking sunlight and the view to the outside. Maybe it's a surveillance-related precaution; maybe it's just routine maintenance. Nonetheless, Nick has cased the room. Satisfied that he's in control of the situation, he agrees to sketch his life story, explaining how he came to be one of the world's most effective corporate spies.

NICK JOINED THE British army right out of school, and he says his superiors in the army noticed that he had a certain potential. He's sharp, he's attentive to detail, and he handles weapons well. His commanding officers steered him toward a career in the special forces, where he became a trained killer and a master of weapons and tactics. More important, Nick says he learned how to match his response to the situation. Sometimes, it is far better not to kill—to defuse a situation long before it becomes violent. And that's a far more nuanced skill than being good with guns once the shooting starts.

Nick won't say what theaters of combat he served in, but he notes, "I was in the British military. And we've only gone a certain number of places in the past fifteen to twenty years." It's likely that his résumé includes stints in Bosnia, Northern Ireland, and the Middle East. Nick says he was often assigned to security details, where he learned the basics of what the British call "close protection" and Americans call bodyguarding.

Generally, special forces units protecting a dignitary or some other high-value target include several bodyguards who stand within two or three feet, each monitoring a different area to the front, side, or rear. You often see them on television. They are mostly big men, unsmiling in the midst of cheerful crowds greeting a president or prime minister. They seldom look up. They are watching people's hands. Nick calls them "big, hairy-assed monsters." But that's not a description of Nick. He was typically assigned to the perimeter of security, working undercover. Dressed as normal members of the public, Nick and the others on his

undercover team watched the crowd from outside the security area around the subject.

Under his jacket, Nick kept a Heckler and Koch MP5 nine-millimeter submachine gun, a lightweight, air-cooled weapon favored by more than forty military forces around the world. With its stock tucked under his armpit and its barrel pointing down toward his waist, the 26.8-inch MP5 barely made a bulge in Nick's street clothes.

In theory, anyone who wanted to attack Nick's subject would be watching the target and the highly visible big men near him. The members of Nick's undercover team—positioned well back from any would-be assailant—could watch without themselves being spotted.

"They're not looking at me," he says. "I'm the little bloke eating ice cream with his girlfriend. When the bad guy pulls out a grenade, that's when we move from surveillance to intervention. If it's in Iraq or Afghanistan and we think it's life threatening, we'll work within our legal remit and take every action necessary." In Iraq, the "legal remit" might include shooting an assailant dead at close range. In a corporate setting, it might mean slapping the hand of a menacing heckler.

When Nick retired from the military in the late 1990s, he returned to England to do the same kind of "close protection" work in the private sector, for private military contractors. It was a logical career move. "You've got all these skills, and not a lot of employment opportunity," Nick explains. But he didn't love the work. So he drifted into corporate intelligence, reaching out to a number of London's biggest spy agencies. He says he was astonished by what he saw there. "Their surveillance capabilities were zero. They were sitting in cars taking pictures of people."

Nick saw a market opportunity. There was demand for top-of-the-line espionage services offered by veterans of the British special forces. He began freelancing for the corporate intelligence firms, picking up surveillance work as needed. He found himself doing a

lot of screening of new hires for large corporate clients. Before offering top management jobs to prospective recruits, the companies wanted to have them followed for a couple of days. *Does this executive have any embarrassing problems the company ought to know about?* Nick tailed them on weekends. *Did they have a secret heroin habit? A weakness for hookers? Perverse sexual tendencies?* Nick would find out. Sometimes, he says, he found that the executives did have problems, but the company hired them anyway. "Think of everything you can think of that goes on in society," Nick says. "I've seen it. I've watched executives picking up transvestites in New York City. What we're doing is the biggest reality TV show there is."

It's not clear how commonly companies conduct surveillance on their own hires. But Nick No-Name and other people involved in the business say it happens most often with a "marquee" corporate hire—any executive who is going to be paid an enormous amount of money or whose name will be linked to the company's brand in the public imagination. Paying Nick's steep fees can be worthwhile if he prevents millions of dollars of public relations damage months later. In some cases, preemployment surveillance seems to verge on entrapment. Nick recalls one case in which he tailed an executive to a midweek golf game. Nick alerted his client that he was observing the executive playing golf, and the client called the executive's cell phone. After some initial chitchat, the client said, "So, what are you doing now?" Not wanting to appear as though he was slacking off, with a lucrative new career opportunity hanging in the balance, the job candidate said, "I'm just heading out to a meeting." The client crossed him off the list for the job. What he minded wasn't that the executive was playing a round of midweek golf—who doesn't enjoy that once in a while?—but that the executive had lied to his future boss. "If he'll lie about the little things," the client later told Nick, "he'll lie about the important things, too."

Soon Nick had developed a network of like-minded surveillance experts who had formerly been in the military. "A couple of us got together and said, 'We've got to make this a viable business.'" They

banded together and incorporated a company. Nick will not reveal its name, except to say that it has a bland corporate title designed to give no hint of its real business—"You can call it 'Harry's Chocolate Factory,'" Nick says elusively. The firm does not have a Web site. It does not have a listing in the phone book. "We're nowhere," he says. But the top corporate intelligence firms in the world know his phone number when they need him.

Nick had stumbled on a key piece of the corporate intelligence business model. Most of the hundreds of firms in the world don't have large staffs. Instead, they serve as a kind of facade that helps connect corporate clients with the netherworld of intelligence, the more shadowy "contractors" who do most of the actual work. Each time a client project comes up, the firms put together teams of subcontractors with the specialties needed for that situation. Need surveillance in London? Insert a contractor. Need linguistic help? Contractor. Need a forensic accountant? Ditto. The teams are assembled for each case and managed by the firm. Nick doesn't need a Web site to publicize his business. The man who pays him already has one. Also, having pictures of himself and his team members on a Web site would devalue their service: "If my face and my operators' faces are all over the Web, we're a blown commodity," he says. "We're useless."

The money's good. Nick says high-end surveillance firms like his charge 1,200 to 1,600 pounds sterling per day per man, plus expenses, plus mileage, and plus the cost of any special equipment. Just to place surveillance on one unsurprising executive in London can cost upwards of 15,000 pounds per day. Nick says he has no idea what the intelligence firms he works for charge their clients for his services, but he suspects they mark up the bill by as much as 20 percent. That's fair, he thinks. The intelligence firms don't know how to do high-end surveillance, he says, but they're charging the client for the one asset they do have: Nick's phone number.

In a typical executive surveillance case, Nick turns over a written report with the details of every place the executive went, the

times he went there, photos of him at each of those locations, and photos of anyone he met with while he was there. Nick's team will also conduct audio surveillance, either with recording devices or by getting undercover operators close enough to hear the conversations in person. With modern equipment, he says, this work can be done almost anywhere.

Nick sometimes uses a laser microphone that can record conversations in a room as much as a kilometer away. Pointing the invisible laser at the glass window of the room in which a meeting is taking place, Nick can record every word that's being said in the room—so long as he has a direct line of sight from his hiding place to the panes of glass in the meeting room's window. The laser is so sensitive that it measures the tiny vibrations in the glass itself, and reassembles those into audible speech.

The downside of this technique is that the lasers don't work as well, or at all, with double- or triple-paned windows, which are increasingly common. And it can be maddeningly difficult to get a good angle for the laser when eavesdropping is taking place on the upper floors of high-rise office buildings—from street level, the angle toward the windows of the higher floors can be so oblique that the devices become useless. With high-paying clients, the way to get around that problem is to rent an office or hotel room in a building across the street at about the same altitude. It's expensive, but it puts the laser in position to record the meeting.

Nick and his team conduct surveillance all over the world, sometimes flying an entire team of nine or ten operators across continents to observe an important meeting or tail a high-value executive. Depending on the laws in the country they're working in, Nick says they can do almost anything: "We'll bug a house, bug cars, put locator devices on vehicles, conduct electronic intercepts of e-mails, whatever it takes," he says. They use encrypted communications equipment to avoid being detected. "But we won't break the law. We retain barristers here in London, and make sure we're on the right side of the law wherever we're operating. Otherwise,

the information we collect is useless to our clients." Illegally gathered material is inadmissible in court—and can't be used in lawsuits. What's more, any lawbreaking by Nick's team could be used
by the other side as leverage in the ongoing business dispute.

Because the skills required for surveillance are so rare, the industry isn't huge. Nick estimates that even in spy-infested London,
there are only enough crews to tail about twenty executives at any
one time. Given the typical nine- or ten-man surveillance crew,
this implies that there are somewhat fewer than 200 surveillance
people working in London. (Another surveillance operative there
gives a higher estimate: 100 executives could be tailed on any one
day, she says. That implies a high-end range of something under
1,000 surveillance operators prowling London's streets.) Clients,
therefore, sometimes have to join waiting lists for surveillance on
a given target, or they have to pay huge fees for an American or
German team to be flown in during a busy time.

As manpower-intensive, and expensive, as professional surveillance can be, it doesn't always work—or at least it doesn't work as
well as Hollywood movies would suggest. Nick and his team can
spend an entire weekend sitting in front of an executive's house,
and the target, perhaps indulging in a DVD marathon, may not
emerge once. One corporate spy recalls a time he hired a surveillance team to tail a subject, left the office, and went home. Around
10 P.M. he got a frantic call from the surveillance operatives in the
field: "Do you have a tuxedo pressed?" they asked. He did. "Great.
Then, quick—run down to this address; the subject has suddenly
gone into a black-tie affair, and we don't have anyone on the team
wearing a tux to get into the event." The spy rushed to the location, bluffed his way past the greeters at the entrance to the ball,
and found the subject enjoying a drink at the bar with a number of
colleagues. His tuxedo saved the surveillance effort. But the episode could just as easily have gone the other way, and the entire
day's effort, costing tens of thousands of dollars, could have been
wasted.

Such unpredictability is inherent to surveillance, and it is why Nick says he encourages clients to consider surveillance only when there is no other way to get information. Clients attracted by the glamour of surveillance operations don't always listen: they hire the team anyway. The clients themselves can be the biggest hurdle to a successful operation. Nick says that in one of the rare instances when he worked directly with a corporate client who had his cell phone number, the man called him forty-six times in one weekend with instructions. "I said, 'All due respect to you, but let me get on with it,'" Nick recalls. In another case, a client wanted surveillance but wouldn't say why. The team followed the subject but had no idea what they were supposed to be looking for. Sometimes business matters are so sensitive that clients are reluctant to share them with the surveillance operatives—who, after all, could leak the details to a competitor for a price. But without details, surveillance isn't particularly effective. "We always need an aim," Nick says. "That way, we can tell what's important and what's not."

Often, clients assume that surveillance means simply hiring someone to tail the subject around town. But the professionals explain that it's much more difficult to execute successful, undetected surveillance than many people think. When tailing someone who's emerging from the London underground—the subway—a surveillance team will have a man behind him, carrying an encrypted radio, to tell the team at which Tube stop he's exiting. As the target steps into the sunlight from the underground, he's got several options for where to go next. He might hail a cab, in which case the team needs to have a motorcycle or car surveillance team ready to follow. Alternatively, the subject might cross the street and enter a hotel, in which case an operative on foot needs to go in right behind him, lest he slip into an elevator or a men's room and vanish from sight. Or he might turn and walk up the sidewalk. A good surveillance team will have operatives stationed at each of the intersections the target might reach next. And each time the target reaches an intersection, the surveillance team leapfrogs ahead,

keeping out of sight, with cars picking up the agents on foot and depositing them ahead of him. There, they reset into positions to cover each of the next set of travel options. Orchestrating all this on the fly without attracting notice, without losing the subject, and without getting into a car crash can be something of an art form.

The team must also consider appearance. The operatives themselves have to be able to fit into every environment. They rarely wear disguises in the Hollywood sense of the term, but they do wear clothes that blend into a variety of situations. If they're tailing an executive at a high-end hotel, that means suits and ties for the men, and business attire for the women. But if they're at a ball game, those suits would stand out. The last thing a surveillance operative wants to do is attract any notice at all. One rule: it's always easier to dress down than it is to dress up. It's easier for a male operative wearing a suit to whip off the tie and jacket and appear "office casual" than it is for an operative to go from shorts and a T-shirt into an executive outfit. Quick costume changes are part of the surveillance operative's day.

At the highest end, where targets, such as executives, might be suspicious of surveillance or might have been themselves trained in counterespionage techniques, the operation becomes the proverbial game of cat and mouse. Take the example of the target getting off the London underground. If he suspects he's under surveillance, he knows an operative will be in the same train car with him. But he doesn't know who it is. Surveillance people are good at not looking as though they're paying attention. The wary target needs to flush out the surveillance team.

One way to do that is to be alert as the train pulls into the station. London underground stops have "Way Out" signs that point toward the exits. The subject can spot the signs from the train as it slows down for the stop. Knowing that the direction of the arrows is the direction that foot traffic will move on the platform, a savvy target will move toward the rear of the train car, getting off through

the last set of doors, and proceeding toward the subway exit, thus forcing any followers from the same train car ahead of him.

This maneuver puts the surveillance operative in a dilemma. A person can be observed, of course, from the front, but that means having to turn around to make sure the subject is still there. A huge part of defeating surveillance is maneuvering in various situations to place the "follower" in front of the subject. Then, the trick is to identify which person ahead is the surveillance operative.

Once the canny subject steps onto the train platform, he can walk with the crowd, not letting anyone from the same car with him fall behind, and make his way to the escalator. On escalators, people face in the direction they're traveling. They almost never turn around and look behind—they're in a rush to get somewhere, and most of them have traveled this route hundreds of times before. No need to be curious. But as the subject approaches the escalator, he knows two things: the surveillance operative is probably in front of him, already on the escalator, and the operative will turn around at about the time that the target steps on the first stair. Even though the operative doesn't want to give himself away, he must watch and make sure the subject gets on the escalator instead of heading for a different exit.

Once spotted, the surveillance team has to scramble. Now they need to rush operatives to the other exit, cover the elevator, and replace an operative who has been compromised. The subject may not have eluded the team this time, but he's made life a lot more complicated for the operatives. That's why high-end surveillance can cost tens of thousands of dollars per day. Following a trained or canny subject can be complicated work; it requires hiring a number of highly trained operatives, and such operatives are hard to find.

Countersurveillance, too, is a good business for Nick, who is just as happy to be paid by a company trying to keep its executives from being spied on as by a company doing the spying. Because the surveillance scene in London is so small, he's sometimes paid

to spend his time trying to outwit the espionage activities of his competitors, men and women he knows well. "In that case, our job is to identify the surveillance, and neutralize it," Nick says. He reverse-engineers everything he would do as a surveillance operative and scans the streets for people doing the same thing. It may be arrogance, but Nick says he almost always spots the rival teams in action. Generally, he says, a stern warning to the opposing surveillance team is enough to scare them off. "I walk up to them and say, 'Hey, guys, I'm not being funny here, but my friend over there is getting bored with you following him.'"

Nick knows that a warning like this will cause a problem for the other surveillance team. After all, their cover has been blown. He also knows that the other company will send in a replacement crew—that's the same thing Nick would do—but for the moment his client will be free of surveillance, and Nick will have earned his fee.

This game of corporate spy versus spy can get expensive for clients, and there's plenty of room for abuse. Sometimes, Nick says, his company gets calls from corporate clients who want countersurveillance on a subject that another company already had paid Nick to spy on. In those cases, he says, he can't reveal that he's the one doing surveillance. Instead, he'll tell the prospective client that he's busy on the date involved. But not everyone in the industry is as careful to avoid conflicts of interest as Nick seems to be. Some firms have been known to accept fees from one client to put surveillance on, say, an executive and fees from another client to conduct countersurveillance on the same person. In effect, these firms are getting paid to spy on themselves.

Why are all these spies lurking about the city? Nick says that the length to which companies go will depend on the amount of money involved. The more money is at stake in a given transaction, the more effort by all parties in the deal. Companies use surveillance when the enormous expense is justified by the even more enormous stakes involved. One expert says that in every transaction

involving more than $1 billion anywhere in the world today at least one of the parties involved is using surveillance operators.

Nick sees all kinds of variations. "We were hired once when Bank One was doing a negotiation with Bank Two," he says. "But Bank One suspected that Bank Two was secretly dealing with Bank Three and talking to Bank One only to drive down its deal price with Bank Three. So we put the top executives at Banks Two and Three under surveillance during the entire negotiation."

Although much of business life these days is conducted by phone and e-mail—which are not easy surveillance targets—Nick remains convinced that when a lot of money is changing hands, people still meet face-to-face. And when they do, he's ready to document it all. "That's the advantage we have as ex-military operators," he says. In the case of the three banks, "We had a guy who was able to swim forty meters to the island where the subject's house was and have a look." Once there, Nick's man dug a hole in the ground just outside the banker's house—and lived in it for days while he watched everything that went on. In the end, Nick's team discovered that Bank Two was conducting talks with Bank Three, and tipped the client off to the deception.

If such spying can save a company millions of dollars, executives reason, it more than justifies the tens of thousands of dollars paid to uncover the information. And if a banker on the other side of a deal objects to having former soldiers from the British special forces living in holes in his backyard, so what? It's nothing personal. It's just business.

NOT EVERYONE IN the surveillance industry is as low-profile as Nick No-Name. Another British operative, Emma Shaw, works in an unremarkable office complex in the bedroom community of Old Woking, in Surrey, about half an hour from London by fast train. The other tenants in the complex are small businesses, accountants, and one-man consulting shops. Emma Shaw's office has the

atmosphere of a suburban dentist's office, and she herself doesn't look anything like a secret agent—but that's the point. A veteran intelligence operative, Shaw appears youthful, spending a casual Friday in her office clad in a pink Abercrombie and Fitch sweat top and fashionable jeans. Her blond hair has highlights, and she's got high cheekbones, giving her an athletic appearance. She looks like a young mom on her way to football practice.

But Emma Shaw is the real deal, as well trained as Nick No-Name, though with a different business philosophy. Shaw feels that surveillance is a legitimate part of the business process and that surveillance operators like her shouldn't hide in the shadows. Her office has a sign on the front door. Her company, "esoteric," has a Web site (www.esotericltd.com), and she hands out slick marketing materials detailing her services, with the tagline: "A specialist security and covert investigations company."

Shaw is a manager now, and doesn't do much actual snooping herself, so she's less concerned than Nick No-Name about her identity becoming public. It's not bad for her career, and in the right context, publicity may even help. She lays down one condition, though: she won't discuss the exact details of surveillance techniques she uses on behalf of her corporate clients. They're by and large the same techniques used to this day by the British intelligence service MI5 and by British military intelligence. Providing too detailed a description, she fears, could give vital intelligence to the terrorists who are trying to elude British intelligence every day.

Emma Shaw was born in Yorkshire, the coastal county in northern England, and at age eighteen joined the army, where she was assigned to the military police. As a teenager in the army, she learned the basics of overt investigations, and then moved on to undercover missions, helping the top brass work against drug use among British forces. She tailed suspects, posed as a regular soldier, and helped support police investigations of soldiers suspected of smuggling or selling drugs. Shaw found her picture on the front pages

of newspapers across Britain. But by that time she'd left the unit, so her undercover status wasn't compromised by the publicity.

Next assigned to Northern Ireland, she served in a garrison township outside Belfast in 1993 and 1994. There, she did undercover intelligence work, but she's vague about what it entailed—saying only that it "related to the problems of the time." And at that time there were problems aplenty for the British army in Northern Ireland. Shaw's job was to support the Royal Ulster Constabulary (RUC), the largely Protestant police force that patrolled a land bitterly divided between Protestants and Catholics.

After Shaw had spent eight years in the army, MI5 recruited her. MI5 focuses on counterintelligence and domestic security. Shaw says she left the military on a Friday afternoon, and reported for duty at the intelligence agency on Monday. She worked on covert operations and intelligence gathering, then left the service toward the end of the 1990s. Like many retiring spies, Shaw saw the allure of the private sector—and wanted to leave the government before she was too old to make the transition to corporate work. "I wanted to go on and do other things," she says. "To get out and get a second career."

She soon went to work for a private company as a security manager, and before long turned to the private sector to find operatives she could trust. And like Nick No-Name, Emma Shaw found that the market lacked military-grade surveillance expertise, and executives had almost no knowledge of the state of the art in the trade. In 1998 she set up shop as a consultant advising companies on how to hire surveillance operatives. That business eventually developed into "esoteric," which provides surveillance services to companies and to spy firms.

For a fee, her company tails executives, and provides covert, but legal, video and audio surveillance. It also helps discover and destroy the same devices planted by a company's opponents. Shaw's employees offer electronic sweeping services, searching out cameras and listening devices in offices, executives' homes, and corporate

jets and yachts. Esoteric says it can set up microwave-transmission cameras to watch specific locations for long periods of time, allowing the images to be monitored from a remote location. It advertises live vehicle tracking services, which are handy for companies that want to keep covert tabs on the whereabouts of their own sales staffs and vehicles. All her services, she says, are legal. And all of them are expensive. Electronic sweeps of a set of six offices costs between 4,000 and 5,000 pounds sterling. Surveillance costs 1,000 to 1,500 pounds per person per day—with teams that can be nine or ten strong. The costs add up.

Sitting at the conference table in her office, Shaw sounds more like a corporate marketer than a spy. "What we set out to do was provide our services to very high-end corporate organizations," she explains. In fact, she herself is working on an MBA.

One of the few indications that there's anything out of the typical corporate experience here is a small trapezoidal white box mounted on the ceiling, with a single blinking green light on the surface. The device, called E-room, was designed and built by Shaw's team. It monitors radio frequencies inside the room. It sounds an alarm if it detects any unauthorized transmissions. E-Room can also send an e-mail to a designated computer, alerting the user of illicit eavesdropping attempts. Shaw says she knows there are no bugs in a visitor's briefcase, because if there were any, the E-room system would have identified them already.

Shaw spends her day largely immersed in the ugliest side of the global economy, investigating theft, fraud, insider trading, breach of contract, and harassment on behalf of lawyers and corporate clients. She also handles straight competitive intelligence cases, in which her client is spying on another company to determine its secrets. Shaw says companies use surveillance for "anything where there is either a risk to employees, or a risk to the company or the intellectual property of that company."

In one case, Shaw's company went to work for a large research and development company that suspected a member of its senior

management was providing details of products to a competitor. Esoteric describes the results in its brochure:

> Through the use of a covert tracking device and other surveillance resources, it was established that the director was collating highly confidential product and client information in order to assist him in any future employment, with a long-term view of setting up his own business in direct competition with his current and past employers and selling their products as his own. Although difficult to quantify the potential loss of revenue to the company, had the director successfully stolen products and client information the financial stability of the company would almost certainly have been affected.[1]

In another case Shaw discusses, her company went to work for a real estate development firm at which several employees had recently quit at the same time. The bosses suspected that the departing employees had stolen client lists and client information. What's more, the company suspected that the former employees were setting up a new business based on those stolen details.

Shaw began surveillance on the former employees with teams following four subjects for six to eight weeks. The surveillance operatives tailed the ex-employees to a printing shop, where one of the employees photocopied site plans. Esoteric's operative, wearing a baseball cap in which a covert imaging device was embedded, approached the photocopier, getting close enough to take clear pictures—with the camera in his cap—of the site plans that the unwary ex-employee was busy photocopying.

Over the next few weeks, the spies discovered that the ex-employees were visiting potential real estate development sites, that they had leased space, and that they had hired people to work for their fledgling firm. On one day, one of Shaw's surveillance teams followed an ex-employee to the bank, and using the same

camera cap, photographed the bank account manager. The operative moved in to get pictures of the documents on this manager's desk, images which when enlarged revealed bank account numbers, financial figures, and transaction details. "We can get in quite close," says Shaw, even in a security-conscious environment like a bank, but "not in all circumstances, not in all banks."

The team leader phoned the client while the subject was still in the bank, reporting, "This is what's going on right now. Is this of interest to you?" In hard-fought legal battles, there can be injunctions or prohibitions in place against certain activities. The surveillance team's client may swing into action in real time to stop the suspicious transaction. In this case, all the details gathered were invaluable information for the client's lawyers when the ex-employees' former firm filed suit against their new company for breach of contract.

In every case, a surveillance operation produces a detailed log, in which the operatives note the dates, times, and addresses where surveillance took place. At the end of each day, the team members gather for a debriefing session. They go over the logs to check for any inconsistency, or add details that couldn't be noted down on the fly. Each operative signs the log with a coded number, and stands ready to serve as a witness in a client's court case, verifying in court that the activity noted in the report took place. "The client may have a summary report, but if they want it, they have access to and they can have a copy of the surveillance log itself," says Shaw.

In the cases she describes, Shaw portrays her operatives as coming to the aid of a company that's been wronged in some way. But she concedes that her firm also works for clients seeking, within the bounds of the law, to do harm to a competitor's business, typically by ferreting out important information. In such cases, the surveillance isn't defensive, to preserve the client's standing in the market; it is offensive—to bring a competitor down.

To her credit, Shaw is unflinching in discussing this less

genteel side of her business. Industrywide, she estimates that the division between defensive and offensive intelligence gathering is about fifty-fifty. "Surveillance is a fact of life," she says. "We're all recorded I think an average of 300 times a day in the United Kingdom through [closed circuit television]." Indeed, in 2002 one report estimated that Londoners—who live in one of the most surveillance-heavy cities in the world—are monitored every day by more than 500,000 closed-circuit television cameras: about one camera for every fourteen people.[2]

What's more, Shaw says, there's an enormous and growing demand for competitive intelligence in the global economy. "Some companies want to find out what their competitors are doing; everybody does. And I think anybody that says they don't want to know what their competitors are doing are not actually being truthful about it." In Shaw's mind, there's nothing untoward about using veteran intelligence operatives to spy on the competition. Asked if spying on people's business lives feels illicit or even creepy to her, she replies, "Generally, no. We deal with very legitimate investigations."

The limits Shaw puts on herself are broad, but they are definable. Her company won't do anything illegal, she insists. "If you can observe somebody in public space, in public activity without infringing on their privacy or without going illegally into their premises, by breaking and entering or stealing and things like that, then people will be prepared to do that. There are also people who will be prepared to go that little bit farther and do that breaking and entering, but that's not something we're involved in."

Shaw also restricts her team from placing families of subjects, particularly children, under surveillance. And she insists that if in the course of following a subject her operatives come across information that's not relevant to the business question at hand—say, if a subject stops off at a hotel for a quick tryst before heading home to his wife—her investigators will not record that information or

provide it to their client. "You don't go recording that person when they're with their family in their private space; you don't go trying to put cameras inside their house whilst they're inside their own home. That's certainly not the work that we get involved in." She may have her limits, but not everyone in her industry does.

SOMETIMES, SURVEILLANCE IS used not for business, but for pleasure. In one case, several sources say that a high-living hedge fund executive used a corporate spy firm to conduct intelligence operations against a Hollywood actor. Why did he do it? Reportedly, the hedge fund executive had fallen in love—or lust—with the actor's model girlfriend.

The financier—who will remain nameless in this account—was up against some steep competition, and he'd need every advantage he could get. The Israeli model who caught his eye was Bar Refaeli, a globe-trotting beauty who was dating the Hollywood actor Leonardo DiCaprio, who had starred in *Titanic* and *The Departed*. Soon DiCaprio would become a target of corporate spies, the sources claimed.

Bar Refaeli, the first Israeli model featured in *Sports Illustrated*'s famous swimsuit issue, was born in 1985 in Hod HaSharon. She began dating DiCaprio soon after she attained stardom, and tabloid reporters reveled in the details when the photogenic couple strolled along Paris's beautiful Champs-Élysées holding hands.

At the same time, the financier, too, began to take an interest in Refaeli. In late 2005 or early 2006, recalls Bar's mother and manager, Tzipi Refaeli, the money man met the model, and asked her to lunch. Tzipi says she spent one entire evening at the financier's side, and came away unimpressed: "He's nothing to write home about," she says. She found him shallow and materialistic. "All he can do is buy, buy, buy. Not many people will say no."

According to her mother—who, like many mothers, may not have all the details—Bar Refaeli is one person who did say no to

the financier, rebuffing his romantic overtures and telling him that she'd rather just be friends. Undeterred, the sources claim, he hired a well-known private spy firm to dig up dirt on DiCaprio that could be used to drive a wedge between the actor and the model. *Does DiCaprio have any bad habits? Is he sleeping around?*

According to one account, the spy firm conducted surveillance on DiCaprio in Cape Town, South Africa, where he was filming the movie *Blood Diamond* in the spring of 2006. According to another story told by insiders, the spies tried to get photos of DiCaprio with other women during a trip to the Caribbean. The ultimate prize would be a photograph of DiCaprio in the arms of anybody other than Bar Refaeli, which could be leaked to the media or mailed to Bar. Presumably, if she was confronted with evidence of DiCaprio's treachery, Bar would be more easily lured into the waiting arms of the financier.

It is important to note that one spy in a position to know denied the existence of the project. In any event, the project, if it existed at all, seems to have fizzled, and DiCaprio and Refaeli continued dating until their reported breakup in the spring of 2009. For as much as two years longer, though, the financier continued to send e-mails to Bar Refaeli, although her mother says she gave up replying to them. "She's very loyal," Tzipi Refaeli says. Tzipi says that Bar never received suspicious photographs or other evidence against DiCaprio, and was never aware that the spy team was interested in him. But Tzipi doesn't doubt the story, either.

"I am not objective," Tzipi says; but "she is beautiful. She is really a very good girl. She's pretty, nice, intelligent, young, Jewish, Israeli, and successful. It's very easy to be in love with her."

CHAPTER TEN

They're All Kind of Crazy

A collection of random facts—even random secrets—isn't worth much unless you can put it together so as to understand what the data tell you about the real world. Beckett Brown faced that problem with the reams of data coming in from its surveillance of Mars, Inc. How do you know what's important, and what's not? Which information is going to move markets, or affect the competitive picture?

One company that specializes in the analysis side of the private intelligence business is Verbatim Advisory Group, based in Boston. Verbatim's squadron of analysts gather information and weave it together to produce what the government calls "actionable intelligence." The firm's theory is that investigators need enough data points confirming a thesis before they'll recommend any action. It's not enough to have one source telling you something. You want to hear it over and over again from people in the know before you act on it.

In September 2006, four different steel buyers around the world got calls from Verbatim's analysts. The analysts were fishing for specifics: *What's the Arcelor Mittal steel company up to now? What kind of capacity does it have? And what about pricing?* That fall, Arcelor Mittal, a London-based company with roots in India, faced

uncomfortably high steel prices—and Verbatim's analysts wondered what Arcelor would do about this.

But the steel buyers already knew the answer. They did business with Arcelor every day. The word was that it was on the verge of scaling back its output to drive up prices—a move that Wall Street would welcome and that would boost the company's stock price. Verbatim passed the intelligence on to a hedge fund client in late September. As it turned out, this was just a few days before Arcelor announced that it would idle two blast furnaces: one in Cleveland and the other in East Chicago, Indiana. As a result of this news, trading volume was nearly triple that of the previous day and the stock closed $1 per share higher, at $35.54. Anyone on Wall Street who knew about the move in advance could have raked in a tidy profit.

Verbatim, founded in 2001, gathers data on companies for more than twenty hedge fund clients by interviewing as many customers of the companies as its operatives can reach. Most of the companies that are being scrutinized have no idea what's going on.

Verbatim's techniques are based on the training that its managing partner John Strehle received as an intelligence officer in the U.S. Navy aboard the aircraft carrier USS *Dwight D. Eisenhower*. He says the challenges he faced as a young lieutenant in the 1980s and 1990s and his present work gathering intelligence on global companies have a lot in common: "You have to make sure you prioritize intelligence properly, you have to be used to changing deadlines, and you have to be able to reach conclusions based on less than complete information."

Verbatim's team members are analysts, the corporate equivalent of the CIA's employees in Langley who pore over data trying to predict trends. For instance, they scrutinize economic and crop data to predict the next famine in the third world and its resulting political instability. Predicting is one of a spy's most valuable skills. To do it, Strehle wants to hire smart, sociable people and trains them in elicitation techniques.

The software manufacturer Salesforce.com, which is based in San Francisco, makes so-called "customer relationship management" computer programs to help salespeople keep track of their accounts and contacts. A hedge fund client asked Verbatim to predict Salesforce's quarterly earnings. In 2006 the company had released a new software product, and it was getting only tepid reviews in the press. Wall Street was betting that the quarterly earnings would be grim.

But Verbatim built its own prediction of what those earnings would be, going from customer to customer, and asking them all how many units they'd purchased that quarter, and matching the information against data it had gathered in previous cycles. Verbatim's team took a systematic approach, calling large and small customers, and getting a wide geographic spread. They talked to the people at big companies who were responsible for buying Salesforce's software. Unlike some of the other corporate intelligence outfits, Verbatim says it doesn't engage in deception. The company insists that its analysts tell sources who they are and what they're doing.

Although Verbatim doesn't pay for interviews, Salesforce's customers were motivated to talk anyway. Sometimes Verbatim's interviewers knew more about what was going on at Salesforce than a customer did, and the customer could pick up valuable information of its own by chatting with them. *What new products are coming out next? Are other customers getting discounts that we're not?* The interviewers probed for specifics in return: *How many users at your company are working with the Salesforce software now? Which of Salesforce's competitors have approached you—and what are they offering? What kind of discounting are the Salesforce reps offering?*

The results were surprising. The customers liked Salesforce better than Wall Street thought they did. Verbatim turned over a report to its client, several weeks before the end of the quarter. The hedge fund managers saw aggregate results, answers to all the questions, and the names and phone numbers of Salesforce's

customers who had agreed to be identified to the hedge fund. The software company reported an unexpectedly strong quarter, and Verbatim's client was well positioned when the quarterly numbers were officially released.

SPIES OFTEN SAY that 90 percent of a good intelligence operation is open-source information—stuff that's in the newspapers, in government documents, or easily available with a phone call or two. Corporate spies also know that. And they know that the best material of all can exist in the narrow zone somewhere between public and private information.

On the afternoon of November 15, 2005, day traders chatting on Yahoo.com were scrambling for information. They couldn't figure out why there was so much action in USG Corporation, a Chicago building-materials company that was mired in asbestos lawsuits. Its stock was trading at double the normal daily volume and would gain $2.12 to close at $61.55. But there didn't seem to be any major news to motivate this.

The day traders exchanged anguished messages trying to figure out what was going on: *I do not understand the volatility lately; is it the market-makers trying to get me to capitulate?* wondered a trader going by the name ethylene_orion on the Yahoo! Finance message board for USG, where individual investors traded tidbits, opinions, and tips about the stock.

What ethelyne_orion and the regulars on the Yahoo! message board didn't know was that behind the scenes, then-Senate Majority Leader Bill Frist of Tennessee (a Republican) had decided to override the qualms of the budget committee's leaders and press ahead with a bill to create a $140 billion fund to relieve companies such as USG of their asbestos liabilities.[1] It would be huge news in the small community of traders who bought and sold shares of companies affected by asbestos litigation—and almost any piece of

news in that world tended to move the market. Frist wouldn't announce his decision until November 16, but the news had gotten to key Wall Street traders a day early via a little-known pipeline: a small group of firms specializing in "political intelligence" that mine the capital for information and translate Washington wonkspeak into trading tips.

The industry started with a couple of cottage firms in the early 1970s. But now it's been propelled to new levels of intensity as information-hungry hedge funds hire squadrons of former lobbyists and journalists to ferret out tidbits of information, such as the details of Frist's decision. "What hedge funds do is look for inefficiencies in the market," says one hedge fund manager who buys several firms' reports. "And Washington is the world's greatest creator of [market] inefficiencies."

Unlike lobbyists, political intelligence outfits are not required to disclose their clients or annual revenues, so the size of this very quiet business is masked. One veteran estimates that there are more than half a dozen contenders collectively raking in $30 million to $40 million a year. The business stretches well beyond Capitol Hill, into every aspect of the federal government. "We analyze public policy—macroeconomics, the Fed, budget, trade, currency—that affects overall financial markets, sectors, or companies," says Leslie Alperstein, a founder of the firm Washington Analysis. And although leaks such as Frist's news about asbestos are welcome, Alperstein says his business is mostly about explaining trends. "If we only dealt in [hot tips], I wouldn't be living in Potomac," he says, referring to a pricey suburb in Maryland. "It doesn't happen often enough."

It happens enough, however, to trouble some legislators. A few days after the rise in USG stock, Representative Brian Baird of Washington (a Democrat) asked the House ethics committee to issue guidance for staffers sitting on some of the capital's most valuable information. "The possibility of direct kickbacks [is]

enormous," says Baird. He worries that the trafficking comes "very close" to insider trading.

But experts in ethics say no one's breaking the current rules. Staffers on Capitol Hill and government employees are forbidden to profit personally from confidential data and can't share information that's classified or deemed secret by their employers. But within those loose guidelines, political intelligence is just another legal way for investors to perform due diligence. The intelligence operatives say that Congress, where decisions are made publicly, is fair game. It's what's known in intelligence as an open source— where information is available to any member of the public.

In theory, ethelyne and his day-trading colleagues could have called Frist's office and asked staffers what was going on, too—just as one of the hedge fund intelligence shops did. But of course that's not how the world really works. An individual investor trying to get information out of the Senate Majority Leader's office is far more likely to end up in voice mail hell than he is to get a hot tip. It takes trained insiders like former Frist staffers, veteran journalists with Capitol Hill rolodexes and other players to really work Washington's open sources: *Hey, buddy, what's going on today?*

Ethelyne_orion and his pals don't stand a chance, and that hasn't escaped the notice of some very shrewd players around the world: As the value of their product rises, the political intelligence firms themselves are becoming fair game. Alperstein sold Washington Analysis in July 2005 to China's Xinhua Finance, which is partly owned by an entity controlled by the communist government: Xinhua News Agency. Xinhua picked up Washington Analysis for an undisclosed amount just as the bidding war between Chevron and China's CNOOC over the acquisition of Unocal was reaching its apogee in the summer of 2005. Chevron outmuscled CNOOC for that deal. The failure indicated that the Chinese didn't fully understand life inside the Beltway.

Maybe that's why the Chinese were interested in a savvy Washington firm. Years ago, foreign governments depended on their

embassies and their networks of spies to obtain inside information on the latest maneuverings in the American political and economic scene. Today, they can hire a private firm to do the work.

The most dangerous people aren't always the ones working for the other side. Sometimes, they're the ones who are supposed to be on your side. Defending against them is called counterintelligence. Companies, too, are constantly looking within for signs of treachery from their own employees. To do that, they lean on counterintelligence experts fresh out of government agencies.

Doctor Eric Shaw was sitting in his office in Washington, D.C., when he got a call from a distraught client at a large oil company several years ago. An unbalanced executive at this company had begun making sinister comments to colleagues about his AK-47 assault rifle. The man's wife was dying of cancer, and he was going on long drinking binges and getting into fistfights. The client was worried. Clearly, this man's mental health presented a potentially explosive situation. The client reached out to Shaw, a clinical psychologist and a veteran of the CIA's psychological profiling shop who now consults for a private investigative firm, Stroz Friedberg. Shaw specializes in finding internal threats to companies: leakers, drunks, disgruntled employees, and staffers on the verge of a violent outburst. The work gives him a cool, unemotional bearing, in stark contrast to the people he studies. "They're all kind of crazy," he says. "But I usually don't get called unless they're totally crazy." Shaw's work is the corporate equivalent of counterintelligence: the shoe leather that goes into spotting and stopping the threats coming a company's way.

Shaw dug into the details, trying to discern just what type of dangerous personality this man had. As with any other kind of intelligence, the key to detecting a threat, Shaw says, is information. There are dozens of different kinds of threats, and each one calls for a different response. Act too soon, or on too little information,

and a situation can spiral out of control. After talking to the unstable executive's colleagues, and reviewing detailed reports of the incidents, Shaw concluded that the man was going through a temporary crisis. If handled correctly, he wouldn't pose a long-term threat. In the end, Shaw's advice to the oil company seemed counterintuitive. He told the company not to fire the man and not to go to law enforcement. Instead, the man's bosses should tell him he couldn't come back to work until he had completed a course of therapy, which the company would pay for.

As it turns out, the crisis passed and the executive went back to work, with no harm done to the company or its employees. Soon afterward, he landed a new job at a labor union working against the company—not a great situation for management, but a healthy channel for the man's anger. It was a far better outcome than the violent outburst that might have ensued if the company had fired him. Shaw says most companies don't handle internal threats this well, and their ham-fisted efforts to respond to minor problems can set off even more damaging outbursts. When a manager spots a problem and leaps into action, reprimanding or firing the employee, that event can trigger a blowup.

Doctor Marisa Randazzo is an expert in assassins, stalkers, and school shooters. She spent ten years with the United States Secret Service as chief research psychologist at the National Threat Assessment Center, developing elaborate profiles of potential killers. Today, she heads Threat Assessment Resources International, a firm based in Sparks, Nevada, just outside Reno. It offers a threat assessment training package for companies to help protect themselves from internal threats. The training includes walking executives through case studies of workplace shootings and insider sabotage, showing them the basic principles of threat assessment in the workplace, and conducting a mock emergency drill to hone crisis-response skills.

Shaw and Randazzo describe several key traits of dangerous insiders. Many have a medical issue, such as a psychiatric problem,

alcoholism, or a high level of anxiety. Others are on the extreme end of the personality spectrum—the office oddballs who are extremely shy, who require high maintenance, or who otherwise cause their colleagues to be uncomfortable around them. And many people who cause problems have a history of minor rule violations preceding a major incident. They may have broken rules regarding technology, or personnel. Many dangerous insiders are already on the radar screen of the human resources department even before they do major damage. And in about one-third of serious cases, a dangerous insider has a social network in place—other people who know in advance what the person is planning.

People who fit this pattern don't always cause problems—they can do their jobs for years without trouble. It's when people with these characteristics hit a problem in life that they start displaying what psychologists call "concerning behaviors." They may have a personal or professional disappointment. A demotion, the death of a spouse, or a move to a new location can all trigger damaging behavior. And when that cycle starts, there's no sure way to tell just how much damage will be done.

That's why the services of intelligence specialists like Shaw and Randazzo can be so valuable: it's much cheaper to head off a problem early than it is to pay to clean up the mess.

CHAPTER ELEVEN

Is This a Great Country, or What?

In April 2008, about a dozen lawyers and investment bankers gathered over muffins and coffee in a small room on the third floor of the Princeton Club on West Forty-third Street in Manhattan to hear from a spy.

They were there for a briefing sponsored by Veracity Worldwide, a one-year-old corporate intelligence firm with close connections to the CIA. And although the people in the room represented some of the top American investment banks, they weren't there for anything to do with the New York Stock Exchange or the NASDAQ stock market. They were concerned about markets on the other side of the globe: the Tokyo Stock Exchange in Japan and the Korea Exchange in Pusan, South Korea.

The American corporate reps wanted to know what was going on in North Korea, the unpredictable communist enclave just across the Sea of Japan from the Tokyo market. The North Korean ruler Kim Jong Il had been acting increasingly erratically as his country's economy collapsed and famine stalked his people. North Korea's pursuit of nuclear weapons was an open secret. No one knew how stable Kim Jong Il's control over the country was.

For the western businesspeople, those weren't just interesting political issues. They were important business concerns. A collapse

of the North Korean government, a surprise nuclear test, or a mass
famine could destabilize the region and cause capital to flee from
the Japanese and South Korean stock exchanges. An adroit banker,
though, would be well positioned to get his money out first. Or, better
yet, he could bet in the markets that the Japanese and South Korean
exchanges would decline, hoping to profit from political disaster.

All the participants that morning were Americans, but their
business and intelligence interests spanned the globe. This multinational mind-set is increasingly the norm in the private-sector
intelligence business. Today's corporate intelligence industry has
firms operating in nearly every country and finds clients all around
the world. Old political enemies can find themselves working
closely together in the private sector, and traditional allies sometimes become bitter rivals. The ethical question in this, as it always
is for spies, is where true loyalty lies. Is it loyalty to a country? To
a company? Or to any client that can pay the fee?

The stories of six corporate intelligence operations around the
world show how intelligence is becoming increasingly intercon-
nected with the global economy:

- Veracity, which hosted the meeting in New York, does
  business for clients all over the world.
- TD International, an intelligence firm that is run by several veterans of the CIA and is based in Washington, D.C.,
  represents a sheikh who is based in Dubai.
- Johann Benöhr is a private investigator in Berlin, where he
  deals with strict government regulations and the German
  public's angst about spying of any sort.
- Hakluyt, a firm based in London, once hired a German spy
  to penetrate Greenpeace on behalf of global oil companies.
- Hamilton Trading Group is a small consultancy founded
  by a former CIA officer and a former KGB operative who
  ran into serious trouble with the Putin government in
  Russia.

• Trident Group, based in Virginia, also has ties to Russia: it was founded by a former Soviet military intelligence officer. It works for some of the largest American companies and law firms.

In each case, the activities of the investigators span continents. And each operation has a "hall of mirrors" quality. Take the Russians, for example: can men who were loyal communists and rose through the ranks of the Soviet establishment truly embrace working for capitalist corporate titans? Or take the former CIA officers: how do patriotic spies who once served their country feel about working for an unelected hereditary billionaire? Such questions do not necessarily involve a conflict of interest, but they may involve a conflict of values. Do spies in the global economy ever feel a disconnect between who they are and who they work for? Does that question even matter?

ONE THING MOST of the people in this industry have in common is that they didn't start their careers with the goal of becoming private spies. When they began their careers in government, most of them didn't know there was an international corporate intelligence industry. They wanted to be soldiers, spies, or diplomats. But somewhere along the way, they became operatives for hire.

That's the story of Steven Fox, who founded Veracity. Fox is thirty-nine, and with his slicked-over hair, aquiline nose and deep voice, he could pass for Hollywood's version of a 1920s society man. The industry trade publication *Intelligence Online* reports that Fox is a veteran of the CIA's Directorate of Operations. And although a bio Fox once used in the private sector described him as having once worked "on counterterrorism in the U.S. intelligence community," he denies he was ever in the CIA. As he tells it, he's a veteran of the State Department, and he took some time off to be an Internet entrepreneur during the dot-com boom in the early

2000s. Still, in his private-sector career he has surrounded himself with lots of alumni of the CIA.

Fox's description of his background—which may or may not be a cover story—goes this way. He is a native of Manhattan, speaks French, and graduated from Princeton University in 1991. He landed a job in the State Department and soon was as far from New York society as it gets—at Bujumbura, the capital city of Burundi in central Africa.

Situated along the Great Rift Valley on the shore of Lake Tanganyika, Bujumbura has, since Burundi's independence in 1962, been a scene of terrible fighting between the majority Hutu ethnic group and the ruling minority, the Tutsi. This ethnic rivalry escalated into open genocide in 1994 in Rwanda, the country just to the north.

In 1996, the Hutu and Tutsi were slaughtering each other again. More than 150,000 Burundians had already died. And when Tutsi paratroopers took up positions at key government outposts, the capital city's television station, and its radio station, the Hutu president of the country, Sylvestre Ntibantunganya, knew he couldn't cling to power much longer. Burundi didn't have much history of peaceful transitions of government—both of Ntibantunganya's predecessors had been assassinated. To avoid the same fate, the president headed for the U.S. embassy and into the arms of Steven Fox, who says he was then a young State Department officer.

The United States agreed to give Ntibantunganya sanctuary, and it became Fox's job to figure out how to get him safely out of the American facility. For eleven months, Fox worked out the logistics of the former president's new life: Where would he live? How could he be kept safe? The American ambassador secured a commitment from the new military government that Ntibantunganya wouldn't face prosecution if he left U.S. custody—and even more important, that the new Tutsi leadership would guarantee his safety.

With that assurance in hand, Fox's work came down to the little things. Fox found a house that had been owned by the local

Heineken brewery. He arranged for cars. He worked with Ntiban-tunganya on security, settling on a thirty-man detail of trusted former officers and men from the Hutu tribe. But the ex-president balked at moving into his new home, announcing that he didn't approve of the furniture the government had agreed to provide for it. Fox scrambled to find suitable furniture from the embassy's own surplus, and obtained approval from Washington to have movers install it in the new home.

Fox and Ntibantunganya passed long hours together. The cooped-up, bored ex-president was happy to have someone atten-tive to talk to. Over the months, he gave Fox a tutorial on central Africa, from the inner workings of the coffee industry to Burun-dian politics.

The episode was a success, as such things go. Ntibantunganya was transferred from the American compound into the former Heineken house. He was not killed, and he began a new life in exile. In 1999, he published a memoir in French, whose title loosely translates as *A Democracy for All Burundians.*

Fox was moving on as well. After the stint in Burundi, he trans-ferred to the U.S. embassy in Paris. Although Paris has always been a favorite posting for American diplomats, Fox found it stifling. He also found that there wasn't much for him to do. Soon he applied for and was accepted by the prestigious INSEAD MBA program in Fontainebleau, France. That city, just under an hour's drive south of Paris, is the site of the celebrated château of Fontainebleau, which was built by French kings and used as a home by Napoleon. In 1999, Fox spent a year there, as a member of a 300-person class that included students from forty countries. Some of the people he met there form the core of his European business contacts today. He didn't know it yet, but his experiences overseas were laying the groundwork for an excellent résumé in the world of international financial consulting.

Fox briefly left the government to work on an Internet start-up, but after 9/11 he decided he had to get back into government

service. He still held his security clearances, which made it relatively simple to reapply to the government. He says he worked as
a State Department desk officer on Israeli-Palestinian issues and
counterterrorism. Fox went to Algeria in 2003, after its civil war,
running the political and economic section of the U.S. embassy.
There, he roved the North African country in an armored Chevy
Suburban with two bodyguards.

But soon Fox left the government again. This time, he did a
stint in the New York office of Diligence, learning the ropes of
the private intelligence business. Then in 2007, along with another
veteran of Diligence, the dapper Charles Garnett (who was also
a veteran of the British army), Fox started Veracity. It would be
similar to Diligence, but would take a new approach to this kind
of work: eschewing much of the traditional investigative work in
place of high-end, emerging-market due diligence. Fox lined up a
single investor who provided start-up funding and opened doors—
but whom he declines to name.

Fox began lining up distinguished international spies and
business executives to serve on Veracity's board of directors. He
soon landed two impressive names. One was Sir Richard Dearlove, who served as the chief—known as "C"—of the British
Secret Intelligence Service (SIS) from 1999 until 2004. The SIS
is commonly known in Britain as MI6, and its head is the nation's
top spy. Dearlove is a British knight, and a member of the Most
Distinguished Order of Saint Michael and Saint George, a class
of knighthood generally reserved for foreign-service officers and
diplomats. Fox also brought in an American, Stuart Eizenstat. A
partner at the law firm Covington and Burling, Eizenstat heads
the international trade and finance practice, and could provide an
invaluable connection to the top of the international corporate
world. Eizenstat was a deputy secretary of the treasury under
President Clinton and helped negotiate the Kyoto Protocol,
among other international agreements.

And Fox began hiring intelligence veterans. The former CIA

intelligence analyst Josh Mikesell became a partner. As senior advisers, Fox brought in Frank Anderson, the former chief of the CIA's Near East Division; Mel Gamble, former deputy chief of the CIA's European Division; Flynt Leverett, a veteran of the CIA who served as senior director for Middle East affairs at the National Security Council; and another CIA veteran, Art Brown.

THOSE CONNECTIONS LED Fox to Veracity's briefing in New York on North Korea. Like any other businesses, corporate intelligence firms have to hustle for new clients. But this can be tricky when the work product, and the techniques that produce it, are confidential. Often the secret is to show prospective clients just a glimpse of what a firm can do—and dazzle them with behind-the-scenes tales of spycraft.

As the audience members noshed on bagels and poured themselves cups of coffee, Fox welcomed guests from the prestigious law firm White and Case, the investment banks Morgan Stanley and Credit Suisse, and two private equity firms. The main attraction on this morning was Art Brown, who had retired from the CIA in 2005 and whom Fox had recruited as a senior adviser for Asian issues. With a bullet-shaped bald head and eyeglasses, Brown looked like Hollywood's idea of a CIA officer. His credentials are impressive. During his twenty-five years in the CIA, Brown lived in Asia for more than twenty years, served as a chief of station in three Asian capitals, and rose to become the chief of the Asia Division for the CIA's clandestine service. He advised the president of the United States in person on Asian issues, and testified in closed-door sessions of Congress about national security and economic and regional stability in Asia.

Brown sat at the head of the table at the Princeton Club and gave the same insights he'd given to presidents and senators, but this time to the paying clients—and prospective clients—of Veracity. He was joined at the head of the table by the former U.S.

ambassador to South Korea, Stephen Bosworth. Today, Bosworth is dean of the Fletcher School of Law and Diplomacy at Tufts University and sits on the advisory board of Veracity Worldwide.

Together, the two men gave a short presentation on North Korea. In deference to protocol, Bosworth spoke first. He alerted the bankers and lawyers that the North Koreans thought a deal was at hand in the protracted talks with the West about their rogue nuclear weapons program. He also laid out North Korea's two goals for diplomacy with the outside world: removal of North Korea from the State Department's list of countries that sponsor terror, and removal of economic sanctions imposed by the Trading with the Enemy Act, a law which limits American companies' ability to conduct business with designated enemies.*

Next, Brown laid out his somewhat controversial vision for future relations between the United States and North Korea. Although the United States had up to that point focused on preventing North Korea from building a nuclear weapon, Brown said that either the North Koreans already have one, or it's only a matter of time until they do. Continuing U.S. policies designed to stop that from happening would be pointless, he said. Instead, Brown argued, the United States should tolerate a nuclear-armed North Korea. "My vision is we should just belly up to this," he said. Then, tailoring his pitch to the audience in the room, Brown told the bankers and lawyers that even such a radical departure from U.S. policy wouldn't have a shock effect on the stock market in Seoul. The market there has probably already priced in an expectation that North Korea would develop a nuclear bomb.†

The group then fired questions at the speakers. What's the status

---

*Two months after this briefing, in fact, the North Koreans got their second wish. The Bush administration removed North Korea from the list of enemy countries under the law, leaving Cuba as the only nation in the world still subject to the Trading with the Enemy Act.

† Brown was right: in May of 2009 the North Koreans detonated a bomb as powerful as the atomic weapon that destroyed Hiroshima.

of the relationship between China and North Korea? (Bosworth: Not as close as we think.) How does the North Korean leadership interact internally? (Brown: Kim Jong Il is not a madman, but no one on the outside really knows how the government there works.) How big is the gray market in consumer goods? (Brown: The gray market is bigger than the legitimate market.) And what about lifting those sanctions? (Brown: North Korea could have a lot to trade with the rest of the world, including seafood and minerals.)

The businesspeople were energized as they left the room, some still munching their breakfast. They'd gotten what they came for: business information and spy stories. Now they, and their hosts, would try to make money from what they'd learned.

That kind of business development takes place around the world in corporate intelligence, just like any other business. In Germany, though, the business of corporate intelligence is especially delicate.

On a warm fall afternoon in Berlin, Johann Benöhr sips a latte and smokes cigarette after cigarette at the Shan Rahimkhan Café, which overlooks a scenic cobblestone plaza, the Gendarmenmarkt. He's there to offer a reporter a glimpse into life as a corporate investigator in Germany, speaking in nearly flawless English honed during a stint as a corporate investigator in London. With his shaved head, two-day stubble, and sleek suit, Benöhr could pass for a slimmer version of the actor Vin Diesel.

In this city, you're never far from a reminder of its years as the center of cold war espionage. The café is just a short walk from Checkpoint Charlie, where East German and western troops faced off at one of the few passages through the Berlin Wall. That wall is long gone, and although Benöhr is sitting several blocks inside what used to be East Berlin, you'd hardly know it. The nearby boulevard Friedrichstrasse is now a fashionable shopping district, featuring luxury brands and a BMW Mini auto dealership. As the city has

changed, so have its spies. Benöhr is a different kind of intelligence
player: he gathers information for companies, not countries.

In recent years, Germany has been racked by corporate spying
and bribery scandals: In 2005 and 2006, Deutsche Telecom hired
a spy firm to obtain phone records of journalists covering it, and
of the members of its own supervisory board. One of the firms
Deutsche Telecom worked with was the German office of Control Risks Group, an investigative firm based in London. Control
Risks in turn hired out some of the Deutsche Telecom work to
Desa, a firm led by onetime informants for the East German secret
police force, Stasi. When investigators from Germany's Federal
Office of Criminal Investigation decided to visit the Control Risks
office in May 2008, they didn't have to go far—the private intelligence firm is located in the same Berlin office building as the
federal investigators.[1] The list of German spying cases goes on: in
2008, the retailers Lidl and Schlecker were revealed to have been
spying on their own employees, too.[2]

The climate of scandal makes it difficult for Benöhr to talk
about his industry. Today, he says, he's taking some time off between gigs. He brushes off requests to discuss specific cases, and
proclaims that the investigative business is rather boring: "There's
very little James Bond, and a lot more librarian work," he says.

Benöhr didn't get his training in an intelligence school. Instead,
he's a lawyer and an MBA. He started his business intelligence
career in Frankfurt, at the headquarters of Kroll, the American
investigative firm. There he learned that with regard to conducting business intelligence operations, Germany was a different place
from what many of his American and British colleagues at Kroll
expected. For one thing, most court records are sealed—even routine civil matters. That makes due diligence investigations much
more difficult than they are in other European countries. Gathering information for a routine background check on an executive takes a few seconds in the United States, and can be done by
anybody with a computer. In Germany, it takes much longer. To

find out if an executive has ever been sued, gone bankrupt, or been arrested, Benöhr can't just dip into an online database. He's got to tap into his long-developed network of German business and legal contacts. Connections are everything in Germany.

Culturally, too, Germany is a trickier place to conduct investigations than other western democracies. The country has recent, searing memories of life under a police state. People have an aversion to anything smacking of intelligence, informants, or secret files. "Because of German history, when it comes to anything to do with intelligence, people are very sensitive," says Benöhr. Calls to an executive's former colleagues—a standard part of a background check in other countries—often meet with grim silence or even a disconnection. All this also makes corporate investigations in Germany much more expensive than elsewhere.

As a result, Benöhr says, the investigations industry in Germany is dominated by financial firms: "They have huge pockets, and when there's a big deal pending, there's so much at stake that they will spend what it takes. And if you do it right, it's going to be expensive."

Ironically, two American business trends are driving the German corporate intelligence market: the increasing aggressiveness of the Securities and Exchange Commission (SEC), and the ratcheting up of prosecutions under the Foreign Corrupt Practices Act (FCPA), which prohibits American companies or their foreign subsidiaries from engaging in bribery overseas.

"Until 1999, German companies could deduct bribes they paid abroad from their taxes," says Benöhr. In Germany, executives have a "different mind-set when it comes to what constitutes criminal activity." Now that so many multinational companies come under the provisions of the American FCPA, Benöhr says, companies that have had problems with bribery are increasingly investigating themselves. Also, American private equity investors that own pieces of German companies need to make sure the German employees aren't bribing third-country officials to ease

environmental, customs, or other regulations. Investigators like Benöhr are brought in to make sure executives know what happened in a bribery case, and what the company's legal exposure is. They ask basic questions: *Who knew? Was upper management involved? Was it a one-off case? Was this the usual method of doing business?* "You have to be particularly thorough," says Benöhr. "Your job is to make certain that you've really looked into this and that everybody who was involved is gone."

There's an additional international wrinkle for investigators doing business in Germany: American private equity companies own many German companies, making them subject to the SEC's disclosure regulations. The burdens of disclosure are much higher in the United States than in many other places, and Benöhr says American investors like to pore over German companies when they're making a purchase. "As an investor, you want to make sure that the company you have bought is not toxic waste."

FOX AND BENÖHR are willing to explain their industry openly to a reporter, but not everyone in the global intelligence business is equally willing to talk about what he does. Take Sheikh Mohammed Bin Rashid Al Maktoum, who is the ruler of the fast-growing city-state of Dubai and the prime minister of the United Arab Emirates. He's worth an estimated $18 billion, likes to race thoroughbred horses and camels, and owns the world's biggest yacht, a glistening white, 530-foot behemoth called *Dubai*.

Sheikh Mo, as he's known, has a firm staffed by CIA veterans on his payroll in Washington.

That fact is buried in obscure U.S government filings, so it has not been discovered by the media and the public. If it were widely known, it could be controversial. In 2006, the effort by a company called Dubai Ports World to buy a company that managed six American ports caused an uproar throughout the United States, in the mainstream media, in the blogosphere, and among the political

elite. How could a company from the United Arab Emirates—a federation to which several of the 9/11 terrorists had ties—be given access to the American shipping infrastructure? Republican congresswoman Sue Myrick sent an angry letter to President George W. Bush that read in part, "Hell no!" Would politicians like Myrick be pleased to learn that Sheikh Mo had hired—through several cutouts—some of the most sophisticated CIA-trained talent available in the private sector?

It's not clear what services these former CIA people offer to the ruler of Dubai, but their work on his behalf has left something of a paper trail in federal disclosure records. The documents are difficult to find, but they are the only clues in the mystery: the CIA veterans aren't talking, and the embassy of the United Arab Emirates does not respond to an inquiry about the matter.

This case is particularly interesting, since it illustrates the way many private intelligence firms are hired. The entire industry is hidden from public view through the clever application of attorney-client privilege, aggressive use of nondisclosure agreements, and creation of elaborate cutout schemes.

Whenever an American company signs on to lobby the government on behalf of a foreign country, it has to file a document with the U.S. Department of Justice Foreign Agents Registration Unit. The law that gives the unit its authority was passed in 1938, and was designed to make life difficult for Nazi sympathizers working in the United States. In all the decades since, the Department of Justice has been accumulating registrations at its small facility in Washington.

Its offices are tucked into the first floor of a nondescript building just a block or so from the White House on New York Avenue. After pressing a buzzer to be let in, visitors enter a filing room overflowing with years of old papers, books, and directories. Three worn-looking computers sit on a table, available to any member of the public for a search through electronic copies of the files. Invariably, young paralegals from some of Washington's high-powered

law firms occupy these computers, searching the records for details to support ongoing litigation.

The documents they're searching through typically include copies of any contracts signed by American companies working to advocate for foreign governments. They detail names of American officials the firms met with, and the dates and times of those contacts.

The disclosure forms show that the government-owned Dubai Holding (which, because Dubai is a monarchy, thus belongs to Sheikh Mohammed Bin Rashid Al Maktoum) hired the American law firm DLA Piper to work on its behalf. The law firm in turn hired the public relations firm Levick Strategic Communications. And the PR firm hired TD International (TDI), a private intelligence firm that is based in Washington, D.C., and employs a number of CIA veterans.

The founder of TDI is William Green, who is described at the firm's Web site as "a former U.S. diplomat specializing in multilateral affairs." Several sources say he is a former CIA officer. A partner at the firm is Ron Slimp, who is described as a "former U.S. diplomat and trade negotiator," and who once described himself in an e-mail to a colleague as a "former spy."*

The contract with Levick called for TDI and its stable of former spies and diplomats to receive $25,000 per month, after an initial start-up payment of $40,000. According to the filings of one of the firms involved, team members in Dubai were working on something they code-named "Project Voss." The work involved building a document sharing system and a Web site that would serve as a public relations vehicle for the firm's client in Dubai.

The entire effort—lawyers, Web masters, and spies—was

---

*Slimp also worked for a time in the London office of Enron before its spectacular collapse in late 2001. On October 16, 2001—this was shortly after 9/11 and three months before Enron filed for bankruptcy—Slimp sent an e-mail to a colleague at Enron in Houston, looking for a new job. "I'd appreciate any ideas you may have on where things are going," Slimp wrote. "And where a former spy/bandwidth trader might want to position himself."

designed to fend off a class-action lawsuit against Sheikh Mo in south Florida. The suit was filed on September 7, 2006. In it, a group of parents alleged that their sons had been kidnapped and forced to work in the United Arab Emirates, as jockeys in camel races.

Camel racing has been popular in the bedouin desert regions of Arabia for hundreds of years. The oil produced in the region in the twentieth century provided wealth for this sport, which grew ever more competitive and deployed ever more resources, as sheikhs battled for prize money and glory. The sheikhs realized that small boys—who weigh very little—made the best jockeys for these races. That fact, plus the oil money, quickly created a market for children to work in the growing camel-racing industry. Boys from as young as three up through adolescence worked in the racing circuit.

But there may have been a dark underside: the lawsuit alleged that the boys riding the camels were not paid athletes but slaves:

> This Complaint seeks redress against individuals who abducted and trafficked thousands of small boys from South Asia and Africa to the United Arab Emirates and other Arab states and enslaved them to work as camel jockeys, camel trainers and camel tenders in the desolation and heat of the Arabian Peninsula. Boys as young as two years old were stolen from their parents, trafficked to foreign lands, and put under the watch of brutal overseers in camel camps throughout the region.

This had the potential to embarrass Sheikh Mo. It also looked as though it might get expensive, even for a billionaire: the lawsuit didn't specify an amount of money sought by the plaintiffs, but it asked for compensatory damages, punitive damages, and the cost of the lawsuit itself. And it listed as plaintiffs "Minors John Does 1–10,000, Mother Does 1–10,000, Father Does 1–10,000, along

with Mother Roes 1–1,000 and Father Roes, Individually and as Survivors of Deceased Children."

That meant potentially tens of thousands of impoverished third-world parents suing one of the richest men on the planet and invoking the images of their enslaved, and in some cases dead, sons. Whatever the merits, it would be a tough case to defend. Sheikh Mo's phalanx of Americans went to work to mitigate the damage.

It's possible that TDI became involved because executives there saw Sheikh Mo's troubles as an opportunity for profit—that's how the competitive intelligence industry works. There is also a possible hint of something more: for the United States, the lawsuit was extraordinarily sensitive. The United Arab Emirates is a crucial ally of the United States against Al Qaeda, and it borders the Strait of Hormuz, a strategic point separating the Persian Gulf from the Gulf of Oman. The twenty-one-mile-wide strait is the sole transit point for as much as 40 percent of the world's oil, which is transported by tanker to the Indian Ocean and the rest of the world beyond. Across the strait is a hostile nation, Iran. The United States military has used the United Arab Emirates as a launching point for operations in Iraq and the Horn of Africa, where two volatile nations—Ethiopia and Somalia—are situated.

For the American government, and by extension the CIA, Sheikh Mo isn't just a billionaire with expensive tastes in yachts. He may be one of the very few men in the world who can keep the U.S. economy from disaster and its military from defeat. The CIA had a motive to help him in the case of the camel jockeys. But it's not at all clear whether TDI's involvement was sanctioned by the CIA itself to help protect a valued friend in the region from embarrassing and costly legal disclosures. The disclosure documents don't detail motive, and TDI declined to respond to repeated requests for an interview.

That's a frequent problem with asking questions in the world of global private intelligence. Sometimes it's impossible to know the truth.

ANOTHER FIRM THAT shies away from publicity sits at the pinnacle of London's corporate spies: Hakluyt and Company. This intelligence firm specializes in dealing with the global corporate elite—CEOs of multinational corporations and their boards of directors. Hakluyt cultivates a tony, upper-crust image derived from the days when English gentlemen sipped tea served from silver platters and divvied up the world's resources over dinner. The company has a butler, a former Gurkha,* who greets visitors at the door, and meetings are sometimes held alongside a crackling fireplace.

In 1995, Mike Reynolds and Christopher James—both veterans of the British intelligence agency MI6—combined forces to start the firm. Reynolds had served British intelligence in Berlin during the cold war, and James was a veteran of the British special forces as well as the intelligence agency. James—who has been described by a friend as "hale, hearty, and well met"—hit the London cocktail party circuit in the mid-1990s looking for connections to help launch his firm. He already had plenty of experience in the corporate world. As a spy for MI6, James headed the section of the agency in charge of liaisons with British companies. And now his contacts were about to get even better. At a cocktail party, he was introduced to Sir William Purves, then the group chairman of the global bank HSBC Holding, and a pillar of the City, London's financial district.

Tapping into Purves's Rolodex, James came to know almost everyone important in the industry, and put together the Hakluyt

---

* Gurkhas are the tenacious Nepalese soldiers who have fought alongside the British army since the 1800s.

Foundation, an advisory board of glittering corporate names. In time, a stint at the Hakluyt Foundation became known as an exit station for captains of British industry entering their retirement years. It soon included luminaries such as Sir Fitzroy Maclean,* who many thought was Ian Fleming's inspiration for the fictional spy James Bond; and Baroness Smith, who was married to the Labour Party leader John Smith. Also serving on the foundation was Sir Peter Holmes, a former chairman of Shell. Such contacts put Hakluyt in touch with the boards of directors of scores of multinational companies. All this was good for business.

To name their firm, James and Reynolds reached deep into British history, choosing as a namesake Richard Hakluyt, an author who specialized in navigation and exploration in the late sixteenth and early seventeenth centuries. Hakluyt was more than just a mild man of letters. He was by turns a savvy businessman, persuasive government lobbyist, and daring undercover spy—a perfect role model for the international corporate spies of today.

Hired by the explorer Sir Walter Raleigh, Hakluyt produced propaganda papers on the glory and fortunes to be made in America, hoping to persuade Queen Elizabeth I to support Raleigh's expeditions there. During a stint in Paris as a secretary to the British ambassador, Hakluyt was asked to covertly gather information about French and Spanish activities, and their intentions and capabilities in the New World. For all this, Hakluyt was well compensated by his benefactors, accumulating a small fortune by the time he died in 1616.

Today, Hakluyt and Company's Web site, www.hakluyt.co.uk, includes none of the traditional marketing boilerplate that other firms post on the Internet. The site has only the firm's logo and

---

*During World War II, Maclean parachuted behind enemy lines in Yugoslavia with orders from Winston Churchill to link up with Tito's communist partisans and "find out who's killing the most Germans, and how we can help them kill more." Years after Maclean's death in 1996, his widow, Lady Veronica Maclean of Dunconnel, denied to *The Scotsman*—a newspaper in Edinburgh—that Maclean had ever been a spy, but admitted that he had loved the rumors that he was the inspiration for James Bond. And, she noted, "we always had a travelling vodka set wherever we went, and that was very Bond-like."

contact information, which convey a subtle message of discretion. But despite the firm's secretive, upper-crust image, its executives have to hustle for clients just like everyone else.

In the summer of 2001, Christopher James made a rare mistake, approaching Enron—then one of America's leading companies— with a business proposition. James's sales effort would prove embarrassing for Hakluyt on several levels. First, this well-connected spy appears not to have known that Enron was only a few months from collapse. Second, the man Hakluyt approached, Jeff Skilling, was about to become a symbol of corporate bad behavior. At this time, Skilling was a few weeks away from leaving the company. Worst of all, Hakluyt's sales pitch to Enron became public knowledge after the U.S. Federal Energy Regulatory Commission made public 200,000 of Enron's internal e-mails from 1999 through 2002.

Buried within that mountain of communication was a letter of July 8, 2001, from Hakluyt's Christopher James to Enron's Jeff Skilling. A few months earlier, the two men had been introduced by a longtime oil industry executive, Phil Carroll, then the CEO of the giant engineering firm Flour Corporation.* Carroll was a perfect point of contact: he was a former CEO of Shell Oil, and he lived in the same apartment building in Houston as Enron's chairman, Ken Lay. Carroll, Lay, and their wives regularly dined together, sharing meals where the talk was more social than business. Now, James was following up with Lay's man, Skilling, hoping to win Enron as a high-paying client:

---

*Carroll's Flour Corporation would later receive billions of dollars in contracts for reconstruction in Iraq from the U.S. government. In 2003, Carroll himself was named chairman of the U.S. effort to rehabilitate the post-invasion Iraqi oil industry. In Iraq, he got caught in a struggle between neoconservatives in the U.S. government and American oil companies over what to do with the Iraqi oil industry. Carroll sided with the oil companies. In 2005, he made this revealing comment to the BBC: "Many neoconservatives are people who have certain ideological beliefs about markets, about democracy, about this, that, and the other. International oil companies, without exception, are very pragmatic commercial organizations. They don't have a theology."

Dear Mr. Skilling,

Your office has asked me to outline Hakluyt's services. . . . I would say simply this; Hakluyt is what you make of it—it places an unparalleled private intelligence network at the personal disposal of senior commercial figures.

. . . Although we work for divisional directors on tactical issues, we have found our most rewarding work in personal dealings with CEOs who wish—for whatever reason—to have a confidential agency at their own disposal. It was this, which prompted Phil Carroll to write to you about us in April. . . . We look at people and the issues, which often drive them to make the decisions or act as they do. All our work is unattributable.[3]

The work is unattributable, that is, until the e-mails are revealed in a high-profile, years-long legal investigation.

In another e-mail, James told Skilling that Hakluyt had already done some low-level work for Enron, and he hinted that it was looking for a much bigger piece of Enron's spying business. Enron had connections to former CIA officers, and wasn't afraid to deploy their talents on its own behalf. Since Enron was using American CIA veterans operating out of London for its flights over European power plants, James may already have been aware of the extent of Enron's interest in the spy game.

Hakluyt was already developing a reputation as a rough customer in the global economy. Earlier that year, the *Sunday Times* of London had broken an embarrassing story: Hakluyt had hired a German agent to spy on the environmental group Greenpeace. The plan had all the hallmarks of spy fiction, but it was real. Also, the spies didn't work for queen and country battling evil empires, they worked for the oil companies Shell and British Petroleum, and they battled environmentalists.

The *Sunday Times* laid out the details. In 1996, Hakluyt's cofounder Mike Reynolds had hired a German spy, Manfred Schlickenrieder. With his shoulder-length hair and impeccable liberal

credentials, Schlickenrieder was a natural infiltration agent. He'd once been a member of the German communist party, and he was a voracious reader of Marxist literature. Schlickenrieder had a documentary film company, Gruppe 2, that was based in Munich; and he was well-known in European activist circles for his work on sympathetic documentaries about leftist groups. He had already spent years on an unfinished documentary about the Red Army Faction, a left-wing German terrorist organization. Apparently, no one on the political left asked why Schlickenrieder's documentaries never seemed to get finished and never seemed to appear on television.

Schlickenrieder billed heavily for his services, submitting one invoice to Hakluyt in June 1997 for more than 6,000 pounds, with the heading "Greenpeace research." The money upgraded his lifestyle: Schlickenrieder drove a BMW, not generally the car of choice among communist activists.

At the time, the oil companies were concerned about firebombing at gas stations in Germany, which they suspected were masterminded by left-wing activists. They also worried about a protest by Greenpeace at the British Petroleum (BP) Stena Dee oil rig off the Shetland Islands. Reynolds told Schlickenrieder that he wanted to know what Greenpeace was doing to prepare for an expected lawsuit from the oil companies. Hakluyt also wanted inside information on the location of the ship *Greenpeace*, which the group often used for elaborate and embarrassing publicity stunts against companies.

Hakluyt gave Schlickenrieder the code name "Camus," after the author of *The Stranger*. Using his cover as a documentary filmmaker, Schlickenrieder approached environmentalist groups and liberal activists, and tried to glean whatever information he could.

Greenpeace was snookered. Speaking to a reporter for the *Sunday Times* after the affair had come to light, the communications director of Greenpeace Germany said, "The bastard was good, I have to admit. He got information about our planner Arctic Frontier campaign to focus on the climate change issue and the responsibility of BP. BP knew everything. They were not taken by surprise." The

spokesman added, "Manfred filmed and interviewed all the time, but now we realize we never saw anything."

That was surprising enough. But Schlickenrieder had one other revelation left. After his cover was blown, another detail came to light. All the time that Schlickenrieder had been a paid spy for Hakluyt working for BP and Shell, he was also in the service of the German government. Schlickenrieder worked for the BND, the German counterpart of the CIA, which paid him the equivalent of more than 3,000 pounds per month in expenses, noted the *Times*.

So the corporate spy was also a government spy, and he was paid by both sides at the same time. It was the ultimate nexus between government intelligence and corporate spying.

IN THE WORLD of international corporate intelligence, such over-lapping loyalties can be profitable, but they can also be dangerous.

In one little-known case, a partnership between an American veteran of the CIA and a former officer in the Soviet Union's KGB ended when the KGB man—who had made enemies for himself in Putin's Russia—vanished. What happened to him, and whether he's alive or dead today, is uncertain. His partner is still trying to solve the mystery.

Today, Jack Platt lives in a small house in leafy Great Falls, Virginia, a suburb of Washington. During the cold war, he served as a CIA officer recruiting spies within the KGB to funnel information to the United States. He spent a large part of those years trying to lure Gennady Vasilenko, a KGB officer who worked in the Soviet Union's embassy in Washington, D.C., in the 1970s and 1980s, to spy for the United States. Of course, Vasilenko was also trying to lure Platt to spy against the United States.

As Platt tells it, neither man succeeded, but the two spent a lot of time together. And although they worked for rival services, they became friendly. They went target shooting and fishing together, and once took in a Harlem Globetrotters game in Washington.

In 1980, they found a way to work together—which Vasilenko recalled years later in an interview with the *Atlanta Journal Constitution*. That year, the Olympic Games were being held in Moscow, and the Soviet Union was concerned about the prospect of terrorism at the games. The United States was boycotting the Olympics to protest against the Soviet Union's invasion of Afghanistan. But even so, the CIA had valuable intelligence the Russians needed: a rare photograph of an international terrorist known as "Carlos the Jackal," who was one of the world's most wanted men. It could be of enormous value to Russian agents working to protect the Olympics. With approval from his bosses, Platt slipped his Russian friend a copy of the precious picture.

Being friends with a CIA officer wasn't a good career move in the KGB during the Soviet era. Neither man could know it, but as their friendship was growing, a corrupt FBI agent, Robert Hanssen* was passing tidbits of inside information along to his Russian handlers. One of those tidbits was the name of Gennady Vasilenko. Hanssen thought Vasilenko had been spying for the Americans, because he had seen CIA references to Vasilenko with the code name "Glazing."

By 1988, the situation was coming to a head. Oblivious of Hanssen's treachery, Vasilenko was ordered to Cuba for what he thought would be a run-of-the-mill meeting. But as he stepped onto the veranda of an apartment building in Havana, two men jumped him. "They beat the shit out of him," Platt recalls. Vasilenko was packed off to the KGB's Lefortovo prison in Moscow, where he was accused of being a traitor. He waited to be executed. But there was no evidence that he had passed any evidence to Platt—Platt says this is because he never passed any—and the Soviets let him out of prison after six months. "He talked his way out of there," Platt says, with a note of pride.

When the cold war ended, Platt reconnected with his old friend

---

*Hanssen spied against the United States for the Soviets for more than two decades. The story of his capture was told in the movie *Breach* in 2007.

Vasilenko, who had been fired from the KGB and had struggled in his career since his arrest in Havana. They went into business together—this time as spies for hire to western businesses that wanted to operate in Moscow. Amid the rush toward privatization in Boris Yeltsin's Russia in the mid-1990s, companies needed intelligence. *What's going on? Who should we deal with? Where are the best deals?* Together, the two ex-spies profited, offering services ranging from investigations of global criminals to checking out the credentials of potential business partners for their clients.

Business was good, until recent years, when Vasilenko ran afoul of Putin's government. Former KGB men dominate the current Russian hierarchy. Actually, as Vladimir Putin himself told a gathering of Russian spies in 2005, when he was president of the Russian Federation, "There is no such thing as a former KGB man."[4] Many of these officers never gave up their dark red KGB identity cards when the Soviet Union collapsed. To this day, Platt says, they can flash the cards to win all sorts of special favors in Russian society—from getting a speeding ticket fixed to being offered career opportunities. The powerful ex-KGB men never quite gave up the idea that Vasilenko had been a secret spy for the Americans. "There were those that never believed that I didn't recruit him," Platt says. Vasilenko was arrested in Russia and sent to prison. He's still in jail today, and Platt says it is once again just a misunderstanding. "He didn't spy, no matter what they said about him. He just got caught in a power struggle."

That leaves Platt without a valued colleague at his firm, the Hamilton Trading Group. Today, Platt works primarily for corporate clients, law firms, financial firms, and hedge funds. Mostly, the work involves figuring out who the people on the other end of a business transaction are. Who are the owners of the firm? Who do they know? Platt explains this with a Russian metaphor, *krysha*, meaning "roof." In the old days, Russian intelligence services used it as slang to describe the cover story of a spy operation. Today, though, the Russian Mafia uses *krysha* in a different way, to mean

"godfather" or, more loosely, "protection." *Krysha* can thus refer to a network of musclemen who protect a businessman, or a company that has paid protection money to the mob. Platt says he's in the business of finding out who provides a company's *krysha*—who backs the firm, who's connected to it, who's looking out for it.

Depending on the case, this service is not always expensive. Corporate investigators like those at Hamilton Trading Group might charge as little as $75 per hour, plus expenses and a premium for difficult work. They know, of course, that the law firms pass those bills along to their corporate clients at upwards of $125 per hour—and pocket the difference. Platt explains that his firm and others like it typically work for law firms that are in turn working for the corporate client. That way, much of the investigative work is concealed behind attorney-client privilege and can't be revealed to the other party in a transaction.

But there are always leaks—the corporate equivalent of Robert Hanssen—and a veteran spy like Platt knows this all too well. "At the top of every report that I send to somebody, I say 'privileged and confidential.' But the bottom line is that doesn't mean shit," Platt says.

Platt doesn't want to discuss Vasilenko's disappearance. He says publicity wouldn't be good for Vasilenko's chances of getting out of prison, but he is bitter about the way the Russian government is being run under the supervision of KGB veterans such as Putin. "These secret police guys have no fucking idea what an economy is," Platt says dismissively. That's going to prove disastrous for the Russian people in the long run, Platt believes. And with a government run by Putin—even if he's officially now in Russia's number-two political job—Platt knows he may never see his old friend and partner again.

Not all stories about Russian corporate intelligence have such a grim ending. One example is the story of Yuri Koshkin, a former

Soviet military intelligence officer who relocated to the United States when the cold war ended. Today, at age forty-nine, he operates a small intelligence firm, Trident Group, in Rosslyn, Virginia, not far from his former enemies at the Pentagon.[5]

On May 26, 2007, a Russian agent working for Trident slipped unnoticed into a movie theater in Moscow showing Disney's *Pirates of the Caribbean: At World's End*. He donned night-vision goggles, scanned the theater, and spotted his target. This maneuver was no cold war spy scenario: the agent was a former Russian cop, and he was searching for real-life pirates making illicit copies of the film. On the Internet, a single copy of this blockbuster film could cost Disney millions in lost sales. Disney wanted the pirates caught— and fast.

That day, the culprit was the projector operator. He was given away by a telltale stream of light seeping out of the projection room. *Hey—what's going on in here?* As the agent burst into the room, the startled operator looked up and offered him a $1,000 bribe to keep quiet about what he'd seen. The agent turned the bribe down, and radioed Trident Group's 24-7 operations center in downtown Moscow, an office staffed by former KGB officers, veterans of Soviet military intelligence, and ex-cops.

Founded in 1996, Trident specializes in helping American companies like Disney navigate the Russian market. Trident consulted with Disney about the bribe offered to its employee, and Disney authorized a $1,000 bonus to the agent for turning down the bribe. This was a successful clandestine operation, and typical of what's going on in the global economy as spies help companies feel their way into tricky emerging markets around the world. It's a sign of the urgency those companies feel that they're overriding years of corporate history. In this instance, Walt Disney himself was a virulent anticommunist who testified before the infamous House Committee on Un-American Activities in 1947 that the Screen Animators Guild was dominated by communists. Today, his namesake

company is working hand in glove with a firm founded by men who were educated as Soviet Marxists, some of whom spent the better part of their early careers spying on the United States. Says the former general counsel of the CIA, Robert M. McNamara, Jr.: "Is this a great country, or what?"

Yuri Koshkin was born in 1958 in Moscow, into what he describes as a "typical family of the Russian intelligentsia." In 1975, he says, he enrolled in the Military Institute of the Soviet Ministry of Defense. He studied the English and Cambodian languages on his way to becoming an intelligence officer in the Red Army. "Cambodian was boring," Koshkin recalls, "but you didn't get to choose which languages you studied. It was the military." After graduating in 1980, Koshkin served as a military adviser to Tanzanian forces in Africa.

The advent of perestroika allowed Koshkin to leave the military before completing the customary twenty-five years of service. In 1989 he became a civilian, working for an American documentary film company in Moscow. From there he bounced into a job at a public relations firm in San Francisco, where he says he first spotted a big gap in perception between American and Russian businesspeople. "I saw lots of companies that were going into Russia didn't really know who they were dealing with," Koshkin says. "They couldn't tell the good guys from the bad guys."

Trident once represented Kenneth Dart, an American investor who is heir to the Styrofoam cup fortune generated by his family's Dart Container Corporation. For several years in the late 1990s, Dart battled with the Russian oil giant Yukos in a dispute over the dilution of shares of Yukos subsidiaries in which Dart held an interest. That fight ended in a confidential settlement.

It was the kind of battle that can become physically dangerous in Russia. Koshkin says Trident was threatened so many times during its work with Dart that one of the firm's employees was getting ready to evacuate his family from Moscow when the two

sides settled the dispute in 1999. The Russian oligarch Mikhail Khodorkovsky, who was the founder of Yukos, later ran afoul of the Russian government and is now serving an eight-year jail term for tax violations.

Today, Koshkin says, Trident has fifteen employees, including Vladimir Joujelo, a KGB veteran who helped the Russians provide security for world leaders, including Mikhail Gorbachev, Boris Yeltsin, and Ronald Reagan; Alexander Trifonov, a former KGB officer; and Alexander Vinogradov, a retired Russian army colonel who specialized in military intelligence. "They're good at what they do, but they charge a lot of money to do it," says Raelynn Hillhouse, who blogs about corporate intelligence for thespywhobilledme.com. "Legally, Russia remains the Wild West. It's convenient to be able to hire people who have experience in that environment."

Koshkin won't discuss most of Trident's clients. Nor will he reveal the firm's billing rates or annual revenues, but he seems to have made a good living from it. He bought a house from a former executive of AOL, Bob Pittman, in Great Falls, Virginia, and an apartment on the Upper East Side in Manhattan.

From his office in Arlington, Virginia, high above the Potomac, Koshkin can see the glint of the white walls of the Russian embassy across the river in Georgetown. "Sometimes I sit back and contemplate and wonder about the quirks of life," he says. "We were trained that the United States was enemy number one."

Koshkin's old enemy is now his number one client.

In from the Cold

I first met Yuri Koshkin over coffee at a Starbucks in suburban Rosslyn, Virginia, just a few blocks from the Key Bridge over the Potomac River into Georgetown. He's a charming and fascinating character, and I enjoyed our wide-ranging discussion immensely. Our meeting got me thinking about the implications of the industry Koshkin came from and the one he's in now.

Washington, D.C., has always been a special target for spies—the first ones probably arrived soon after the capital was founded on July 16, 1790. Their stories are epic, sometimes bizarre, and frequently tragic. This is the city where Allan Pinkerton chased after the confederate spy "Rebel Rose" Greenhow during the Civil War. And it's also the city where Allen Dulles oversaw the CIA's surreal experiments with amphetamines, sleeping pills, and LSD to develop new interrogation methods for the cold war.[1] It was here that the veteran FBI agent Robert Hanssen betrayed his country to the Russians, and the young FBI agent Eric O'Neill helped bring him down.

Today, intelligence services from all over the world send operatives to Washington, D.C., to try to pry secrets out of the government. Spying is so much a part of the fabric of the town that when

a neighbor at a barbecue says he works "for the government," most people know not to ask any further questions.

But as I sat at the tiny table at Starbucks sipping my latte, it struck me that Koshkin and his spying colleagues in the private sector represent something new in Washington. For they are extending the espionage culture of the cold war into the global economy. For good or ill, the heirs of Allen Dulles and his rivals at the KGB are hanging out their shingles and selling their services to clients around the world.

That's the reason why Washington is a hub of their global private intelligence industry. The spy firm Diligence once had its headquarters here, and today it maintains an office just two blocks from the White House. Three blocks on the other side of the executive mansion is the headquarters of TD International, where several intelligence veterans offer what the firm blandly describes as "strategic advisory and risk management" consulting services. Kroll's office is just outside Georgetown. From there, it's a short walk to the offices of Investigative Group International, which is headed by Terry Lenzner, the man who became known as Bill Clinton's private investigator during the scandal over Monica Lewinsky. There are more: Executive Action, Fairfax Group, and Corporate Risk International all have headquarters in this area, offering some combination of risk management, investigative, and intelligence services. The offices of Koshkin's Trident Group are in Rosslyn, Virginia.

A fifteen-minute drive away in northern Virginia, the firm Total Intelligence Solutions operates what it calls a "global fusion center"—a data gathering operation—at its bland corporate offices. I toured the facility with Matthew Devost, who was the company's president in 2008—an unassuming guy who on that day was wearing a blue polo shirt and khakis. Devost is something new in the intelligence world: he has spent his entire career in the private sector—not in the government. His career is a sign that the private-sector intelligence business has reached its next stage of

evolution. The industry is now incubating the careers of intelligence professionals from entry level to executive rank.

Devost told me he'd worked on a dramatic intelligence operation in Lebanon in 2006. Total Intelligence Solutions worked frantically during that year's thirty-four-day war between Israel and Hezbollah extremists. The corporate clients had employees trapped in Lebanon when the shooting started, and needed to get them out. Devost and his colleagues used real-time satellite images and a network of private informants on the ground to determine which bridges had been bombed, and where heavy fighting might block evacuation routes. It was the kind of work a CIA officer might once have done for Americans stranded during a coup in a banana republic. But this was a completely private-sector intelligence operation, with no government agents involved at all.

One level below such organized, corporate, and official spy firms is an enormous network of sole practitioners and small operators. These are private intelligence operatives who are available for hire on a case-by-case basis to anyone with the cash to pay for a few days—or a few hours—of work. They come from diverse backgrounds. I've met former FBI agents, former investigators for the SEC, and former investigative reporters who sell their services to clients. In March 2009, two reporters I admire greatly—Glenn Simpson and Sue Schmidt of the *Wall Street Journal*—announced their resignations. They formed SNS Global, LLC, a firm that will do what Simpson described as "some public interest work and some consulting."[2] Both are well known in the world of investigative reporting: Schmidt won a Pulitzer Prize after breaking the story of the corrupt lobbyist Jack Abramoff; and Simpson has made a career out of probing the darker reaches of money laundering, financial crime, financing of terrorists, and all sorts of corporate misconduct. Now their skills are available for hire on the private market, too. The quest for an information edge goes on.

But where does it stop? We live in an age when technology is increasingly blurring the line between what was once thought to

be private and what is now public information about our most intimate selves. That's causing wrenching adjustments in the way we think about the boundaries between ourselves and our society. In England, for example, the introduction of Google Street View provoked a firestorm of controversy. The company dispatched camera-equipped cars to photograph street scenes for its mapping software, but many people feared it would catch them in compromising situations. The rock star Liam Gallagher of the band Oasis was forced to deny that one image was of himself drinking at a streetside café.[3] The increased intrusiveness of technology has made us a society struggling to sort out the villains from the victims. In the United States, a fourteen-year-old girl in New Jersey was charged with child pornography after posting nude pictures of *herself* on the social networking Web site MySpace.com.

Such evolutionary leaps in technology have unsettling implications for privacy. And the exploding growth of the private intelligence industry represents yet another trend in the 100-year balance of power between private and government intelligence. In an increasingly fragmented geopolitical environment, the balance seems to be shifting away from governments and toward corporations and even private individuals, who have access to more intelligence and information-gathering ability than many governments in history ever had.

What comes next?

I asked Peter Earnest, a retired CIA officer who serves as the executive director of the International Spy Museum in Washington, D.C. Earnest sees corporate espionage as a natural outgrowth of increased globalization and an ever-increasing demand for information. Over the coming years, he says, intelligence operations will be ever more effective. "Spying doesn't change; the tactics have been the same throughout human history," he says. "But the technology keeps getting better and better."

Even after meeting many of the top corporate spies in the world, exposing operations that many of them did not want exposed, and

poring over the history of their industry, I'm still conflicted about whether all this is headed in a positive direction for society. As a journalist, I'm a strong believer in the importance of gathering information. And I'm a fundamentalist when it comes to the First Amendment. But what separates me, and reporters like me, from the corporate spies is that we believe in making sure the information we report reaches the widest possible audience. Spies do the opposite: they make sure the details they harvest reach only a very narrow—and very high-paying—audience.

I don't think that's always good for society. So I'll offer one modest suggestion. The spy firms must be dragged farther into public view, where citizens can keep an eye on whether what they're doing is constructive or destructive.

There's one way this could be done. Today, American lobbyists must register with Congress, revealing to the public how much they're getting paid, who their clients are, and what they're trying to accomplish. When they were put into place in the mid-1990s, the regulations were hotly resisted by Washington's lobbying community. But they have helped to clean up an industry, and made it easier for the media and the public to spot the problem firms before these firms can do too much damage.

A spy registry modeled on the lobbying disclosure rules could be coordinated by the SEC, which already processes millions of pages of public disclosure documents from public companies every year. Free markets do work best without friction, and a big source of friction in the economy is misinformation. The ability of investors and corporate leaders to stamp out confusion in the market by finding out the truth of a situation helps boost confidence, speed transactions, and prevent prices from spiraling too high or too low.

It's time for the spy firms to come in from the cold.

Acknowledgments

I'll start where everything begins for me: my wife, Maureen, who decided not to move back to Minnesota and gave me a chance instead. Thanks, babe. And to our children, Declan and Evelyn, whose curiosity and intelligence give me confidence that each generation is an improvement upon the last.

My parents, Ron and Eileen Javers, gave me license to ask impertinent questions of powerful people over dinners each night in the Philadelphia home of my childhood. My dad, who is still the best journalist I've ever known, diligently proofread early versions of this manuscript, policing them for clichés and redundancies—some of which, you may have noticed, I managed to slip past him. My kid brother, Quinn Javers, is a real historian, and I should probably apologize to him for imitating one in these pages.

Professionally, I have to thank the team at *Politico*, particularly Jim VandeHei, John Harris, Craig Gordon, and Jeanne Cummings, who gave me a home while I wrote this book. They are inventing a new kind of Internet journalism for an era in which the survival of even the greatest news institutions is in doubt. The journalism they're creating is new and exciting, but the values they bring to the project are old and good.

At *Business Week*, where I did my early research into the nexus between intelligence and the economy, former editor in chief Steve Adler carved out an important space for investigative reporting, giving his reporters the time to dig deeper into the stories that

captivated them. It's a rare and important gift for a journalist. The magazine's Paul Barrett is both brilliant and demanding, and taught me to continually challenge my material and myself. My former colleague Dawn Kopecki, who knows a good story when she sees one, also gave me an invaluable early boost on this project.

My old bosses at CNBC, Alan Murray of the *Wall Street Journal* and Gloria Borger, who is now with CNN, made heroic efforts to turn a print guy into a television correspondent. Give them credit for trying, anyway. Both have gone far beyond what's required of a boss, and for long after they stopped signing my paychecks. I'm proud to call them both friends.

My agent, Rafe Sagalyn, is a true gentleman, and my editor at HarperCollins, Ben Loehnen, was a pleasure to work with.

In writing this book, I had the help of a huge number of sources, both on the record and off. I'm grateful to the people who gave me their time to explain an industry that's largely shrouded in mystery.

Secret keepers don't often talk candidly with secret tellers, but I'm glad so many did.

Thanks.

Notes

Chapter 1: Code Name: Yucca

1. Project Yucca was first detailed by the author in "Spies, Lies, and KPMG," *Business Week*, February 26, 2007. It can be found online at www.businessweek.com/magazine/content/07_09/b4023070.htm.
2. Burt's bio can be found on the Web site of the International Institute for Strategic Studies, available online at www.iiss.org/about-us/regional-offices/washington/board-of-directors/ambassador-richard-burt.
3. Barbour Griffith and Rogers' contract with Eritrea is on file with the U.S. Department of Justice's Foreign Agents Registration Act Registration Unit Public Office. It is available online at www.fara.gov/docs/5430-Exhibit-AB-20060203-22.pdf.
4. The case was filed in United States District Court for the District of Columbia, number 1:05-cv-02204-PLF-AK. It was unsealed and made available for public view on January 26, 2006.

Chapter 2: A High and Honorable Calling

1. "Tapping the Wires for Stock Operations," *Sacramento Daily Union*, August 12, 1864.
2. The Pinkertons' entire statement on Homestead can be found online at www.explorepahistory.com/~expa/cms/pbfiles/Project1/Scheme40/ExplorePAHistory-a0j7g3-a_707.doc.

Chapter 3: For the Money

1. John F. Fox, "The Birth of the Federal Bureau of Investigation," Federal Bureau of Investigation Office of Public/Congressional Affairs, July 2003. This official history of the FBI is available online at www.fbi.gov/libref/historic/history/artspies/artspies.htm#_ftn8.
2. Sam Dash, *The Eavesdroppers* (New York: Da Capo, 1959), p. 86.
3. Edward V. Long, *The Intruders: The Invasion of Privacy by Government and Industry* (New York: Praeger, 1967), p. 193.
4. "Two Men Are Seized in Wiretap Case, a Third Gives Up," *New York Times*, February 20, 1955, p. 1.

5. Long, *The Intruders*, p. 195.
6. Patent no. 2,699,054. Documents available online at: www.pat2pdf.org/patents/patz699054.pdf.
7. "Anticipating the 21st Century: Competition Policy in the New High Tech Global Marketplace," Report by Federal Trade Commission Staff, May 1996. Available online at www.ftc.gov/opp/global/report/gc_v1.pdf.
8. "Broady Outburst Marks Testimony," *New York Times*, December 7, 1955, p. 23.
9. "Broady Sentenced to 2–4 Years; Judge Hits 'Dirty' Wiretapping," *New York Times*, January 14, 1956, p. 38.
10. Patricia Holt, *The Bug in the Martini Olive: And Other True Cases from the Files of Hal Lipset, Private Eye* (Boston: Little, Brown, 1991), p. 11.
11. Transcript of Hearings before the Subcommittee on Administrative Practice and Procedure of the Committee on the Judiciary, United States Senate, Eighty-Ninth Congress, First Session, February 18, 1965, p. 14.
12. Holt, *The Bug in the Martini Olive*, p. 69.
13. Ibid., p. 79.
14. Ibid., p. 154.
15. "Disappearing Witnesses," *Time*, September 12, 1977.
16. Edith Evans Asbury, "DeCarlo Witness Describes Fears: Zelmanowitz Tells of Talks with Defense Lawyer," *New York Times*, January 22, 1970.

Chapter 4: The Man Is Gone

1. George O'Toole, *The Private Sector: Rent-a-Cops, Private Spies, and the Police-Industrial Complex* (New York: Norton, 1978), p. 40.
2. Jim Hougan, *Spooks: The Haunting of America—The Private Use of Secret Agents* (New York: Morrow, 1978), p. 332.
3. Robert Maheu and Richard Hack, *Next to Hughes: Behind the Power and Tragic Downfall of Howard Hughes by His Closest Advisor* (New York: HarperCollins, 1992), p. 115.
4. Ibid., p. 122.
5. History of the OH-6A Cayuse available online at http://www.boeing.com/history/mdc/cayuse.htm.
6. Unclassified transcript of testimony of Robert A. Maheu before the United States Senate Select Committee to Study Governmental Operations with Respect to Intelligence Activities, Tuesday, July 29, 1975, 10:50 A.M., p. 28.
7. Maheu and Hack, *Next To Hughes*, p. 2.
8. "Statements by Hughes and Two Publishers in Autobiography Controversy," *New York Times*, January 10, 1972, p. 23.
9. "The ITT Affair," *Time*, March, 1972. This thorough summary of the Dita Beard scandal is available online at www.time.com/time/magazine/article/0,9171,903331-2,00.html. A more in-depth account can be found in the Senate Watergate Report, p. 206. It is available online at http://books.google.com/books?id=x7nMs-JwAikC&pg=PA206&lpg=PA206&dq=dita+beard+affair&source=web&ots=-leJC8aX3C&sig=06FakbStYMUIUT-fNsY01LnPTOE&hl=en&sa=X&oi=book_result&resnum=1&ct=result#PPA208,M1.
10. Jack Anderson, *Peace, War, and Politics: An Eyewitness Account* (New York: Macmillan, 2000), p. 230.

11. J. Anthony Lukas, "The Hughes Connection: What Were the Watergate Burglars Looking For?" *New York Times*, January 4, 1976.

CHAPTER 5: THUG BUSTERS

1. Arthur Meier Schlesinger, *Robert Kennedy and His Times* (New York: Houghton Mifflin Harcourt, 2002), p. 585.
2. Charles D. Ellis and James R. Vertin, *Wall Street People: True Stories of Today's Masters and Moguls* (New York: Wiley, 2001), p. 136.
3. Jon Nordheimer, "Financier Avoids Jail in Deal to Aid Homeless," *New York Times*, February 13, 1988.
4. Fred R. Bleakley, "Wall Street's Private Eye," *New York Times*, March 4, 1985.
5. Daniel Pedersen, Ruth Marshall, and Jane Whitmore, "On Saddam's Money Trail," *Newsweek*, April 8, 1991.
6. Celestine Bohlen, "U.S. Company to Help Russia Track Billions," *New York Times*, March 3, 1992.
7. L. J. Davis, "International Gumshoe," *New York Times*, August 30, 1992.
8. Christopher Byron, "High Spy: Jules Kroll's Modern Gumshoes Are on a Roll," *New York*, May 13, 1991.
9. Bryan Burrough, "Pirate of the Caribbean," *Vanity Fair*, July 2009.
10. "How Kroll Signed Off on $7 Billion Fraud," *Intelligence Online*, July 15, 2009.

CHAPTER 6: THE CHOCOLATE WAR

1. "Nestlé S.A. to Acquire Spillers Petfoods," Vevey, February 4, 1998. Press release. Available online at www.Nestlé.com/MediaCenter/PressReleases/AllPressReleases/SpillersPetfoods4Feb98.htm.
2. "Suggestions for Nestlé's Public Relations Response," obtained by the author.
3. Neil A. Lewis, "Giants in Candy Waging Battle over a Tiny Toy," *New York Times*, September 28, 1997.
4. "Nestlé Announces Plans to Voluntarily Withdraw Nestlé Magic," *Business Wire*, October 1, 1997.
5. "International Briefs: Nestlé to Buy Spillers from Dalgety," *New York Times*, February 5, 1998.
6. The ratio of lobbying spending to earmark return was first calculated by the author in "Inside the Hidden World of Earmarks," *Business Week*, September 17, 2007. Available online at www.businessweek.com/magazine/content/07_38/b4050059.htm?campaign_id=rss_daily.
7. Roald Dahl, *Charlie and the Chocolate Factory* (New York: Puffin, 1964), p. 19.
8. James Ridgeway, "Exclusive: Cops and Former Secret Service Agents Ran Black Ops on Green Groups," *Mother Jones*, April 11, 2008. Available online at www.motherjones.com/news/feature/2008/04/firm-spied-on-environmental-groups.html.
9. "There's Something about Mary: Unmasking a Gun Lobby Mole," *Mother Jones*, July 30, 2008. Available online at www.motherjones.com/news/feature/2008/07/mary-mcfate-sapone-gun-lobby-nra-spy.html.
10. "Swiss Campaign Group Says Food Giant Nestlé Hired Spy against It," Associated Press, June 20, 2008. Available online at www.iht.com/articles/ap/2008/06/20/business/EU-FIN-Switzerland-Nestlé-Activists-Infiltrated.php.

Chapter 7: Tactical Behavior Assessment

1. Transcripts of the UTStarcom call and the BIA analysis of it come from a confidential report produced by BIA for its client: "UTStarcom (UTSI: $8.54) Q2 Earnings Call August 2, 2005 Rating: Medium-High Level of Concern."

2. UTStarcom's press release from that day is on the company's Web site at http://investorrelations.utstar.com/releasedetail.cfm?ReleaseID=175772.

3. Details of the movements of UTStarcom's stock price can be found online at http://finance.yahoo.com/q/hp?s=UTSI&a=07&b=1&c=2005&d=10&e=1&f=2005&g=d.

4. Details of BIA's activities have been compiled from on- and off-the-record accounts by participants in the events and people who were in a position to be familiar with the events. BIA declined to offer any comment or details of its activities during the research for this book. The backgrounds of its employees are taken from BIA documents obtained by the author as well as descriptions given to him by people familiar with the company.

5. Re-creation of the TBA method is based on interviews with trained practitioners and their trainees. It is also based on written training material produced by BIA and obtained by the author.

6. Descriptions of the founding of BIA are compiled from the on-the-record recollections of its former CEO Don Carlson, as well as off-the-record recollections of others familiar with BIA.

7. BIA's self-description was included in a set of training materials handed out to clients: "Elicitation Skills: Increasing the Flow of Information." The materials were obtained by the author.

8. The article was published on June 26, 2006, and is available online at http://online.barrons.com/article/SB115110330795289453.html.

9. Transcript of the Southwest earnings call used as a source for quotes was produced by Thompson StreetEvents, and is titled "LUV-Q2 2005 Southwest Airlines Earnings Conference Call."

10. Southwest's 2005 annual report is available on the Web site of the Securities and Exchange Commission at www.sec.gov/Archives/edgar/data/92380/000095013406001553/d32370e10vk.htm.

11. An image of Cascade's headquarters can be found on Google Maps at http://maps.google.com/maps?f=q&hl=en&geocode=&q=2365+Carillon+Point,+Kirkland,+Washington&sll=37.0625,-95.677068&sspn=64.497063,108.984375&ie=UTF8&ll=47.657359,-122.206625&spn=0.003418,0.006652&t=h&z=17&iwloc=addr.

12. Information on Cascade Investment LLC is available on the Web site of the Securities and Exchange Commission at www.sec.gov/Archives/edgar/data/1052192/000104746908001369/a2182606z13f-hr.txt.

13. General Scale data available on the Web site of the U.S. Office of Personnel Management at http://opm.gov/oca/08tables/pdf/gs.pdf.

14. BIA's document "Strategic Information Collection for Investors" was obtained by the author.

CHAPTER 8: THE EDDIE MURPHY STRATEGY

1. GeoEye's May 2008 10-Q filing with the SEC can be found online at http://www.sec.gov/Archives/edgar/data/1040570/000095013308001863/w57751e10vq.htm.

2. The National Reconnaissance Office Web at www.nro.gov/corona/corona2.jpg site has a copy of the fist spy satellite picture.

3. This and other quotes from *Trading Places* can be found online at www.imdb.com/title/tt0086465/quotes.

4. The $100,000 annual fee was reported in Ben Paynter, "Feeding the Masses: Data In, Crop Predictions Out," *Wired*, June 23, 2008. Available online at www.wired.com/science/discoveries/magazine/16-07/pb_feeding.

5. The press release is available on the USDA Web site at www.nass.usda.gov/Newsroom/printable/06_30_08.pdf?printable=true&contentidonly=true&contentid=2008/06/0171.xml. The acreage report of June 30, 2008, can be found at http://usda.mannlib.cornell.edu/usda/current/Acre/Acre-06-30-2008.pdf.

6. The history of U.S. commercial satellite imagery was ably laid out in Ann M. Florini and Yahya A. Dehqanzada, "No More Secrets? Policy Implications of Commercial Remote Sensing Satellites," paper written for a Carnegie Endowment conference, 1999. Available online at https://www.policyarchive.org/bitstream/handle/10207/6465/satellite.pdf?sequence=1.

7. Joanne Irene Gabrynowicz, "The Perils of Landsat from Grassroots to Globalization: A Comprehensive Review of U.S. Remote Sensing Law with a Few Thoughts for the Future," *Chicago Journal of International Law* (Summer 2005): 45.

8. The complete list is available at the NOAA Web site, http://www.licensing.noaa.gov/licensees.html.

9. NOAA has a handy fact sheet on satellite regulations on its Web site at http://www.licensing.noaa.gov/faq.html.

10. The BBC account of the U.S. satellite action in Afghanistan, "U.S. Buys Afghan Image Rights," appeared on October 17, 2001. Available online at http://news.bbc.co.uk/1/hi/sci/tech/1604426.stm.

11. *Wilson et al. v. ImageSat International N.V. et al.*, CASE 1:07-cv-06176-DLC-DFE, filed July 2, 2007.

CHAPTER 9: NICK NO-NAME

1. "Esoteric: A Specialist Security and Covert Investigations Company," corporate marketing brochure.

2. Michael McCahill and Clive Norris, "CCTV in London," Centre for Criminology and Criminal Justice, University of Hull, 2002. Available online at www.urbaneye.net/results/ue_wp6.pdf.

CHAPTER 10: THEY'RE ALL KIND OF CRAZY

1. How Senator Frist's decision leaked to Wall Street traders was first revealed by the author in "Washington Whispers to Wall Street," *Business Week*, December 26, 2005. It can be found online at www.businessweek.com/magazine/content/05_52/b3965061.htm.

CHAPTER 11: IS THIS A GREAT COUNTRY, OR WHAT?

1. "German Corporate Spying Scandal Widens," Spiegel Online International, June 9, 2008. Available online at www.spiegel.de/international/business/0,1518,558510,00.html.

2. "Germany's Corporate Spying Scandal," Time.com, May 27, 2008. Available online at www.time.com/time/business/article/0,8599,1809679,00.html?xid=feed-cnn-topics.

3. The e-mails between Hakluyt and Enron can be found online at www.enronexplorer.com.

4. Owen Matthews and Anna Nemtsova, "A Chill in the Moscow Air," *Newsweek*, February 6, 2006. Available online at www.newsweek.com/id/57048.

5. Trident Group was first described by the author in "I Spy—for Capitalism," *Business Week*, August 13, 2007. It can be found online at www.businessweek.com/magazine/content/07_33/b4046052.htm.

EPILOGUE: IN FROM THE COLD

1. Tim Weiner, *Legacy of Ashes: The History of the CIA* (Garden City, N.Y.: Doubleday, 2007), p. 65.

2. Michael Calderone, "Two WSJ Reporters Launch New Company," Politico.com, March 23, 2009. Blog available online at http://www.politico.com/blogs/michaelcalderone/0309/WSJ_reporters_start_company.html?showall.

3. "Rock Star: That's Not Me Drinking on Google," CNN.com, March 28, 2009.

Index